Gender and Sexual Identities in Transition

Gender and Sexual Identities in Transition: International Perspectives

Edited by

José Santaemilia and Patricia Bou

Cambridge Scholars Publishing

Gender and Sexual Identities in Transition: International Perspectives,
Edited by José Santaemilia and Patricia Bou

This book first published 2008 by

Cambridge Scholars Publishing

12 Back Chapman Street, Newcastle upon Tyne, NE6 2XX, UK

British Library Cataloguing in Publication Data
A catalogue record for this book is available from the British Library

ISBN (10): 1-84718-668-8, ISBN (13): 9781847186683

TABLE OF CONTENTS

LIST OF ILLUSTRATIONS

LIST OF TABLES

ACKNOWLEDGMENTS

We are greatly indebted to our students and colleagues at the *Universitat de València* who have given us their support and insights over the last few years, in particular Sergio Maruenda, Barry Pennock and Gora Zaragoza. Our thanks also go to Janet Holmes, Sara Mills and Jane Sunderland for their advice and encouragement.

Introduction

Gender and Sexual Identities in Transition

Gender and language studies is entering a phase of maturity. Gender and language researchers have been increasingly concerned with the ways in which a variety of gender and sexual identities are represented, performed, constructed and (re)negotiated in discourse. With reality as complex as ever, the field is far richer now, enough to allow a healthy theoretical and methodological plurality, and yet also to demand analytical rigour. Gender and language is an empirically-oriented field of inquiry that contiues to generate a wealth of ethnographic and discourse-based case studies from an increasing number of settings and contexts.

The work of language and gender scholars had been traditionally classified into three paradigms, deficit, difference and dominance (Cameron 1995, Bing & Bergvall 1996, Bergvall 1999). More recently it has been classified into two paradigms, difference and dominance (Cameron 2005). The basic components of these paradigms –women as disadvantaged or powerless speakers, men as powerful speakers, and the existence of differing male and female linguistic subcultures– have been recently merged into more nuanced analyses which integrate several dimensions of social identity (gender and sexuality, as well as class, age or ethnicity), and take into account not only linguistic features but also beliefs, prejudices and symbolic-ideological constructs. As Weatherall (2002: 162) contends,

> 'Women's speech' and 'men's speech' are not an empirical reality of how women and men speak. Rather, women's speech and men's speech are symbolic notions that are ideological. They function as standards or norms against which the ways women and men actually talk get judged.

A position that has been heavily criticized over the last few decades of gender and language research is the ideology of gender essentialism –i.e. the 'belief in essences', that is, the conviction that there is some essential, fundamental and fixed property or set of properties which all members of a particular category must share, and by which they are distinguished from the members of other categories (Cameron 1998: 15).

Whether social or biological, a sense of essentialism informed the initial stages of gender and language research (Lakoff 1975, Spender 1980) and continues to do so outside discourse-informed studies. But in spite of the tendency to reify gender differences in essentialist terms, all feminist and gender and language research since Simone de Beauvoir's 'One is not born, but rather becomes a woman' declaration (1949) is committed to the core finding that gender is –to a greater or lesser extent– socially and ideologically constructed (Cameron 2005).

From the 1980s onwards, there has been a shift from looking at the ways gender or sexual identities are *reflected* in language to those in which they are *constructed* in and through discourse (Hall & Bucholtz 1995, Litosseliti & Sunderland 2002, Cameron & Kulick 2003, and countless other publications). Gender is now viewed as plural, multidimensional, related to numerous social and ideological factors. Gone are the days in which masculinity or femininity were singular concepts, seen as a binary opposition of masculinity vs. femininity. Today gender and sexual identities are difficult to delimit or classify, as they are fluid, unstable, and even ambiguous.

From a critical point of view, gender and language researchers no longer analyse gender features in terms of dichotomized oppositional female/male sex differences. Although there seems to be agreement on the fact that this appears outdated and unrealistic, social expectations and personal constraints may force us to take up essentialist positions. In analysing a variety of gender and sexual identities, it would be better to observe a range of masculinities and femininities which may have been constructed by and for a variety of people. But the paradox is that we also need to consider "the socially ascribed nature of gender: the assumptions and expectations of (often binary) ascribed social roles against which any peformance of gender is constructed, accommodated to, or resisted" (Bergvall 1999: 282). Then, although a social constructivist approach seems to be a more thorough analytical tool in gender and language, essentialism remains a popular stance, one which researchers cannot ignore altogether. Historically, language has provided us with a range of gendered/sexualized identities, settings, positions and even discourses (Sunderland 2004). Essentialism is, then, an ideology which has proved to be very resilient, and has been a useful conceptual tool to understand how we assess and construct our gender/sexual identities or others'.

There is, however, a danger that an excessive emphasis on social constructedness can transform identity into an amorphous, endless repetitious category. Here Austin's 1962 concept of 'performativity', popularized by Butler (1990) for gender research, may prove useful. Identities (whether gender or sexual) are practices rather than solid categories. They are actively constructed performances rather than pre-defined roles. Although identities can be constructed internally, what gives gender its real status is its public representation and display. Indeed, identities are in fact (public) performances or displays, but they are not absolutely fluid, but rather the results of (often predictable) situated interactions. The construction of gender/sex identities is a holistic process – "Our gender (and also our sexuality) emerges not only through how we move and dress, but also in our speech habits and our linguistic choices" (Cameron & Kulick 2006: 8-9). 'Man' or 'woman', 'heterosexuality' or 'homosexuality', 'dominance' or 'subordination' are all constructed in interaction, in and through discourse.

Quite often, though, realities are already gendered or sexualized before we even interact with them. There are linguistic features, like the use of tag-questions (Lakoff 1975, 1990), or discourse strategies, like positive politeness (Holmes 1995), which are regularly associated with either men or women. Alice Freed also proposes the existence of settings and activities which may be indexed for certain types of talk, and which may further become "symbolically gendered if they are regularly and consistently associated with either women or men" (Freed 1996: 67). The connection between workplace and gender, for example, and the notion of gendered workplace (Holmes & Stubbe 2003, Holmes 2006, Schleicher, this volume) have become prominent objects of analysis. Sunderland (2004) has studied as well what *gendered discourses* are and do –they are constantly created and abandoned, (re)circulated and disfavoured, legitimised and stigmatised. Gender, then, can be not only a process, a performance, but also "an idea, or set of ideas, articulated in and as discourse" (Sunderland 2004: 18) which may contribute to the production of certain people as women or men, rich or poor, dominating or subordinated.

Hegemonic gender ideologies may be relatively stable and even resilient to change, but ways of being gendered/sexualised are ever-changing processes. At any point in history we have been surrounded by a multiplicity of discourses, in the Foucauldian sense of "practices that systematically form the objects of which they speak" (Foucault 1972: 49). These discourses have always been highly ideological, as they have been fostered by a variety of pressure groups, organizations and institutions which construct the world through language and texts, subject positions and shifting articulations of gender and sexual identities.

These gendered or sexualized discourses are unstable constructions, always in transition, in a perpetual struggle to gain social legitimacy and to counter the workings of opposite discourses. A good example of these contingent discourses is the 'Catholic' discourse in Western Europe. This discourse attempts to impose a highly restrictive view of religion, of gender equality, and of sexual ethics. A case in point in Europe is the Spanish Catholic church, which is orchestrating a media and popular campaign to impose a narrow-minded idea of homosexuality and of homosexual marriages (Santaemilia, this volume).

In some cases, those discourses which are already *gendered* (Sunderland 2004) do not promote certain gender/sexual identities, but rather they try to impose an ideological project, like that found in the perpetuation of hegemonic masculinity in Evangelical universities (Jule, this volume) or in a variety of economic goals. Examples of the latter are the pharmaceutical industry's promotion of biometaphors involving a shopping strategy which revolves around compulsory heterosexuality (Simon-Maeda, this volume) or the consolidation of American TV shopping channels as a setting where middle-class femininity and consumption are linked stereotypically (Garcés-Conejos, this volume).

Gender can also be characterized as a dynamic repertoire of identities, of public displays of self, and of self-representations. But as societies change, the difficult transitional nature of gender/sexual identities is even more evident. The *chattista*, or oral ritual poems sung or recited at traditional social occasions, are a good example of this. Greek-Cypriot men playfully try to perpetuate their sexual superiority over women, both resisting new articulations of femininity and the pressures of society upon men to display traditional forms of male sexuality (Doukanari, this volume). In contemporary Japan, although women's status has significantly increased, linguistic gatekeepers like the mass media and the self-help literature actively promote a stereotypical *women's language* (Lakoff 1975) which is associated with beauty and politeness. Thus, this reinforces the idea of a binary differentiation between male and female languages (Tanaka, this volume). Time-old stereotypes begin to be contested, though mildly and often ambiguously, and a new dialectic between the hegemonic forces of traditional gender/sexual stereotypes and the new forms of resistance to these stereotypes is becoming more and more common.

In our quest for gender equality, we cannot deny that much progress is being made. However, at the same time, we cannot deny that this progress is unevenly distributed across cultures and contexts, with occasional backlashes and giant leaps forward. As Schleicher (this volume) affirms, gender "takes up different meanings in different ages and cultures". Gender is, undoubtedly, a socio-historical construct, which can also be a strategic resource in the configuration of the gender/sexual identities one wishes to adopt. When several cultures coexist, greater complexity ensues. Therefore gender- and sex-related norms are negotiated in order to come to terms with the conflicting identity/identities chosen. One example will suffice to illuminate this complexity. British Bangladeshi girls are, according to a stereotype which is amplified by the popular mass media in the United Kingdom, caught between two cultures, the victims of a culture clash. Through the analysis of spontaneous conversations in a group of girls on the topic of 'arranged marriage', we can see how different traditions of love and sexuality are negotiated in discourse and, accordingly, contradictory sexual identities interactively rejected or taken up (Pichler, this volume). This leads us to the concept of gender as struggle, (re)negotiation, and conflict.

Gender is an extraordinarily labile process. It is highly fluid in the way it gives rise to a multiplicity of identities, but also highly sensitive to historical and ideological determinants. Gender/sexual identities are the result–in Butler's (1990) terms–of the repeated stylization of the body, of a repeated performance of dressing, gesturing and speech rituals that are only apparent or public when they are performed (and understood as performance). Gender is also the site of struggle and conflict over our self-construction as individuals. Identities, affiliations, sexual and moral attitudes are all (re)negotiated, (re)affirmed and challenged within a gender(ed) framework. In some cases, social attitudes on sex-related issues such as abortion and same-sex marriage are played out in a fierce discourse versus counter-discourse scenario (Santaemilia, this volume). In other cases, and in spite of its transgressive character, gender becomes the most reactionary framework of human relations and identities. This, therefore, upholds a rigid and essentialist divide between human beings in terms of sexual behaviour, gender-related characteristics and moral norms. Perhaps the most obvious example is heterosexuality, a time-old "political institution" (Cameron & Kulick 2003: 44) whose function is "maintaining the gender hierarchy that subordinates women to men" (*ibidem* 45). Heterosexuality silently shapes the experiences and behaviours of millions of ordinary people, essentially through heteronormativity. This "encapsulates the insight that sexuality is organized and regulated in accordance with certain societal beliefs about what is normal, natural and desirable" (Cameron & Kulick 2006: 165). Ericsson and Simon-Maeda (this volume) offer insight into the silent workings of heterosexuality, in Sweden and in English-language online advertising.

Other gender and language ideologies are probably created to claim a subliminal, but powerful, status. One of the most popular gendered language ideologies is the recent view of women as expert communicators, particulary suited for interpersonal communication and polite discursive strategies. In particular, this new gendered myth is invoked in workplace settings. In post-communist Poland, globalised costumer service communication is rapidly expanding, and many workers (mainly female) are needed (see Kielkiewicz-Janowiak & Pawelczyk, this volume). What may seem at first a positive step in terms of job opportunities can have different interpretations. Deborah Cameron's warning, for instance, deserves to be taken into account and tested: "all this discourse about women's superiority is intended to distract attention from factual evidence suggesting that in material reality, women are still 'the second sex'" (Cameron 2003: 457). New gendered myths are likely to bring about new forms of subordination and stereotyping. The power of gender and language ideologies lies in their invisibility and social permeability, as well as their commonsensical nature and the fact that they usually remain uncontested.

The aim of this volume is to offer a vast international panorama of gendered and sexualised experiences, with new and original data collected from a variety of cultural settings and sociopolitical contexts. Although Cameron (2005) claims that the gender and language research community is an international one, and that the current issues and directions are well-established within the community, the fact remains that gender studies is a mostly Anglocentric, white and middle-class discipline. We think cross-cultural dialogue in gender and language issues should be reinforced, allowing a variety of methodologies, concerns and even prejudices. Real internationalization is perhaps one of the key issues for the future, which involves giving up absolute certainties and even accepting that there is no absolute certainty, no absolute canon in gender and language studies but rather a multiplicity of canons, research interests, institutional or religious constraints, traditions, needs and rhythms.

To address this imbalance, Kotthoff & Wodak, in their *Communicating Gender in Context* (1997), claim that one of their objectives is to "rectify the lack of international awareness of empirical studies made in non-English speaking European countries" (Kotthoff & Wodak 1997: xii). In their three-volume *Gender Across Languages* (2001-2003), Hellinger & Bußman present a broad investigation of some thirty languages, which tries to "illustrate the diversity and complexity of linguistic representations of gender across languages" (Hellinger & Bußman 2001: ix). They take special care "not to impose a narrow western perspective on other languages" (*ibidem*). In *Women, Gender and Language in Morocco* (2003), Fatima Sadiqi asks herself a number of questions, mainly "what do the terms 'gender' and 'feminism' mean to Moroccans, and to Arabs and Muslims in general" (Sadiqi 2003: xv). This reflects her conviction that "an understanding of gender perception and women's agency can be achieved only within the structures of power in a specific culture" (*ibidem* xvi). In our *International Perspectives on Gender and Language* (2007), we called for a real internationalization of associations like IGALA (International Gender and Language Association), with the progressive incorporation of languages other than English in the running of conferences as well as in the recently-launched *Gender and Language* journal. Undoubtedly, the more languages and cultures are investigated, the more all of us will feel identified with a world-wide gender and language community.

We are happy to offer here a volume whose main asset is diversity, in a world which is global and local at the same time. This reveals a tension between the tendency towards globalising identities and the experience of localised gender/sexual identities. This volume looks at many parts of the world (Japan, Sweden, Poland, Cyprus, Spain, US, Australia, Canada, Hungary) with different assumptions and expectations, often revealing various research practices and traditions. This analytical and geographical diversity will no doubt render gender and language research closer to reality than it is currently. Joan Pujolar (this volume) examines the role of linguistic diversity (a key feature of today's societies) in the production and reproduction of inequalities. A dialogical approach may unearth the dynamics of the conflicts between publicly legitimized language varieties (usually masculine) and subordinated language varieties (usually feminine).

Gender and sexual identities are privileged vantage points from which one can observe and judge power relationships. They are in permanent transition, in a state of flux. New identities are created and reproduced, refused and challenged. They constitute an open, unpredictable catalogue which sometimes breaks free of dominant ideologies, and sometimes falls into a backlash against the search for equality. Often too there are ambiguous phenomena like the current language ideology of female superiority. Cameron (2003: 458) argues this when writing that there is "neither a simple case of successful feminist intervention in a tradition of sexist representations, nor straightforwardly part of a 'backlash' discourse in which feminism 'has 'gone too far', leaving men as the new victims of sexist oppression". In any case, it is hardly possible to imagine a society where gender and sexual identities remain absolutely stable, or where there is absolute gender equality.

The concept of 'transition' thwarts the apparent predictability of gender or sexual identities. Identities, no matter the type, require a great deal of interactional and ideological work –they are not simply fluid or fragmentary categories laying indolently at our disposal but, rather, discursive positions which need to be constantly disputed and performed, whether upheld or feigned. Even heterosexuality, as the unmarked form of sexual identity and the primary site for the reproduction of gender difference, needs to reassert its normative and prescriptive status, maybe through the silent workings of tradition. Both establishing a stereotype and breaking free from it require repetitive, conscious displays or performances. Achieving public recognition for certain identity categories involves a large-scale mobilization of conflicting ideological discourses and counter-discourses. This is clearly in the world-wide debate on homosexuality and same-sex marriage. This debate is staged daily in a variety of religious or institutional publications, in popular magazines and, most importantly, in the media, or "the modern arena for the ritualised transgressions of the very taboos that they also uphold and reinforce" (Harvey & Shalom 1997: 9).

Gender is a social category which quite often indexes not only maleness or femaleness, nor homosexuality or heterosexuality, but rather gender- or sex-related conflict. It is a vital resource which is not simply linguistic, but also cultural, sexual and strategic. Thus it is used (or displayed or performed) differently by different groups of men and women, sometimes playfully (Greek-Cypriot men displaying a contemporary version of traditional masculinity –Doukanari, this volume), and sometimes confrontationally (e.g. the use of male-dominated lecturing at a Canadian Evangelical university to rehearse female theology students in feminine patterns of silence –see Jule, this volume), sometimes persuasively (e.g. Viagra advertisements as an instance of the reproduction of dominant ideologies of male sexuality by the pharmaceutical industry – see Simon-Maeda, this volume), sometimes dialectically (e.g. the negotiation of gendered positions of a group of British Bangladeshi girls on the topic of arranged marriage –see Pichler, this volume). However, it is never displayed neutrally.

By suggesting the concept of transition, we resist seeing the idea of identity as a fixed and definitive category. Gender and sexual identities – which are inextricably linked, as is evident in the construction of male heterosexual and female lesbian identities, where gender is deployed as a resource for constructing sexual identities (Cameron 1997, Sauntson 2005)– are never at rest. One is never finished developing into a woman or a man, or any other gender/sexual identity. Essentially, in more abstract terms, one is always in the process of defining one's identity. This is in part confirmed by numerous labels which have appeared in the last few years. 'New man', 'new lad', 'metrosexual', 'nerd' or 'pomosexual' are just a few examples. Ericsson (this volume) adds a few sex-related identity categories in the Swedish context ('missus', 'cohabitee', 'real babe') whose main discursive function is to render heteronormativity unproblematic and desirable. The variety of labels is perhaps indicative of a permanent gender and sexual instability. In the same vein, the crisis of masculinity we have heard of so much recently is only a reminder that all identities are in a permanent state of crisis. They always constitute unsatisfactory indices of a slippery reality, which cannot be contained within any single name. New realities bring about new categories, which are but feeble translations of the new anxieties. Although the processes of transition seem to be faster today, the traditional categories are subtly there. These categories are transformed into beliefs and prejudices, the foundation stones of a traditional discourse which finds comfort in fixed, immutable, binary categories. But we never know where transitions lead, and this is the most revolutionary aspect of gender. Through new (re)configurations of existing gender and sexual identities, the promise of a more egalitarian future is consistently offered.

Chapter survey

The book contains eleven contributions that explore a variety of gender and sexual identities under construction in different situations and cultural contexts. In chapter one, **Joan Pujolar** explores the connections between gender and other fields of linguistics which show social domination such as bilingualism, a connection that has been neglected so far. The paper begins with a brief revision of the separate historical trajectories of gender studies and bilingual studies, particularly reflecting on their theoretical and epistemological similarities and differences. The few prior studies concerned with both areas show that gender is indeed essential in understanding the influence of linguistic difference on the reproduction of or resistance against inequalities. In the last section of the paper, the author deals with the ways in which bilingual studies could contribute to gender studies. His argument focuses on the need to deconstruct and critique received notions of language following research into gender studies in relation to notions such as femininity and masculinity. Linguistic diversity is necessary in a diverse world, as some human groups (particularly women) are denied access to the social spaces where officially recognised forms of 'linguistic capital' are acquired. This most frequently occurs in schooling.

The next two contributions broach on the notion of masculinity from different angles. In chapter two, **Andrea Simon-Maeda** adopts a Critical Discourse Analysis framework to address how masculinity is treated within Internet advertisements for Viagra and other sexual enhancement products. The author highlights the powerful role that internet advertisements for bodily management play in the representation and reproduction of dominant ideologies of male sexuality. Simon-Maeda argues that the sexual pharmacology pharmaceutical industry depends on advertising strategies that highlight prevalent notions of heterosexual relationships wherein effective hydraulic performance of the 'power tool' is conflated with ideas of 'authentic' masculinity. Advertisers, the author affirms, make use of provocative images, vocabulary and discourse features appealing to the implied sexual needs and expectations of 'consumption communities'. The author concludes that advertisers are currently investing in the appropriation of male bodies and masculinity for the sake of contemporary capitalist enterprises intent on promulgating the slogan 'bigger is better' among consumer and sexual cultures. This paper provides a good example of the power of regulatory discourses on sex: on the one hand, the pharmaceutical industry adheres to hegemonic notions of masculinity and femininity; and on the other hand, advertising is a popular discourse which revolves around a reified, naturalized notion of gender/sexual difference which is embodied by heterosexuality.

In the following chapter, **Allyson Jule** explores masculinity as public performance. Jule investigates the male-dominated teaching discourse (lecturing) used at an Evangelical post-graduate college in Canada and the subsequent linguistic demands that lecturing places on male participants. From the perspective of Lacan's (1968) theory of intersubjectivity, the author suggests that lecturing is a powerful tool for gender performance. In the author's opinion, it is essential in propelling male learners into masculine performance of public speech. She also puts forward that owing to the transference relationship that lecturing presupposes, the silence of female students and the speech of male students affirm the possibility that within 'God-talk' (Ruether 1996), participants perform devout behaviour in gendered ways. After an analysis of students' classroom participation the author concludes that the clash of conservative/spiritual masculinity with pro-feminist/social justice masculinity in pedagogy provokes questions of gender speech performances alongside religious identity

(Clatterbaugh 1990, Skelton 2001). This analysis is only a sample of the manifold ways that religious beliefs may impose and perpetuate identities (e.g. hegemonic masculinity) through teaching rituals and linguistic features. Religious institutions of the kind described here constitute heavily gendered and gender-reinforcing settings. In essence, stereotypical gender identities are upheld, as part of an evangelical message which prescribes male leadership and female silence.

Chapter four brings up issues of heterosexuality and normativity in Swedish conversations. From a social constructivist view of sexual identity as construed and enacted in social interaction, **Stina Ericsson** analyses three types of conversational data so as to show how heteronormativity is maintained throughout. The three data sets include first, examples using non-recognitional person reference forms; second, examples employing the term "sambo" ("cohabitee"); and third, interviews involving pre-adolescents and young adolescents. The author highlights how heteronormativity is sustained thus rendering notions of heterosexual identity as desirable and unproblematic. In Sweden, as in many other parts of the world, new forms of family or sexual relationships are prompting new gender- and sex-related labels, which have become the focus of social debate. The chapters by Simon-Maeda and Ericsson show how situated analyses provide a good way to expose the silent, invisible dynamics of heterosexuality.

Next, **Agnieszka Kiełkiewicz-Janowiak** and **Joanna Pawelczyk** investigate Polish call-centre communication alongside gender identities and stereotypes. The authors analyse three data sources related to call centre interaction: written descriptions of call centre procedures, interviews with call-centre trainers, supervisors and operators, and recordings of customer-operator exchanges. The analysis shows that, although stereotypically feminine communicative behaviour is prescriptive for call centre performance and is thus valued, call-centre operators, however, fail to apply such behaviour in their interactions with customers. The authors conclude that the ideal worker possesses a mixture of communicative features stereotyped in Poland as feminine and masculine. These features become salient in discourse depending on the type of task and the personality of the customer. In times of political and economic changes in Poland, as in other ex-Communist societies, traditional stereotypes and beliefs are likely to be reinforced under the guise of new gender and language ideologies. Thus, the new gendered language ideology of women as expert communicators awaits further study in the Polish context, as it confers both privileges and limitations on women and is contested by the perpetuated historical ideal of the 'Polish mother'.

Chapter six constitutes the first contribution to the study of the construction of gender in a Hungarian workplace, given that most research on language and gender at the workplace focuses on English-speaking worlds. **Nóra Schleicher** aims to analyse Hungarian female managers' representation and construction of their gendered identities at their workplace. She notes two cases of strategic language use that are affected by specific notions of gender. One is related to the use of English words to promote the impression of expertise while the other concerns extensive use of swear words in order to portray an image of honesty. Through her investigation, Schleicher makes the point that it is more useful to think of gender as an area constrained by community-specific meanings of 'man' and 'woman' than as people's attributes.

In chapter seven, **Elli Doukanari** investigates the construction of male sexuality in Kipriaka chattista, or Cyprus rhyming improvisations. The author analyses recorded performances of chattista as well as further supportive conversations and shows how the Greek-Cypriot man projects a socio-culturally bound image of a superior, amorous male protector of family honour. Doukanari underlines the male struggle to demonstrate manliness while emphasising his own sexuality and defending his honour. This, however, depends on the sexual behaviour of female relatives and on his opponent's sexual verbal insults. Although some changes are occurring, we see how in some highly traditional societies, like Cyprus, both morality and sexuality are heavily gendered. In fact they still revolve around female honour and male (hetero)sexual prowess. There is a paradox here: women are also active in the construction of male gender and sexual identities −Connell (1995: 242) terms this as "women's investment in patriarchy", and is confirmed by similar phenomena such as women's loyalty to patriarchal religions, their preference for narratives of romance, and their activism against abortion rights or homosexuality.

The next chapter investigates the rapport building and maintaning strategies (Spencer-Oatey 2000) of male and female hosts of American shopping networks. **Pilar Garcés-Conejos** tests the hypothesis that the role of host in this female gendered domain will determine choice of rapport-creating strategies independently of whether the host is male or female. To test this hypothesis the author analyses six hours of shows from different channels in which three women and three men hosts are represented. Findings indicate that all hosts used the same type of rapport-building strategies, mainly oriented to the establishing of common ground (Brown and Levinson 1987). This, the author argues, could lead to the tentative conclusion that the constraints that the community of practice (Eckert & McConnell-Ginet 1992) poses on participant's roles supersede gender in determining choice of linguistic behaviour. Although gender may not be here a relevant individual resource, it is a collective one. In America and Europe there is a stereotypical association between women, on the one hand, and better communication and politeness, on the other. In Mills's (2003: 204) words, "[a]t a stereotypical level politeness is largely associated within Western countries with middle-class women's behaviour". This paper discursively documents the consolidation of American TV shopping channels as a setting where middle-class femininity and consumption are linked stereotypically. It also provides an example of the repositioning of women in the new social hierarchy of American consumer culture.

Chapter nine also interrogates the stereotypical connection between politeness and women, this time from a Japanese perspective. It raises the topic of the existence and maintenance of a women's language in Japanese. The author, **Lidia Tanaka**, affirms that there are strong societal expectations that adult women continue to employ stereotypically feminine language despite the changes in Japanese society. Tanaka's aim is to investigate whether the traditional image of women and their language are portrayed in contemporary texts. To this end, she analyses self-help books, a magazine and letters to an online newspaper on the topic of women's language. Her findings reveal that although the public perception of women's language indicates diversity, traditional attitudes still prevail, especially in connection with child rearing. While some traditional stereotypes have been altered to include personal success and happiness, contemporary texts promote the use of women's language by associating it with correctness and politeness. The media, as well as the pharmaceutical industry (chapter two) or institutional settings like university (chapter three), and play a crucial role in the reinforcement of normative gender and sexual identities. Sunderland, in particular, emphasizes the discursive importance of newspapers, which provide "valuable sources of data for the study of gender and language, in part because of their frequent and telling exemplification of sexist language, along with wider stereotypical and normative representations of gender" (Sunderland 2004: 124).

The media, though, could be both a fundamental site of discursive legitimation and of stigmatization of new gender and sexual identities articulated as a consequence of more egalitarian legislation and of societal demands for gender equality. This is in part addressed in chapter ten by **José Santaemilia**, who argues that despite Spain's recent modernisation and adoption of legal measures to ensure respect for all gender/sexual identities, a 'war of words' (Dunant 1994) is still being fought over ideologically endowed terms like abortion or family. An analysis reveals that there is still a long way to go with regards to the recognition of (new) gender and sexual identities. Still, church and right-wing policies are oriented to oppose changes in traditional models of family and human relationships. Legislation, mass media and religious and institutional publications are the sites in which new gender and sexual identities are redefined. This is an arena for the enactment of a fierce battle between reactionary and progressive positions on the recognition of diversity. In particular, this paper exemplifies the harsh negotiations on the meaning of 'homosexual marriage'. The author affirms that studies of gender, sex and language shed light on people's views of modernity, democratization and respect for others.

In the last chapter of this volume, **Pia Pichler** also explores the topic of marriage (arranged marriage) in a group of British Bangladeshi girls. The author adopts a discourse analysis perspective to deal with the role of traditional marriage in popular discourses of culture clash as well as to address academic celebrations of hybrid British Asian femininities. Thus, she focuses on the complex negotiations and contestations of ideas, discourses and subject positions that characterise the spontaneous talk of five Bangladeshi girls from London. If the mass media are a fundamental site of legitimation of ideological positions, spontaneous talk offers these five girls with mixed origins and feelings the opportunity to negotiate new discourses on a topic so sensitive as arranged marriage. They acknowledge their own hybrid identities and embrace a variety of (often contradictory) discourses in their personal transitions from one culture to another.

The papers in this volume will hopefully stimulate further studies in the construction of gender and sexual identities across multiple (and sometimes contradictory) contexts and settings, as well as alert gender and language scholars to the richness and diversity of the endeavour. The eleven contributions gathered here give us a glimpse of the variety of goals, approaches and objectives of those researching gender and language.

References

Austin, J.L. 1962. *How to Do Things with Words*. Oxford: Oxford University Press.

Bergvall, V.L. 1999. "Toward a comprehensive theory of language and gender". *Language and Society* 28: 273-293.

Bing, J.M. and V.L. Bergvall. 1996. "The question of questions: Beyond binary thinking". In *Rethinking Language and Gender Research:*

Theory and Practice. Eds. V.L. Bergvall, J.M. Bing and A.F. Freed. London: Longman, 1-30.

Brown, P. and S. Levinson. 1987. *Politeness: Some Universals of Language Usage*. Cambridge, UK: Cambridge University Press.

Butler, J. 1990. *Gender Trouble*. New York/London: Routledge.

Cameron, D. 1995. "Rethinking language and gender studies: some issues for the 1990s". In *Language and gender: Interdisciplinary perspectives*. Ed. S. Mills. London/New York: Longman, 31-44.

—. 2003. "Gender and Language Ideologies". In *The Handbook of Language and Gender*. Eds. J. Holmes and M. Meyerhoff. Oxford: Blackwell, 447-467.

—. 2005. "Language, gender and sexuality". *Applied Linguistics* 26(4): 482-502.

—. ed. 1998 *The Feminist Critique of Language: A Reader*. London: Routledge. 2nd ed.

Cameron, D. and D. Kulick. 2003. *Language and Sexuality*. Cambridge: Cambridge University Press.

Cameron, D. and D. Kulick, eds. 2006. *The Language and Sexuality Reader*. London/New York: Routledge.

Clatterbaugh, K. 1990. *Contemporary perspectives on masculinity: men, women and politics in modern society*. Washington, DC: Westview Press.

Dunant, S., ed. 1994. *The War of the Words. The Political Correctness Debate*. London: Virago Press.

Eckert, P. and S. McConnell-Ginet. 1992. "Think practically and look locally: Language and gender as community-based practice." *Annual Review of Anthropology* 21: 461-490.

Foucault, M. 1972. *The Archaeology of Knowledge*. London: Tavistock Publications.

Freed, A.F. 1996. "Language and gender research in an experimental setting". In *Rethinking Language and Gender Research: Theory and Practice*. Eds. V.L. Bergvall, J.M. Bing & A.F. Freed. London: Longman, 54-76.

Harvey, K. and C. Shalom, eds. 1997. *Language and Desire: Encoding sex, romance and intimacy*. London/New York: Routledge.

Hellinger, M. and H. Bußman, eds. 2001. *Gender across Languages: The linguistic representation of women and men*. Vol. I. Amsterdam/Philadelphia: John Benjamins.

Holmes, J. 1995. *Women, Men and Politeness*. London: Longman.

—. 2006. *Gendered Talk at Work*. Oxford: Blackwell.

Holmes, J. and M. Stubbe. 2003. ""Feminine" workplaces: Stereotype and reality". In *The Handbook of Language and Gender*. Eds. J. Holmes and M. Meyerhoff. Oxford: Blackwell, 573-599.

Kotthoff, H. and R. Wodak, eds. 1997. *Communicating Gender in Context*. Amsterdam/ Philadelphia: John Benjamins Publishing Co.

Lacan, J. 1968. *The language of the self: the function of language in psychoanalysis* (trans. Anthony Wilden). Baltimore: Johns Hopkins University Press.

Lakoff, R. 1975. *Language and Woman's Place*. New York: Harper & Row.

—. 1990. *The Language War*. Los Angeles/Berkeley: University of California Press.

Mills, S., ed. 1995. *Language and gender: Interdisciplinary perspectives*. London/New York: Longman.

—. 2003. *Gender and Politeness*. Cambridge, UK: Cambridge University Press.

Ruether, R.R. 1998. *Introducing redemption in Christian feminism.* Sheffield, UK: Sheffield Academic Press.

Sadiqi, F. 2003. *Women, Gender and Language in Morocco*. Leiden/Boston: Brill.

Santaemilia, J., ed. 2003. *Género, Lenguaje y Traducción*. Valencia: Universitat de València/Dirección General de la Mujer.

Santaemilia, J., P. Bou, S. Maruenda and G. Zaragoza, eds. 2007. *International Perspectives on Gender and Language*. Valencia: Universitat de València.

Skelton, C. 2001. *Schooling the boys: masculinities and primary education.* Buckingham, UK: Open University Press.

Spencer-Oatey, H. 2000. "Rapport management: A framework for analysis." In *Culturally Speaking: Managing Rapport through Talk across Cultures.* Ed. H. Spencer-Oatey. London: Continuum, 98-120.

Sunderland, J. 2004. *Gendered Discourses*. Houndmills & New York: Palgrave Macmillan.

Talbot, M.M. 2003. "'Women Rule as a Natter of Fact': Reproducing and Challenging Gender Setereotypes". In *Género, Lenguaje y Traducción*. Ed. J. Santaemilia. Valencia: Universitat de València/Dirección General de la Mujer, 26-41.

Weatherall, A. 2002. *Gender, Language and Discourse*. London: Routledge.

CHAPTER ONE

GENDER AND BILINGUALISM: CONNECTING EXPERIENCES AND THEORIES[1]

JOAN PUJOLAR, UNIVERSITAT OBERTA DE CATALUNYA

Abstract: In this paper, I argue for the need to strengthen the connections between Gender and Language studies (henceforth G&L) and other fields of linguistics concerned with forms of social domination, particularly with approaches to bilingualism and multilingualism that examine the role of linguistic diversity in the production and reproduction of inequalities. Gender and language studies have made contributions that are important from a wider linguistic and sociolinguistic perspective; but very few studies have focused so far in connecting gender and bilingualism. Here I begin by briefly exploring the separate historical trajectories of G&L studies and bilingual studies. I reflect in particular about their theoretical and epistemological differences and coincidences. The few studies that have addressed the interrelations between gender and bilingualism show that gender is indeed essential to understand how linguistic difference is mobilized in the reproduction of or resistance against inequalities. Is it possible for bilingual studies to make a comparable contribution to gender studies? In the last section of the paper, I reflect on how this could be so, basically by deconstructing or critiquing received notions of language in a way that is comparable to what gender studies have done with notions such as femininity and masculinity, and also to what G&L studies have addressed in relation to linguistic theory.
Keywords: *Gender and language, bilingualism, post-structuralism, social inequalities, Bakhtin.*

1. Introduction

In this chapter, I make the particular case for the importance of studies of bilingualism and linguistic diversity within gender studies. This is part of a wider agenda to strengthen the connections between studies of Gender and Language (G&L) and other fields of linguistics concerned with forms of social domination. So I am trying to respond to the question: how can bilingual studies contribute to an understanding of gender inequalities?

Up to now, feminist linguistics, gender studies and research on language and gender have contributed significantly to the theoretical development of studies of bilingualism. I believe that this view would be corroborated by most scholars who are mainly associated with bilingual studies but are also sensitive to gender issues: Marilyn Martin-Jones, Monica Heller, Kathryn Woolard, Jacqueline Urla, Susan Ehrlich, Aneta Pavlenko, Ingrid Piller, Kathryn Jones, Susan Gal, Adrian Blackledge, Bonny Norton and many others. Pavlenko, together with Piller, Blackledge, Ehrlich and many others have produced solid and weighty arguments (based on an ever-growing body of research) that studies of bilingualism must necessarily address gender issues (Pavlenko *et al* 2001, Pavlenko 2001: 117-51, Piller and Pavlenko 2004: 489-511). Otherwise the findings and the analyses are going to be biased and shallow, and the social problems addressed never adequately understood, as gender is after all a fundamental axis of social differentiation and categorization in all societies.

However, what do bilingual (or multilingual) studies bring into studies of G&L (or into gender studies more generally)? Simply one more dimension of identity, such as class, ethnicity, race, age? Simply the study of another form of cultural capital amongst others? Simply one more attribute of individuals and groups, such as educational background, physical or intellectual skills, tastes, styles of dress?

In this paper, I intend to argue that studies of bilingualism can make an important contribution to studies of language and gender in more fundamental ways. However, to do this, we must deconstruct not only the notion of identity (as gender studies have successfully achieved); but also the notion of "language" that underpins most linguistic and sociolinguistic research. In linguistics, bilingualism has always been considered a marginal or a deviant phenomenon; but what if it was the norm? What if language was intrinsically hybrid and monolingualism and monologism were artifices? And what would the consequences of this be for the study of gender?

Feminist, women or gender studies have made important contributions to the humanities and the social sciences by uncovering the androcentric assumptions of many social practices, including scientific theories and methodologies. By engaging in a critique of relations of domination, many feminists have also explored the connections between gender inequalities and other forms of inequality, such as race, ethnicity or social class. From this viewpoint, they have contributed to illuminate the ways in which domination operates in subtle ways in different social contexts, including the academic and intellectual world, and not only in relation to gender, but also in a more generic way. Feminist scholarship, in conclusion, proposes new ways to understand and study society. Gender and language studies have also made critical contributions to linguistics and sociolinguistics, often uncovering androcentric practices and biases in these fields. They have also contributed to uncover and analyze subtle communicative and social practices that reveal inequalities between men and women and between different gender and sexuality models in many social contexts.

Here I wish to reflect on what the sociolinguistics of bilingualism can actually contribute to feminism, gender studies and G&L in particular. What do bilingual studies have to say about gender domination? In this paper, I explore these questions through various sociolinguistic studies that address in an integrated way issues of gender and multilingualism. I will finally argue that it is through such studies, which combine various dimensions of social categorization, that gender and language studies can do valuable contributions in the struggle against inequalities. To do so, I will begin with a historical overview of theoretical developments in both fields. This entails a degree of simplification which I hope will be seen as justified.

2. Two parallel histories

Up to the 1990s, the sociolinguistics of gender and bilingualism were following parallel lines, although both were sensitive to general developments within the areas of sociolinguistics, discourse analysis, conversational analysis and pragmatics. There were few exceptions to this "non-connection", such as the studies of Schlieben-Lange (1977: 101-8) and Solé (1978: 29-44). The portrait of studies of language and gender is probably more shared and widely known in the field. The movement from the "deficit" perspective to the "Dominance-versus-difference" debate and the later shift towards "post-structuralism" is traceable in the key works and many articles and book introductions up to the present (Cameron 1992, Pavlenko 2001: 117-51). The evolution of bilingual studies has not been critically analyzed to the same extent (although see Williams 1992), which means that I must bear a great degree of responsibility for the portrayal that follows, which is inspired by ideas developed at the Bilingualism Research Group at Lancaster University in the early 1990s.[2]

I see the trajectory of Gender Studies as having largely revolved around a process of deconstruction of the notions of gender and identity. This has been projected onto many studies analyzing the relationship between gender and bilingualism, which I will briefly review. However, bilingual studies as a field have not been equally forthcoming in questioning the epistemological bases of its objects of study. There have certainly been developments in this direction, mainly through works that deconstruct or displace the notions of language and communicative competence through concepts such as "discourse", "language practices" and "linguistic ideologies" (Woolard 1998: 3-47). However, I believe that there is still the need to reflect more explicitly about what language is and what languages (in plural) are. In this paper, I sketch some ideas as to how this could be done, basically by adopting Bakhtin's (1981, 1986) dialogic perspective.

Studies of Gender and Language are said to begin with the publication of "Language and woman's place" (Lakoff 1975). It was later framed as the "deficit perspective" because it portrayed women's talk as "tentative", "unassertive", as lacking necessary features of mature conversational participants. Later contributors argued that women's features of talk in sex-mixed conversations reflected their inferior position, their status as "dominated" individuals in relation to men. Fishman (1983) observed that many women took peripheral roles in conversation, just providing support for those who were playing leading roles, which were almost always men. At the same time, other researchers sought to build a more comprehensive view of women's talk, particularly in single-sex situations. They drew ideas from contemporary studies on cross-cultural communication, as was the case of Maltz and Borker (1982), who were inspired by Gumperz' approach to bilingualism and communicative competence. It was termed as the "difference" or the "subcultural" approach, as it tended to portray women's forms of talk as simply different, but equally valid, to that of men (Coates and Cameron 1992, Tannen 1984). Critiques to the dominance approach centered on the fact that it problematized women's identities, and implied recognition of men's ways as the norm. The difference approach was critiqued because it reportedly obscured the social domination and deprivation imposed on women. Of course, the dichotomy was useful as a way of triggering programmatic debates; but the two approaches were not mutually exclusive: after all, domination cannot unproblematically be inferred from particular instances of social interaction, and difference does not exclude taking on board issues of domination (Cameron 1992, Uchida 1992: 547-68). To these studies, a fourth strand deserves mentioning, which are the studies on "sexist language," which tended to focus on the asymmetrical forms of representation of men and women in texts.

Cameron (1992) provides a pointed critique of analyses that focus merely on content analyses and issues of representation in texts without considering the ways in which these texts are used or appropriated in particular social contexts. Her book on "Feminism and linguistic theory" provided a very thorough theoretical assessment of this earlier period of Gender and Language Studies. She argued convincingly that the problem lied in structuralist assumptions that took language as a system whose meanings are independent from their use in society. In this way, one ended up with deterministic readings of theories such as the Sapir/Whorf hypothesis or the Lacanian psychoanalytic approach; or conversely, with the naive idea that gender discrimination may be solved just by purifying language from sexist modes of expression, or even by making women speak in an assertive style (Cameron 1992). On the other hand, the alternative is to assume that language use reflects social structure in an unmediated way and, therefore, that "everything about women's behavior can be traced simply to their subordination" (ibid: 73).

The latest period of Gender and Language studies has been widely characterized as "post-structuralist." As Pavlenko (2001) describes it, the new perspective incorporates the fundamental principle that language (as practice) or discourse is the constitutive locus of social organization, identity and power. As the term indicates, the foucaultian notion of discourse is important here, although it gets significantly qualified by the methodological commitment to "context" and "situatedness." To this "paradigm" follows the idea that identities are constructed through language and discourse, which means that language does not "reflect" gender; but rather the opposite, that gender emerges out of language use and discursive practice. Butler's (1990) idea that "identity is performatively constituted by the very 'expressions' that are said to be its results" has provided a powerful metaphorical elaboration for this principle, which has had a wide impact beyond the field too. Connell's (1987) work on the diversity of gender models and their interrelations has provided further depth to the analysis, and it has allowed G&L researchers to detach themselves from gender stereotypes in a definitive way (see Goodwin 1990, Thorne 1993). Within the field itself, the focus on context has led to the elaboration of the concept of "communities of practice" (Eckert and McConnell-Ginet 1999), which allows the reconceptualization of the notion of speech community in a way that emphasizes its situatedness, the contingency of its boundaries and its constructed character. Ethnographers in particular have also become convinced of the need to attend to the construction of multiple identities in social interaction, what Eckert & McConnell-Ginet (1999) also call "co-construction". The idea is that gender is never constructed in isolation from other axes of social relations such as class, ethnicity, age, etc. This resonates on earlier literature on the relevance of feminism for minority women, and it has provided the necessary ground to justify –amongst other things- the interrelations between gender and bilingual practices.

Finally, researchers in the field have kept their interest in social frameworks that might help to adequately conceptualize relationships of domination. In the later years, we find increasing reference (both explicit and implicit) to the ideas of Pierre Bourdieu on linguistic markets, which became widely available when they were translated into English in 1991. From this perspective, gender inequalities are conceptualized in terms of struggles over access to material and symbolic resources, as well as struggles over the legitimization of different forms of cultural and symbolic capital (Bucholtz 2007, Pujolar 2001). One of our present challenges is precisely the need to find ways of connecting our contextualized analyses of situated practices with the wider processes that respond to the logic of Bourdieu's markets.

Research on bilingualism also has a departure point with a conception of identity as fixed and stable, and with an interpretation of language practices as an expression of this identity. In so far as bilingualism has focused mainly on the spaces of contact between institutionalized linguistic varieties (i.e. languages), its main focus has been on language and ethnicity, and on the significance of language in the construction of national identity (e.g. Fishman 1999). The earliest studies were based on structural-functional sociology, which assumed that language contact had to be associated with the functional distribution of language varieties (e.g. diglossia) (Fishman 1967, Fishman 1972). Sociolinguistic ethnographers, however, developed a more complex picture and realized that bilingual speakers made subtle, creative uses of their "linguistic repertoire" (Blom and Gumperz 1972). Thus Gumperz (1982) proposed the study of bilingualism as a "discourse strategy" that could be analyzed from a variety of pragmatic, discursive and conversational analytic perspectives. Attention to context was therefore an important component of studies of bilingualism, particularly of ethnographic ones. The move towards a post-structuralist outlook that incorporates a political economic perspective was anticipated by the work of Gal (1979) and Woolard (1985) and became consolidated with the formulation of a program to examine "linguistic ideologies " (Woolard 1998) and Heller's work on linguistic minorities and modernity (Heller 1999, Heller and Martin-Jones 2001). Issues of gender are also increasingly incorporated into the analyses, particularly in the case of sociolinguistic ethnographers and linguistic anthropologists (see Martin-Jones and Jones 2000).

Despite the different theoretical and methodological orientations, the sociolinguistics of bilingualism has developed an important point of consensus, namely that bilingualism is an expression of the constitutive sociolinguistic stratification of human societies, as well as an important resource for individual creative expression. From his earlier work, Fishman (1972) had already argued that all societies presented forms of linguistic differentiation that could be amenable to functional analysis: different linguistic varieties were spoken even where only a single language was recognized. Researchers of code-switching went further by arguing that bilingual discourse (code-switching, code-mixing, transfer) presented elements of structuration that showed the ability of speakers to use their linguistic resources in ways that formal linguistics could not account for. What these earlier studies were doing was to cast doubts on the monolingual assumptions of linguistics, and to question the legitimacy of the traditional ideologies that served to legitimate monolingual nation states. A certain deconstruction of linguistics was under way.

There has been therefore a convergence between studies of bilingualism and of gender and language in some aspects, particularly in the advances triggered by context-driven, situated, ethnographic studies that often lead to question received ideas about language.

Language and gender studies	Bilingual studies	Timing
Biologically-based categorizations	Structural-functionalism	1970s
The perspectives of: Deficit Domination Difference	Code-switching Language choice as an "act of identity"	1980s-90s
Post-structuralist approaches	The political economy of bilingualism	1990s-00s

Table 1-1: The convergence between language and gender studies and bilingual studies

3. Gender, bilingualism and context

Most publications that address issues of both gender and bilingualism stem from the mid nineties. I am only going to provide a brief overview of their results. There are excellent research reviews by Pavlenko (2001), Piller and Pavlenko (2004), Sunderland (2000) and others. To me, there are three main aspects that these studies document in a rich and inspiring way:

A: Men/Society imposes restrictions on women's access to (BL) linguistic capital

In many communities, women are denied access to the social spaces where particular forms of linguistic capital are developed. The most obvious restriction is to deny or restrict access to schooling, and hence prevent women from learning official languages, languages of religious significance or other prestigious varieties, as may happen in some Quechua communities (Harvey 1994) or amongst the Nahualt (Hill 1987). Women can also have difficulties to learn more languages, dialects or language varieties if their mobility is restricted or they are not allowed to talk with outsiders, as can happen in rural Georgia (Chinchaladze and Dragadze 1994) or in the rural Maghrib (Sadiqi 2003). Of course, in some circumstances, women themselves may develop self-restrictive practices, as happened in Goldstein's (1995) factory in Toronto, where female workers controlled each others' use of English. Some profiles of immigrant women, particularly those that accompany a migrant husband, characteristically suffer from isolation and from tight controls within their own communities, which makes it very difficult for them to learn the language of the host society (Norton 2000).

B: Women's (BL) linguistic capital is devaluated/delegitimized

Women may be constructed as monolingual simply because their competence in other languages is ignored or considered worthless, as happened again in Harvey's Quechua women who tried to use Spanish in formal public meetings. However, when women are bilingual or multilingual, it is not extraordinary that this is regarded negatively as suspicious, demeaning or contaminating, as in cases where women somehow mediate between their community's men and the majority community or its institutions. Tomkin (1994) mentions such roles amongst Native American communities, as well as amongst the English working classes. In Britain, Bangladeshi women who are literate in Bengali are treated as illiterate by educators, and their literacy practices are not considered relevant to the education of their children (Blackledge 2000). It seems as if women present always the "wrong" type of bilingual competence, whatever it is. As McDonald points out, "the power and center of definition always lies elsewhere" (1994: 102).

C: Women construct their subjectivities creatively through their (BL) linguistic repertoire

As Norton (2000) and Pavlenko (2001) argue, bilingual communities offer individuals and groups different types of subject positions connected with each of the varieties or with particular bilingual styles. One such position is typically that of the child-rearer that is supposed to be responsible for the cultural reproduction of the community. Women have been found to negotiate these expectations in different ways. In some rural contexts, they have been found to actively encourage language shift by raising the children (and girls in particular) in the dominant language so that they escape the difficult social conditions in which they live, as Gal (1978) found amongst Hungarian-speaking peasants in Austria, McDonald (1994) amongst Breton speakers in France or Constantinidou (1994) amongst Gaelic speakers in Scotland. In other cases, women resist language shift as in rural Georgia (Chinchaladze and Dragadze 1994) or amongst the Sámi in Finland (Huss 1999). Another interesting aspect is the ways in which some language education policies target specifically immigrant women so that they become agents of cultural change in their communities, by teaching the majority language to their children and adopt local forms of house management. Such policies often meet with various forms of passive and active resistance (Cleghorn 2000, Pavlenko 2005: 275-297). The experience of second language learning can also be markedly different for men and women in different contexts, and influence the learning process quite considerably (Pavlenko *et al* 2001).

4. Deconstructing languages

So far we have seen some of the ways in which issues of gender and bilingualism come together in ways that can help us understand multilingualism better and in ways that reveal aspects of gender inequality that are tied to linguistic diversity. Now I would like to focus on the implications of this research for the way in which we conceptualize language, and languages, as such.

First, it is interesting to note that research on gender and language has been historically more prone than bilingual studies to raise fundamental questions about language as an object of study. Both fields have recognized the universal character of linguistic differentiation, as is shown in Gal's 30-year-old quote: "Sexual differentiation of speech is expected to occur whenever a social division exists between the roles of men and women – that is, universally" (1978: 292). Another meeting point has to do with the explanatory power of notions such as "situatedness", "context" or "activity." Sociolinguists have also regarded "situations" as explaining language or register switching. However, in gender studies, "situatedness" has been used to address more fundamental questions, as when Philips says: "Gender differences in language use are often a reflection of such differences in activity and are associated with the activity rather than the gender" (1987: 7).

This awareness leads to a questioning of the research object itself: what is then gender? How does it connect with language? This is the step that researchers on bilingualism very rarely make in an explicit way, even when the principle of "situatedness" obviously clashes with the notion of language derived from Saussure and Chomsky, where a language is by definition everything that is not linked to *parole* or performance. The necessary issue to address begins therefore by Tomkin's question: "What is a language? And how different must language varieties be for us to talk of bilingualism?" (1994: 186). The first attempt in this direction can be found in Cameron (1992), when she tries to conceptualize language in a way that is relevant to the issues addressed in language and gender studies:

> The social practice of language-using is not defined simply by the act of speaking (or writing or signing). Nor is it completely defined by the structures of the language itself, though these do bear on it. What most crucially defines this social practice, I would argue, is the act of addressing someone, in some context, for some purpose. (Cameron 1992: 186)

If structuralist linguistics was very much about erasing context from language, and hence erasing any connection between language and social issues, then how can one address gender through linguistics? How can one address bilingualism through linguistics? Variationist sociolinguistics sought to solve the contradiction by using statistical calculations, which is what makes Eckert and McConnell-Ginet's statement most revealing.

> The more fundamental problem is that, if we search for patterns in language data unconnected to the practices of particular communities, we can at best get correlational information, and can never offer explanatory accounts. Such practices typically are relevant not only to gender, but at the same time to other aspects of social identity and other relations (1999: 190).

Bilingual studies have only recently sought to question the discipline's fundamental categories. And except for Makoni and Pennycook's (2007) most recent book, the most explicit attempts have come precisely from studies that combine issues of bilingualism and gender, such as Pavlenko (2001) or Pavlenko and Piller (2004):

> While the term 'language' assumes a chain of signs without a subject, produced and seen from an 'objective' position or from nowhere in particular, 'discourse' as 'practices which form the objects of which they speak' (…) involves human beings as agents operating in specific contexts. (Pavlenko, 2001: 121)

> Feminist post-structuralist approaches (…) cease to view language as a set of disembodied structures. Instead, language becomes the locus of social organization, power, individual consciousness, and a form of symbolic capital (…) "a situated process of participation in multiple and overlapping communities of practice. (Pavlenko and Piller, 2004: 492)

Pavlenko and Piller point to the need to develop an idea of language that accounts for the processes of articulation of subjectivity, for the fact that language practices are productive of representations and social relations, and hence intrinsically ideological. Although some studies on bilingualism had pointed out that language choice often responded to the negotiation of social relationships (Scotton 1988), an explicit development of a discursive, constructive and critical conception of language practices had not been developed. Thus, this critical appraisal of the epistemology of linguistics is much more recent in bilingual studies than in gender studies. Most of the quotations presented so far come from introductory comments of books, chapters or articles, except for the case of Cameron (1992) and Makoni and Pennycook (2007). This means that a fully developed theoretical and methodological framework, such as is found in structural linguistics and Variationism, is not yet available. In the last decades, discourse studies have broadened the scope of our research beyond grammar and linguistic structure to include content analysis, ideas from pragmatics and conversational analysis. However, this has been done in a tentative and intuitive way through eclectic practices that integrated concepts and procedures from different traditions. As a result, fundamental theoretical and epistemological questions have not been addressed in depth. In relation to bilingualism, for example, we still do not know how languages and linguistic varieties can be inscribed in a discursive perspective, which means that the very notion of "bilingualism" remains fairly undefined and used with many different meanings. But, if languages

were not really what structuralism made of them, what would they be?
Why are they significant categories for speakers? Why are they the object
of so many struggles socially?

I shall not pretend to have a ready answer to these questions, of course.
But I would like to make some contributions to developing these ideas.
Makoni and Pennycook (2007) have observed how the concept of "a
language" from linguistics has been used as a form of control over
colonized populations as colonial powers delegitimized the cultural
practices that did not fit the programs of "development" and
"modernization." But, do we have any way to register and conceive of
language practices that is not inscribed in this paradigm? Can we analyze
utterances in ways that must not draw upon the traditional categories of
linguistics, always based on formal criteria? I believe that such alternative
linguistics is not yet available, despite the interesting attempts of Harris
(1990), Yngve (2004) and others. It is from this viewpoint that I wish to
suggest that Bakhtin's dialogical conception of language can provide the
basis for a post-structuralist linguistics.

5. Dialogical linguistics

Bakhtin's works created quite a stir when the English translations
appeared in the early 1980s (Bakhtin 1981, 1986), particularly in literary
studies and sociolinguistics up to the 1990s. Now this interest seems to
have died down without leaving a significant imprint in linguistics. In my
view, this is due to the fact that it is difficult to insert his principles within
our own analytical practices and traditions. Some authors have made
attempts in this direction that have not attracted much attention (see
Moraes 1996, Pujolar 2001 and Woolard 2004). In this section, I will
reflect on the implications of some of Bakhtin's ideas to theorize the
spaces of contact between studies of bilingualism and gender.

The fundamental idea of Bakhtin's linguistic thought is expressed
through the notion of "dialogism", which he described in the following
way:

> (...) any utterance, in addition to its own theme, always responds ... in one
> form or another to others' utterances that precede it... The utterance is
> addressed not only to its own object, but also to others' speech about it...
> But the utterance is related not only to preceding, but also to subsequent
> links in the chain of speech communion... [T]he utterance is constructed by
> taking into account possible responsive reactions, for whose sake, in
> essence, it is actually created. (Bakhtin, 1986: 94)

Dialogism means that language is inherently responsive and this that it acquires value, or meaning, only in the context where it is produced. As I see it, this idea is what opens up the possibility of a post-structuralist linguistics. One important implication of dialogism is that subjectivity emerges in ways that are intrinsically ambivalent and dispersed within the utterance. For Bakhtin, "Each utterance is filled with echoes and reverberations of other utterances to which it is related by the communality of the sphere of speech communication." (Bakhtin, 1986: 91). The utterance is therefore hybrid by definition, as it "is filled with "'others' words, varying degrees of other-ness and varying degrees of 'our-"own-ness'" (ibid.: 89). The speaking subject assimilates, reworks and re-accentuates these words and voices which we take from others, from the environmental dialogue (Bakhtin, 1986: 89). The speaker manipulates the voices thus incorporated and constructs and negotiates her relationship with the different subjectivities that make up the utterance, which does not form a unified voice.

Another fundamental tenet of traditional linguistics that Bakhtin questions is the separation between form and content: "Form and content in discourse are one, once we understand that verbal discourse is a social phenomenon" (1981: 259).

Thus, for Bakhtin, linguistic form and content converge in the utterance. They become inseparably linked to context and to the subjectivities, representations and social relationships that they contribute to construct. This is what shapes speech genres, and what explains the "heteroglossic" character of language.

Genres are "relatively stable types" (*ibidem* 60) of utterance that can be described in terms of both content (a particular range of topics, a particular ideological perspective) and form (length, intonation, compositional structure). Genres become associated to the situations and forms of expression of different social groups:

> Society, in fact, is always linguistically diverse, stratified or heteroglossic. The social stratification of language is parallel to the diversity of social groups (classes, generations, professions, groups of friends, etc.). As each social group is associated with particular activities, social relations and ideologies, each develops its own speech genres which, at the same time, gradually fashion differentiated accents, styles, dialects and languages. (Pujolar 1995)

Thus, linguistic varieties emerge out of complex repertoires of speech genres, and they involve not only formal features but also ideologies.

How these principles may be applied to particular research projects and to concrete analytical needs may not be directly obvious. At present, we have got used to the idea that the significance of a particular linguistic or discursive feature must be anchored to a context; but we still feel safer when we use purely formal criteria to identify these features (be they phonemes, adjacency pairs, languages or some ideational configurations). We would not know how to frame their association with a "genre" and why we should do so. For one thing, we should need to know what a genre exactly is from a dialogical perspective, and not only conceptually but also methodologically, that is, how to operationalize it in research practice.

What I shall attempt here is to explore some of the ways in which dialogism can be relevant to the study of gender identities. Ideas from Bakhtin and Voloshinov (or the Bakhtin Circle) often crop up in many studies, and the work of Kristeva has been very influential amongst Critical Discourse Analysts (Fairclough 1992). Jean Mills' observations in her study of Punjabi mothers in Britain are a good example:

> In Bakhtinian terms, subjectivity is social in nature, since individuals only come to understand themselves through interaction with others. (...) speakers signaled through a dialogue with themselves, or by reporting the words of others, that they had come to terms with, or were coming to terms with, a significant aspect of themselves. (Mills 2004: 168)

In my own research, I have shown how particular forms of linguistic alternation clearly reveal a juxtaposition of genres that are connected with different speaking subjects and social locations. The following extract comes from an interview to a Catalan young woman (italics express a switch from Catalan to Spanish):

Patrícia: es una escola de pago • i el curs val unaa- • tot el any • són unes
It is a private school. And the course costs a-, for the whole year, it's about

cent mi- • quasi doscentes mil peles • *lo pagas a codo- cómodos*
a hundred th- almost two hundred thousand ptes. *You pay in cof-comfortable*

plazos dee ochoo o diez mil pelas al mes però • • però són deu bitllets [pica a la taula, somriu]
***installments oof eeight or ten thousand ptas. per month* but, • but it's ten papers! [She knocks the table and smiles].**
(Extracted from Pujolar, 2001)

Here Patricia expresses her stance in relation to the payment of a training course. Her own voice is represented in colloquial Catalan; but she also incorporates an institutional voice that draws from phraseology of marketing in Spanish. Here the two voices do not only mark a topical change, but also two differing ideological perspectives, subject positions and networks of relations. In Catalan there is the woman who must struggle to earn money for her and her family; in Spanish she is the client seen from the perspective of a bureaucratic organization that constructs subjects in terms of their financial capabilities. Each voice brings in its own criteria of evaluation and it is the speaking subject that organizes the narrative in a way that establishes, in this context, which voice is given more validity. The narrative is therefore not just a representation; but constitutes also a claim for the legitimacy of a particular discursive formation over another. The hybrid character of the segment is made obvious by the easily perceivable contrast between Catalan and Spanish; but it would also apply to a context where just one institutionalized language of reference would be used. The utterance could also be seen as revealing a form of resistance to the social position of the speaking subject, who lacks the resources to access a particular mode of education. Thus a connection with social structures and inequalities is also possible, although more contextual elements should be brought into the picture.

There is, in any case, another example from a text by Jean Mills that provides an even clearer indication of the ideological underpinnings of linguistic varieties. The narrative is similar in many aspects; but more explicit. It is an interview transcript of a Punjabi woman that reflects on the fact that her duty as mother involves the passing of religion onto the children and that this must be done in Urdu:

> One of the things, one that we are taught in Islam or in Urdu, that heaven is at the foot of the mother, mother's feet… so, respect your mother and your life after will be, you know, rewarded and so on. Now if you say that to them in English. 'Son, heaven is at your mother's feet', they just look at you and say 'Mom are you alright?' sort of thing because it just doesn't make any sense to them… I know you can say it in English but it doesn't seem to have the same meaning (extract from Mills 2004: 180)

Now the interview turned to a discussion about translation. However, what is interesting here is the fact that the speaker represents her challenge in terms of a dialogue with her child where she would adopt the voice or the genre of the scripture (Urdu translated into English) whereas her son is represented through a markedly colloquial English turn of phrase that bespeaks a juvenile skepticism. The juxtaposition of the two genres is meant to deliver the effect of their ideological incompatibility. On the one hand, the translated Urdu text that draws legitimacy from its historical location in generations and networks of Punjabi texts inserted in particular spiritual and socioeconomic practices. On the other hand, the voice of English youth that does not have a "mother", but a "mom"; and whose spiritual commitment will be probably leaned towards a realistic empiricism only qualified by his participation in fantasies delivered and legitimized by transnational cultural industries and local peer-groups. What is obvious here is that the problem is not the "linguistic" aspect of translation; but the fact that the two voices draw from differing sources of legitimacy, they connect with different conversations, different textual-ideological practices. The mother's challenge is how she can create a space for Punjabi/Urdu social practices for a son that largely leads an English life.

This is where the important message comes. Language varieties are not simply made up of linguistic features; they are made up of complex sets of genres that incorporate formal and ideological elements in an inextricable way. They are made up of verbal-ideological material, whose value or expressive potential is anchored not only in context, but also in history. The choice between different linguistic varieties involves a choice between different historical trajectories of complex networks of dialogues and voices, real and fictitious, from different speaking subjects. The utterance is always a meeting point, or a collision point, of these trajectories in which the speaker seeks to construct a position according to her interests. All language varieties are anchored in particular contexts and social subjects constituted by ideological struggles and inequalities; they carry with them the dialogical relationships that draw upon their own sources of legitimacy.

Thus, linguistic varieties are more than simple tools for communication that can be mastered better or worse. They are also more than abstract capital assets, whose value fluctuates according to the dynamics of each market. They are also the very sites where ideologies acquire and lose their legitimacy. Linguistic diversity is therefore a necessary outcome of a world where different human groups and subgroups within them construct differing forms of social relationships and identities, and enjoy differing forms of access to resources and power. And not only this; but also a world where social subjects draw from their inherited linguistic resources, through which they reproduce and transform inherited social structures.

In this context, we can begin to hypothesize what languages are from a dialogical perspective. Languages, as traditionally understood, are hegemonic varieties anchored in the ideological legitimacy of particular genres and social practices. Hegemonic languages "rule" over a complex and unstable range of other varieties with which it can share (or not) many resources and with which it engages in many forms of relationships. Varieties are not systematically differentiated from each other; but normally have ample spaces of overlap unless a given social group has interest in constructing and maintaining their boundaries.

As Bourdieu pointedly observes, the acquisition of hegemonic languages does not automatically accord legitimacy to those who speak them. The legitimacy derives from the recognition accorded to particular groups to assume the expected subject positions and to perform the legitimate genres and to reproduce their constitutive ideologies in particular contexts and moments. Individuals, moreover, need not and usually do not acquire or use a single variety; but a range of them. As we have seen, language diversity can appear within single hybrid utterances in the negotiation of conflicts and contradictions. However, speakers have to grapple with the ideological implications and the material consequences of using various languages. The language skills, their associated ideologies and sanctions are, in any case, inscribed in embodied dispositions that constitute what Bourdieu calls the linguistic habitus.

The implications of this dialogical outlook of languages for gender studies can be profound and manifold. Here I shall merely attempt some brief reflections that connect with the studies of bilingualism and gender. To some extend, it involves rephrasing some of the questions addressed in these fields. The question is not to wonder why women always speak the wrong variety. Rather, we can ask ourselves about the character and dynamics of the conflict between women's languages, on the one hand, and publicly legitimized (typically masculine) varieties, on the other; and we can also explore the role of these varieties in the production and legitimization of traditional femininities and masculinities.

Thus, studies combining a focus on gender and bilingualism could document women's appropriation of formerly masculinized varieties (i.e. their genres, ideologies and identities), a process that bespeaks women's assumption of roles and relationships traditionally associated with men. This creates incongruences between historically constituted linguistic and social categorizations: women who take up roles and forms of expression traditionally associated to men. A classical example would be the debates on assertivity amongst women (Cameron 1995).

In a way, the experience of women and men connected with non-hegemonic gender identities involves the negotiation of dualities, the need to make contradictory ideologies compatible. From a (dialogic) linguistic perspective, this could be a kind of conflictive bilingualism in so far as it places the subject between two polarized position, that is, positions that are defined one in opposition to the other. The experience of this tension can only be recognized and negotiated if we adopt a critical outlook over linguistic and social processes. That is, if we recognize that any established order is unstable in a context in which some social groups strive to maintain it while others seek to dismantle it or redefine it. And also if we recognize the ample scope for ambivalence and negotiation that exists in social practices in relation to meaning. If, on the contrary, we conceive of language and subjectivity on the basis of closed, essentializing categories independent form context, it is impossible to understand how people mobilize their linguistic resources to achieve their expressive projects, projects not necessarily inscribed in a pre-manufactured linguistic code. Actually, one aspect that explains and enables ambivalence is the multiplicity of unpredictable combinations of different dimensions of social belonging (class, race, age, profession), with their accompanying subjectivities, patterns of relationship and modes of expression.

Thus, studies of bilingualism or –more properly speaking– heteroglossia should recognize this open character of language in a way similar to what studies of gender have done with its definitory concept. Of course, there will always be the danger to slide into an anecdotal and socially innocuous relativism that is contented with simply documenting forms of expression and gender models without reference to the power relations that constitute them. This danger shall always be there; but I believe it is necessary to recognize the open character of both gender and language if we wish to understand by whom, how and when they get closed down to result in structures of domination.

It may well be that, seen from this dialogical perspective, researchers of bilingualism do not recognize their object of study any more, as the discipline is genealogically linked to attempts to sustain the boundedness and legitimacy of institutionalized languages, and particularly of minority languages in front of dominant languages. Probably, researchers on bilingualism have a natural mistrust for approaches that resonate with relativism because the unbalances of power between dominant and dominated languages are very visible. Maybe this mistrust can also be useful to gender studies, in order to develop a post-structuralist outlook that does not bypass the problem of hegemony.

Notes

[1] I am grateful to Josep-Anton Fernàndez for his comments to an earlier draft of this paper.

[2] Many of the ideas henceforth exposed on bilingual studies owe much to the teachings of Marilyn Martin-Jones, although the responsibility for the final shape that they take in this article, particularly the shortcomings, must naturally fall on the author.

References

Bakhtin, M. 1981. *The Dialogic Imagination*. Austin: University of Texas Press.

—. 1986. *Speech Genres and Other Late Essays*. Austin: University of Texas Press.

Blackledge, A. 2000. "Power relations and the social construction of 'literacy'and 'illiteracy'. The experience of Bangladeshi women in Birmingham." In *Multilingual Literacies: reading and writing different worlds*. Ed. by M. Martin-Jones and K. Jones. Amsterdam: John Benjamins, 55-70.

Blom, J.P. and J. Gumperz. 1972. "Social meaning in linguistic structures: code-switching in Norway." In *Directions in Sociolinguistics: the Ethnography of Communication*. Ed. by J. Gumperz and D. Hymes. New York: Holt, Rinehart and Winston Inc., 407-434.

Bucholtz, M. 2007. "Shop talk: Branding, consumption, and gender in white middle-class youth interaction." In *Words, Worlds, and Material Girls: Language, Gender, Globalized Economy*. Ed. by B. McElhinny. Berlin: Mouton de Gruyter, 371-402.

Butler, J. P. 1990. *Gender Trouble: Feminism and the Subversion of Identity*. New York: Routledge.

Cameron, D. 1992. *Feminism and Linguistic Theory*. London: The Macmillan Press Ltd.

—. 1995. *Verbal Hygiene*. London: Routledge.

Chinchaladze, N. and T. Dragadze. 1994. "Women and Second-Language Knowledge in Rural Societ Georgia: An Outline." In *Bilingual Women: Anthropological Approaches to Second-Language Use*. Ed. by P. Burton, K. Dyson and S. Ardener. Oxford/Providence: Berg Publishers, 80-84.

Cleghorn, L. 2000. *Valuing English: An Ethnography of a Federal Language Training Program for Adult Immigrants*. University of Toronto Master of Arts.

Coates, J. and D. Cameron. 1992. *Women in their Speech Communities: New perspectives on Language and Sex*. London: Longman.

Connell, R. 1987. *Gender and Power*. Cambridge: Polity Press and Basil Blackwell.

Constantinidou, E. 1994. "The 'Death' of East Sutherland Gaelic: Death by Women?" In *Bilingual Women: Anthropological Approaches to Second-Language Use*. Ed. by P. Burton, K. Dyson and S. Ardener. Oxford/Providence: Berg Publishers, 111-127.

Eckert, P. and S. McConnell-Ginet. 1999. "New generalizations and explanations in language and gender research." *Language in Society* 28. 185-201.

Fairclough, N. 1992. *Discourse and Social Change*. Cambridge: Polity Press.

Fishman, J. 1967. "Bilingualism with and without diglossia: Diglossia with and without bilingualism." *Journal of Social Issues* 23: 29-38.

—. 1972. "The relationship between micro- and macro-linguistics in the study of who speaks what to whom and when." In *Language in Sociocultural Change*. Ed. by A. Dil. Stanford: Stanford University Press, 244-267.

—. 1999. *Handbook of Language and Ethnic Identity*. New York: Oxford University Press.

Fishman, P. 1983. "Interaction: the Work Women Do." In *Language, Gender and Society*. Ed. by B. Thorne, C. Kramarae and N. Henley. Rowley, Massachussets: Newbury House, 89-101.

Gal, S. 1978. "Peasant men Can't get wives: Language change and sex roles in a bilingual community." *Language in Society* 7: 1-16.

—. 1979. *Language shift*. New York: Academic Press.

Goldstein, T. 1995. "Nobody is Talking Bad: Creating Community and Claiming Power on the Production Lines." In *Gender Articulated: Language and the Socially Constructed Self*. Ed. by K. Hall and M. Bucholtz. New York: Routledge, 375-400.

Goodwin, M. 1990. *She-Said-he-Said. Talk as Social Organisation among Black Children*. Bloomington and Indianapolis: Indiana University Press.

Gumperz, J. J. 1982. *Discourse Strategies*. Cambridge: Cambridge University Press.

Harris, R. 1990. "On Redefining Linguistics." In *Redefining Linguistics*. Ed. by H. Davis and R. Harris. London: Routledge, 18-52.

Harvey, P. 1994. "The Presence and Absence of Speech in the Communication of Gender." In *Bilingual Women: Anthropological*

Approaches to Second-Language Use. Ed. by P. Burton, K. Dyson and S. Ardener. Oxford/Providence: Berg Publishers, 44-64.

Heller, M. 1999. *Linguistic Minorities and Modernity: A Sociolinguistic Ethnography*. London: Longman.

Heller, M. and M. Martin-Jones. 2001. *Voices of Authority. Education and Linguistic Difference*. Westport, Connecticut: Ablex publishing.

Hill, J. 1987. "Women's speech in modern Mexicano." In *Language, Gender and Sex in Comparative Perspective*. Ed. by S. Philips, S. Steele and C. Tanz. Cambridge: Cambridge University Press, 121-160.

Huss, L. 1999. *Reversing Language Shift in the Far North: Linguistic Revitalization in Northern Scandinavia and Finland*. Uppsala: University of Uppsala.

Lakoff, R. 1975. *Language in Women's Place*. New York: Harper & Row.

Makoni, S. and A. Pennycook. 2007. "Disinventing and Reconstituting Languages." In *Disinventing and Reconstituting Languages*. Ed. by S. Makoni and A. Pennycook. Clevedon: Multilingual Matters, 1-41.

Maltz, D. and R. Borker. 1982. "A Cultural Approach to Male-female Miscommunication." In *Language and Social Identity*. Ed. by J. Gumperz. Cambridge: Cambrdige University Press, 196-216.

Martin-Jones, M. and K. Jones. 2000. *Multilingual Literacies: reading and writing different worlds*. Amsterdam: John Benjamins.

McDonald, M. 1994. "Women and Linguistic Innovation in Brittany." In *Bilingual Women: Anthropological Approaches to Second-Language Use*. Ed. by P. Burton, K. Dyson and S. Ardener. Oxford/Providence: Berg Publishers, 85-110.

Mills, J. 2004. "Mothers and Mother Tongue: Perspectives on Self-construction by Mothers of Pakistani Heritage." In *Negotiation of Identities in Multilingual Contexts*. Ed. by A. Pavlenko and A. Blackledge, 161-191. Clevedon: Multilingual Matters, 161-191.

Moraes, M. 1996. *Bilingual Education: a Dialogue with the Bakhtin Circle*. Albany, NY: SUNY Press.

Norton, B. 2000. *Identity and language learning: gender, ethnicity and educational change*. Harlow: Longman. Harlow: Longman.

Pavlenko, A. 2001. "Bilingualism, gender and ideology." *International Journal of Bilingualism* 5: 117-51.

—. 2005. "'Ask each pupil about her methods of cleaning': Ideologies of language and gender in americanization instruction." *International Journal of Bilingual Education and Bilingualism* 8: 275-297.

Pavlenko, A., A. Blackledge, I. Piller and M. Teutsch-Dwyer. 2001. *Multilingualism, Second Language Learning, and Gender*. Berlin.: Mouton de Gruyter.

Piller, I. and A. Pavlenko. 2004. "Bilingualism and gender." In *Handbook of Bilingualism*. Ed. by T. Bhatia and W. Ritchie. Oxford: Blackwell, 489-511.

Pujolar, J. 1995. *The identities of "La Penya". The Voices and Struggles of Young Working-Class People in Barcelona*. Lancaster: University of Lancaster PhD.

—. 2001. *Gender, Heteroglossia, and Power: a sociolinguistic study of youth culture*. Berlin: Walter de Gruyter.

Sadiqi, F. 2003. *Women, Gender and Language in Morocco*. Leiden: Brill.

Schlieben-Lange, B. 1977. "The language situation in southern France". *Linguistics* 19: 101-8.

Scotton, C. 1988. "Codeswitching as indexical of social negotiations." In *Codeswitching. Anthropological and Sociolinguistic Perspectives*. Ed. by M. Heller. Berlin: Mouton de Gruyter, 151-186.

Solé, Y. 1978. "Sociocultural and sociopsychological factors in differential language rettentiveness by sex." *International Journal of the Sociology of Language* 17: 29-44.

Sunderland, J. 2000. "Issues of language and gender in second and foreign language learning." *Language Teaching* 33: 203-23.

Tannen, D. 1984. *Conversational Style: Analyzing Talk among Friends*. Norwood, NJ: Ablex.

Thorne, B. 1993. *Gender Play. Girls and Boys in School*. Buckingham: Open University Press.

Tomkin, E. 1994. "Engendering Language Difference." In *Bilingual Women: Anthropological Approaches to Second-Language Use*. Ed. by P. Burton, K. Dyson and S. Ardener. Oxford/Providence: Berg Publishers, 186-192.

Uchida, A. 1992. "When 'difference' is dominance: A critique of the 'anti-power-based' cultural approach to sex differences." *Language in Society* 21: 547-68.

Williams, G. 1992. *Sociolinguistics: a sociological Critique*. London: Routledge.

Woolard, K. A. 1985. "Language variation and cultural hegemony: Towards an integration of sociolinguistics and social theory." *American Ethnologist* 12: 738-48.

—. 1998. "Introduction: Language ideology as a field of inquiry." In *Language Ideologies: Practice and Theory*. Ed. by B. B. Schieffelin, K. A. Woolard and P. V. Kroskrity. Oxford: Oxford University Press, 3-47.

—. 2004. "Codeswitching." In *A Companion to Linguistic Anthropology*. Ed. by A. Duranti. Oxford: Blackwell, 73-94.

Yngve, V. 2004. "An Introduction to Hard-Science Linguistics." In *Hard-Science Linguistics*. Ed. by V. Yngve and Z. Wasik. New York: Cotinuum, 27-35.

CHAPTER TWO

'BIGGER IS BETTER': MASCULINITY AND CONSUMERIST DISCOURSES IN VIAGRA ADVERTISEMENTS

ANDREA SIMON-MAEDA, NAGOYA KEIZAI UNIVERSITY

Abstract: Drawing on a critical discourse framework to examine the interconnectedness of language and sexuality, this paper explores the visual and textual construction of masculinity and consumerist discourses. How a universal standard for male performance framed by heterosexual desire is discursively fashioned and exploited for marketing purposes is illustrated through an analysis of Internet advertisements for vasoactive agents. The sexual pharmacology industry depends on advertising strategies that highlight prevalent notions of heterosexual relationships wherein effective hydraulic performance of the 'power tool' is conflated with ideas of 'authentic' masculinity. In addition to provocative images and vocabulary, advertisers appeal to the implied sexual needs and expectations of 'consumption communities' through the use of particular discursive features that create a simulated sense of solidarity with the reader of the text. A considerable investment is now being made by advertisers in the appropriation of male bodies and masculinity for the sake of contemporary capitalist enterprises intent on promulgating the slogan 'bigger is better' among consumer and sexual cultures.

Key words: *masculinity, consumerism, heteronormativity, critical discourse analysis.*

1. Introduction

Internet advertisements for bodily management play a powerful role in the display and reproduction of dominant ideologies of sexuality. Drawing on Critical Discourse Theory (Fairclough 1989, 1995), poststructuralist understandings of male sexuality (Bordo 1999; Foucault 1975, 1978), and analyses of the interconnectedness of language and sexuality (Cameron & Kulick 2003a, 2003b), this paper explores the visual and textual construction of masculinity and consumerist discourses in advertisements for vasoactive agents (e.g., Viagra, Cialis). The use of biometaphors to describe masculine sexual potency ('throbbing member') and (hetero)sexist depictions of function/dysfunction ('Can't perform in bed?') problematize aspects of male biology which can be repaired or enhanced with medications offered to the consumer in 'the friendly voice' of advertisements ('I've been there, and trust me, I understand and empathize with you.'). The sexual pharmacology industry depends on advertising strategies which highlight prevalent notions of (hetero)sexual relationships wherein effective performance of the 'power tool' is conflated with ideas of 'authentic' masculinity. To send this ideological message to consumers, advertisers employ visual and textual types which, sustained by dominant views of sexuality, construct an idealized version of manhood. In addition to provocative images and vocabulary, advertisers appeal to the implied sexual needs and expectations of 'consumption communities' (Fairclough 1989: 201) through the use of discursive features (e.g., overwording, declaratives, direct address) creating a 'synthetic personalization' (p. 62) and simulated sense of solidarity with the reader of the text. Although the commodification of women's bodies continues to predominate discourses of the 'sex sell,' a considerable investment is now being made by advertisers in the appropriation of male bodies and masculinity for the sake of contemporary capitalist enterprises intent on promulgating the slogan 'bigger is better' among consumer and sexual cultures.

2. The Study

2.1. Conceptual Framework

In his 1989 book, *Language and Power*, Norman Fairclough outlines the link created between advertising texts and 'consumption communities' wherein the subject positions of consumers are constructed through the ideological messages of advertisements prescribing the 'ideal' lifestyle as defined by contemporary capitalism (Fairclough 1989: 199-211). Likewise, in the current study, an analysis of Viagra ads illustrates how the male reader of Viagra ads is positioned as being a 'good consumer' if he makes the 'right choice' and takes advantage of a product which promises a life-altering change in his sex life. Female readers are also positioned as good consumers if they encourage their partners to buy the products, thereby supporting the restoration of a healthy erection. On the other hand, women are positioned as 'bad consumers' if they, for reasons that would be labeled as pathological by normative psychoanalytic discourses, resist the idea of a viagrified penis[1]. In sum, the pharmaceutical industry's marketing strategies are designed to exploit the heterosexual norm of male/female desire and performance with a variety of ideological messages. In so doing, their primary goal is to inflict shame on the sexually deficient man and reduce what is otherwise a complex human condition to a simple matter of chemistry. At the same time, by defining erectile dysfunction (ED)[2] as a malfunctioning of a man's chemical and biological equipment that can be fixed with a 'simple' pill, Viagra ads in effect absolve men of their inadequacies and thus offer a very narrow definition of masculinity, i.e., a penis that responds when it's *supposed to*, rather than taking into broader consideration the complex intersection of cultural norms and socioeconomic pressures concerning masculinity.

Poststructuralist interpretations of the discursive and ideological construction of sexualities within heteronormative[3] cultures (e.g., Bordo 1999; Cameron & Kulick 2003a, 2003b; Foucault 1975, 1978) highlight the complexities of male/female desire that cannot be understood apart from broader socio-historical contexts. Michel Foucault described how medical discourses and practices, what he called 'the clinical gaze' (1975: 120), historically constructed the body in dichotomous terms of normal/abnormal, healthy/sick, thus creating universal standards against which individuals could be compared. For Foucault, the crucial point concerning the ways in which 'power mechanisms' (1978: 23) at the beginning of the 18th century produced discourses on sex was that

> there emerged a political, economic, and technical incitement to talk about sex. And not so much in the form of a general theory of sexuality as in the form of analysis, stocktaking, classification, and specification, of quantitative or causal studies . . . . one had to speak of it [sex] as of a thing to be not simply condemned or tolerated but managed, inserted into systems of utility, regulated for the greater good of all, made to function according to an optimum. Sex was not something one simply judged; it was a thing one administered . . . it called for management procedures; it had to be taken charge of by analytical discourses (*ibidem* 24).

These types of regulatory discourses have facilitated modern-day pharmaceutical companies' attempts to convince male customers of their need to 'measure up' to an idealized version of phallic manhood. As a consequence, rather than challenge dominant conceptualizations of masculinity that demand ultimate performance of the penis for heterosexual penetration[4], medical discourses, in collaboration with the pharmaceutical industry, continue to reinforce the significance of stamina and control. Relatedly, Susan Bordo comments that 'Viagra for men, like diet pills and cosmetic surgery for women, is not about restoring sexual pleasure – but about meeting and keeping up with the cultural standards and expectations of masculinity and femininity' (1999: 42-43). The crucial role of language in the construction and manifestation of societal norms concerning sexualities has been described by Cameron and Kulick (2003a) as follows:

> To say that sexuality is 'discursively constructed' is to say that sex does not have meaning outside the discourses we use to make sense of it, and the language in which those discourses are (re)circulated . . . . the 'reality' of sex does not pre-exist the language in which it is expressed; rather, language *produces* the categories through which we organize our sexual desires, identities and practices (italics in original, pp. 18-19).

Furthermore, our 'desires may feel private, but are unavoidably shaped through public structures and in public interactions' (ibid., p. 113). Hence, in the context of the current study, the deconstruction of discursive elements in Viagra ads reveals the interconnectedness of language and ideological presuppositions on the part of pharmaceutical industries that reflect and reproduce heteronormative ideas and practices concerning masculinity.

3. Analysis

Over a one-year period (2003-2004), approximately 100 Internet advertisements for Viagra and other vasoactive agents/sexual enhancement medications were collected and classified according to the scheme outlined below. Irritation with a daily bombardment of direct to the consumer (DCT) advertisements (junk mail), coupled with parental concern over heteronormative ideologies the author's teenage son was receiving from the ads constituted the impetus for this report.

3.1. Classification scheme and representative samples

The most distinguishing feature of the ads is the way in which a 'synthetic personalization' (Fairclough 1989: 62) is created between the addresser (copywriter) and addressee (reader of ads) through the use of the following discursive devices.

3.1.1. Direct address in a friendly voice

o   I've been there, and trust me, I understand and empathize with
    you.
o   I'd like to tell you about a great product that I tried and fell in
    love with. I know you're thinking that I'm just some salesman,
    which is true but I have also used this product myself and had
    great results, and that is why I am selling it today!
o   How do you think all those porn stars got so huge? Trust me,
    God didn't bless them any more than the rest of us. They simply
    went out and MADE their members bigger.
o   You've heard about these pills on TV, in the news, and online
    and have probably asked yourself, 'Do they really work?' The
    answer is YES! IGF2 is a powerful erection enhancing product
    that will create erections so strong and full that over time your
    penis will actually grow as a direct result! If you would like a
    more satisfying life then IGF2 is for you!

The advertisement's bonding techniques are designed to reassure
insecure male consumers that ED is a common problem among 'us guys'
and a physical condition that can be easily rectified. A similar discursive
use of 'you' constructions in advertisements for women's skin products
was analyzed in Justine Coupland's (2003) article on consumerism and
ageist ideologies. The author noted that the authorial voice of the
advertiser is designed to merge with and stimulate the 'inner voice' of the
consumer's conscience urging oneself to follow the sociocultural,
consumerist imperative of ageless beauty.

The voices of testimonials (real or fictional) are also a form of address
meant to create a sense of camaraderie among those seeking help:

o   I suffered from erectile dysfunction for over 5 years before I
    asked my doctor for advice. It was tough to talk about my
    problem because I was only 38. I was not one of those old men I
    used to think of when I thought about ED. Coming to terms with
    this issue is not always easy. It can cause anger, embarrassment,
    and frustration. Being so young, I feel it was that much harder.
    Luckily my wife played an important role in my treatment. She
    surprised me one day and handed me one of the tablets I got
    from my doctor. I understood what she was suggesting.
    Spontaneity issues went away after that, and VIAGRA had a
    positive impact on my marriage. Thanks to VIAGRA I was able
    to have sex again. My wife and I were recently given the best
    gift of all – our first son. (Darrell – Age 43)

> o   I'm in my 40's. I've always enjoyed an active sex life. Maintaining an erection was never a problem for me. But the stress of my everyday life was beginning to take a toll. At times I found myself unable to perform. This frustrated me to no end. Instead of looking forward to sex, I found myself avoiding it. In fact, I was avoiding all forms of intimacy – period. What a downer. And what a job it was doing on my head, not to mention my marriage. There were times when I just wanted to give up. But I'm glad I didn't. Instead I talked to my doctor, who told me to try VIAGRA. My wife suggested we rent a romantic video and light candles. This helped me to relax. After that, everything else played out just the way I wanted. (David – In his 40's) (Testimonials on Pfizer's Confidential web page, April 2004)

Another aspect of the testimonials, which I will develop further in a later section, is how sexuality is constructed along heteronormative conventions wherein successful penetration of a female partner is deemed the preferred outcome of male/female sexual desire and performance. The ads thus reinforce the ideological message that a fully functioning penis is not only the ultimate marker of male sexuality but also of female sexuality as well. In other words, failure of the man to have an erection signifies a loss in the female partner's desirability, which, in a heteronormative culture, is dependent on successful copulation. Also of note is how a sense of shame is inflicted on the man who can't perform while, at the same time, he can feel confident of being exonerated of his sexual deficiencies if he joins the club and buys the 'little blue pill.'

3.1.2. Exclusive use of 'we'

In addition to the use of an inclusive 'we,' as in the above testimonial examples, an exclusive 'we' also appears for the purposes of adding a layer of expertise to the messages, thus allaying customers' fears of unsatisfactory results or harmful effects of the drug:

> o   We do our best to educate our customers.
> o   NEW MEDICAL BREAKTHROUGH: Our Male Enlargement Pill is the most effective on the medical market today with over a million satisfied customers worldwide. Our product is doctor recommended and made from 100% natural ingredients.
> o   Dear friend, thank you for taking the opportunity to look at this ad. Scientific research has discovered a new herbal formula that generates significant increases in penis length and diameter by stimulating the natural production of growth hormones and male sex hormones known as androgens . . . . 69% of women say they

are not satisfied with the size of their lover's penis. So if you
want to be certain your lover is satisfied with the size of your
penis we advise you to read on.

3.1.3. Provocative/sexist language

The level of provocative, (hetero)sexist language varied across the ads
according to the product's manufacturer and intended audience. Susan
Bordo (1999) comments that biometaphors (e.g., proud member, throbbing
manhood) used in ads or pornographic literature reflect modern society's
ideas about the penis that emerge 'not from anatomical fact but from our
cultural imagination' (p. 46). Mechanical and other power-laden penile
metaphors (e.g., power tool, torpedo, fuckstick, blow torch, cockpit) serve
to convince male readers that they can avoid the embarrassment of 'soft
equipment' if they buy the sexual enhancement product:

o   Wouldn't you kill to have a larger rod?   Produce rock-solid
     erections. Turbo–boost your sex drive. Not just for impotence,
     turns normal guys into stallions!

Bordo further explains that this type of metaphorical language also
implies that an erect penis

has a soft being living inside itself too, like a snail within a shell . . . . A
human organ of flesh and blood is subject to anxiety, ambivalence,
uncertainty. A torpedo, rocket, or power tool . . . in contrast, would never
let one down. Boys talking to each other, using these terms, can identify
with a state of bravado and toughness that they don't really feel. (p. 48)

Hence, advertisers strategically deploy biometaphors alongside other
provocative images ('Make women drool when they see the massive
member you are packing') to convince men of their need to live up to
cultural standards of male sexuality.

3.1.4. Imperative/Question modals

Fairclough (1989) explains how power relations between addresser and
addressee are established through an asymmetric distribution of imperative
and question modals. That is, 'asking, be it for action or information, is
generally a position of power, as too is giving information – except where
it has been asked for' (p. 126). In the ads, both question and imperative
modals position the addressee (male reader) as a compliant recipient of
what the authoritative addresser (writer of the ads) has to offer:

o   Tired of having a small penis? Change it!
o   Feel more confident. Expand your manhood. Never question your size or ability again. Men, don't be afraid. Be a GOD in the sack!
o   Do your weener a favor. Face the facts: Your penis is small.

3.1.5. (Hetero)sexist descriptors of function/dysfunction

As mentioned above, current notions of erectile dysfunction involve 'phallocentric imperatives constituting hegemonic masculinity -- imperatives that are reproduced and reinforced in a variety of discursive fields (e.g., medicine, sexology, psychiatry, pornography, popular culture, and the media)' (Potts 2000: 88). Ads for vasoactive agents are complicit in these dominant imperatives, restricting male sexual expression to performance, size, stamina, and control:

o   Perform like a Porn Star in the sack! It's a fact, a bigger member leads to a bigger orgasm for your partner. 'It's not the size that matters' . . . WHAT A LOAD OF CRAP! Women don't want their men to feel insecure, so they aren't going to come out and say 'Hey, your penis is small.' However, 67% of women fessed up in a recent survey that bigger is better. Those are just the ones that confessed it!
o   When those panties come off the last thing you need is soft equipment.
o   In a society where 'performance is everything' and 'size does indeed matter,' below par sexual performance is a very painful thing . . . a true self confidence crusher.
o   Let me briefly explain why so many males suffer from sexual dysfunction. From a biological anthropological standpoint, the male's job is to impregnate as many females as possible, which increases the chance that he will successfully pass his genes on to the next generation. It is therefore of benefit if ejaculation occurs rapidly so he can move on to the next mate. Now what this means is that once the job is done, there is no need for further sexual interaction. Unfortunately, this usually leaves the female unsatisfied and displeasured. This is because biologically, women are programmed completely differently than men. Their job is to ensure that the male's semen is passed on, otherwise, child rearing would be impossible. This is why women have such an insatiable appetite for orgasms . . . continuation of the human race depends on her lasting as least as long as the male!

Needless to say, for the female partner in a heteronormative relationship a receptive vagina for the erect penis is the defining criterion for 'healthy' female sexuality[5], and the accompanying photos in the ads of a man and woman in a (presupposed) heterosexual relationship are visual manifestations of traditional gendered roles. Relatedly, in Erving Goffman's (1976) work *Gender Advertisements*, he illustrated how power differentials between men and women are constructed in advertising photographs (see Figure 2-1) with men typically portrayed as bigger or taller than women who are usually positioned in a swooning pose with an enraptured facial expression.

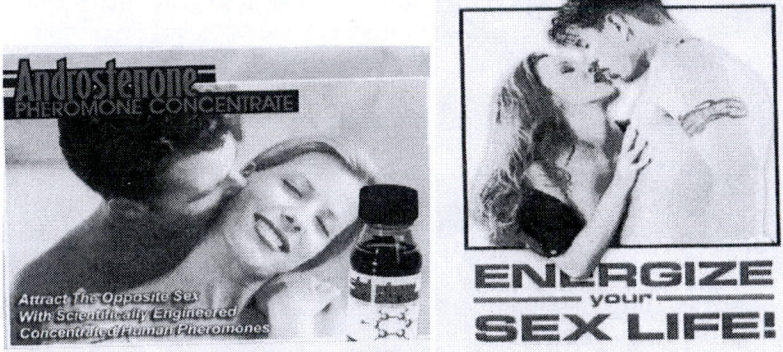

Fig. 2-1: Advertisement photos

The combination of textual and non-textual material (e.g., photos, illustrations) inscribes men and women in hegemonic dualisms of active/passive, strong/weak, aggressive/submissive, and so on. Although early psychoanalytical (e.g., Freud 1905/1981) treatises posited that both active and passive sexuality modes exist in males and females from birth, Kirby and Costello (2004: 218) note, however, that

> [b]y maturation though, instincts have been overlaid with social meanings as the ego tests 'reality' and directs responses to the external environment. In our society, a boy comes to see the penis as representing activity and, through activity, power. In a patriarchal, heterosexist society, a boy must abandon passivity to retain 'masculinity.' But, as Freud shows, what is repressed is not erased, and sexuality for many men is a site of tension and conflict.

The ads thus adjust their textual tropes to fit and perpetuate dominant binaries of male/female sexuality that restrict a man's range of possible alternative modes of erotic performance:

- o So hot! This is a great addition to my bag of tricks for pleasing the ladies. It is crazy to say but this product has not only changed my sex life but my life in general as well! It has given me the confidence and self-esteem to go up to that hot girl in the club and bring her back to my place without feeling a doubt of shame in my mid-section. Even for you married men, you could definitely use this product to your advantage, make your wife start begging you for sex, he he :)
- o How would she feel about herself if you often had the urge to ravage her body?

Not only is the marketing of vasoactive agents constructed along heteronormative conventions concerning sexuality, but there is also a racialized imagery contained in the photographs that are usually either of white/white or black/black couples (see Figure 2-2). This is evidence of advertisers' covert alignment with normative societal sanctions against mixed racial couples. Viagra marketing strategies thus appeal to the needs and desires of a well-to-do social group who can afford the product – 'a reality that reinforces existing race, age, and class-based hierarchies of privilege in relation to medical care and coverage' (Loe 2004: 171).

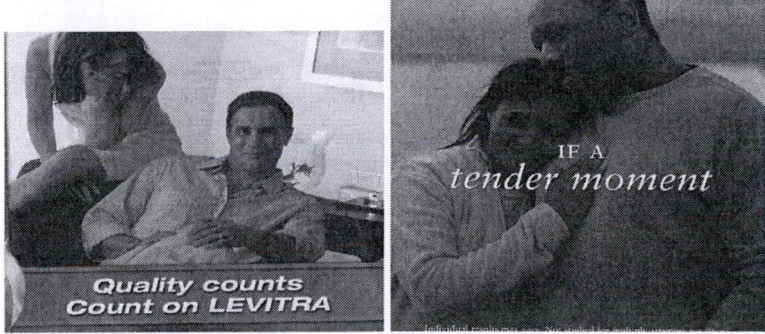

Fig. 2-2: Same racial couples

As Viagra was originally marketed to a mature audience as a treatment for an age-related condition[6] within a stable, monogamous relationship, early ads often contained pictures of white-haired couples dancing. More recently, younger couples are depicted in the ads, or sometimes the partner is missing completely, as in the New York Times newspaper ad below (see Figure 2-3), and Viagra is now being marketed as one more consumerist tool for constructing a sexually functional, ageless body defined by its penile erectility.

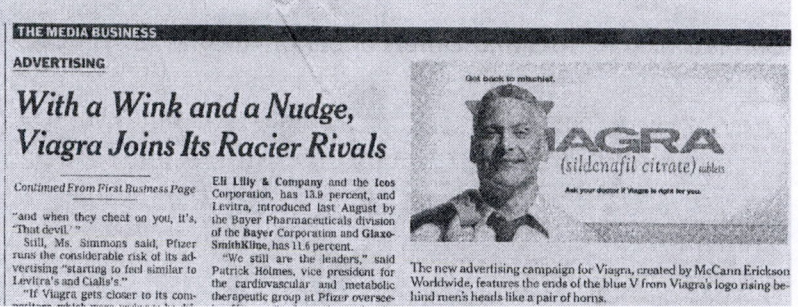

Fig. 2-3: *New York Times* advertising

The above advertising campaign featuring a 'devilish' image of a man with the 'V' of Viagra placed behind his head to portray a pair of horns, was Pfizer's attempt to keep up with its more 'friskier' competitors, Cialis and Levitra. Comments made by a Pfizer consumer marketing executive in the accompanying article attest to the pharmaceutical industry's rationalization and medicalization of sexuality for increased profits:

> Twenty-three million men have tried Viagra worldwide, but there are so many who have not, and our job is to motivate them to go to their doctors and ask for Viagra. We had to find a new way to do it, because there are still so many undertreated and undiagnosed as a result of the stigma and embarrassment in this category. ("With a Wink and a Nudge," 2004)

Although recent Viagra ads are meant to appeal to as wide a consumer base as possible, including the large numbers of the unmarried or married same-sex population, or those only interested in Viagra's usefulness for recreational sex, there is no explicit acknowledgement of these different groups of people beyond the use of gender-neutral vocabulary for one's 'partner' -- a token form of acknowledgment of sexual diversity for the sake of marketing purposes:

> o   Help your partner – Your partner will probably benefit more
>   from treatment than you think. That's because erectile dysfunction

> (ED) can have a serious effect on your partner's self-image. It
> can even make him think that he is less of a man. Studies show
> that ED is associated with a loss of self-esteem and even
> depression. Your partner may be avoiding intimacy so he can
> escape these negative emotions. All these factors can put a strain
> on your sexual relationship. VIAGRA can help by treating his
> ED. (Viagra website 2006)

In sum, men's bodies and their sexual (dys)functions have been exploited and medicalized through the interplay of 'the cultural valorization of an erect penis in definitions of healthy and normal heterosex' (Potts 2000: 87) and the proliferation of consumerist discourses in advertisements for sexual enhancement aids.

4. Discussion

This report adopted Fairclough's early (yet seminal) critical discourse analytical approach to deconstruct ideological formations of masculinity and consumerist discourses found in ads for Viagra and other sexual enhancement formulas, and the derivative analysis mainly highlighted the more obvious linguistic features of the advertisements. A more in-depth analysis following up-to-date versions of CDA or Systemic-Functional Linguistics (SFL) would have served to further complexify the interplay of advertising texts, images and social norms; however, this was beyond the scope of the present paper. Nevertheless, the report addressed a not-as-yet fully explored socially significant issue involving heteronormative constructions of masculinity within consumerist cultures. The inscription on male sexuality of a consumerist, biomedical mandate to be always in control of (hetero)sexual response severely limits the range of bodily pleasures obtainable through a more holistic expression of one's sexual self. A socially constructed, static binary of active/passive roles for men and women hinges on a counter-intuitive expression of sexual desire[7]. Pharmaceutical industries have a vested interest in maintaining hegemonic definitions of sexuality that reduce a psychologically and socioculturally complex condition to a 'hydraulics malfunctioning' and thus market and distribute their products accordingly. An examination of Internet ads for vasoactive agents brought to the fore the textual and visual tropes invoked by marketing strategists to construct a phallocentric consumerist culture wherein the little blue pill 'has become a cultural signifier of virility, bioperfection, potentially unlimited sexual performance and a new era in sexuality' (Marshall 2002: 132). Sexual enhancement drugs have quickly become a 'capitalist fetish' (Mamo & Fishman 2001: 17) prevalent among privileged users who 'have disposable income for these non-insurance-covered medications, and are more likely to try these drugs in an effort to maintain youthful appearance, activities and lifestyles' (p. 18).

In addition to the construction of masculinity and consumerist discourses, the ads reinforce hegemonic processes (see, e.g., Gramsci 1971) that permeate and organize our sociocultural beliefs and language practices concerning sexual behavior. It is not through direct coercive force that pharmaceutical industries and the medical establishment have managed to wield a pervasive influence on consumers but rather through a carefully orchestrated application of conceptual binaries that people have come to accept as 'the way things are.' Moreover, a 'compulsory heterosexuality' (Rich 1980) is being reinforced through the diffusion of vasoactive agents and their marketing ideologies that exclude 'the possibility of linking maleness with anything other than vaginal penetration (and likewise femaleness with anything other than receptivity)' (Mamo & Fishman 2001: 24).

Notwithstanding the promulgation of discourses of heteronormativity and consumerism through advertisements for vasoactive agents, alternative uses of the technology are also conceivable. That is, members of heterogeneous sexual categories (e.g. LGBT) who experiment with Viagra and other sexual enhancement formulas are resisting normative inscriptions of erotic desire and performance and are thus constructing sites of resistance to the regulation and commodification of bodies[8]. Recent gender and language studies (most notably, Cameron & Kulick 2003a, 2003b; Bucholtz, Liang & Sutton 1999) have stressed how discursive expressions of sexuality do not constitute static, mutually exclusive categories but rather a continuum of gendered identities and linguistic choices enacted both within and against traditional norms for men and women. Choosing to be different and inciting 'gender trouble' (Butler 1990) at exclusionary borders artificially created by dominant medical and consumerist discourses may hopefully lead to the continuing destabilization of heteronormative ideologies and the (re)appropriation of biotechnology to serve, rather than regulate, our sexual lives.

Notes

[1] Loe (2004) reports that for senior women in particular, attitudes towards their elderly male partners' use of Viagra include anxiety over 'harmful sexual norms and expectations, prohibitively expensive prescriptions, a quick-fix ethic, and an underemphasis on romance and emotions' (p. 121). While ads for Viagra and other vasoactive agents primarily emphasize highly sexualized masculinities, female partners oftentimes resist these biomedical and societal inscriptions on their erotic

lives and hence place themselves at risk of being labeled 'deviant' by mainstream psychoanalytical standards.

[2] The widespread appearance in the '90s of Viagra, along with the newly coined term 'erectile dysfunction' (in lieu of the stigmatized 'male impotence'), was a result of Pfizer Pharmaceuticals and the medical establishment's coordinated efforts to redefine a physical condition and consequently widen the range of potential users. That is, while medical discourses concerning erectile dysfunction had previously included an emphasis on psychological factors, a shift in expectations about lifelong sexual performance and penis size, coupled with the proliferation of pharmaceutical treatments, created a huge market of male consumers convinced that Viagra would take care of their 'hydraulics' malfunctioning.

[3] Cameron and Kulick (2003a) define heteronormativity 'as those structures, institutions, relations and actions that promote and produce heterosexuality as natural, self-evident, desirable, privileged and necessary' (p. 55).

[4] Fausto-Sterling (2000) comments that in decisions concerning male genital surgery for intersexed individuals (born with both male and female genitalia) that 'what counts especially is how the penis functions in social interactions – whether it 'looks right' to other boys, whether it can 'perform satisfactorily' in intercourse. It is not what that the sex organ does for the body to which it is attached that defines the body as male. It is what it does vis-à-vis other bodies' (p. 58).

[5] It is beyond the scope of this paper to elaborate on discourses surrounding female sexual dysfunction (FSD); however, an examination of ads for creams, pills, etc. to treat FSD reveals the same hegemonic pattern found in ED ads wherein bodily functions are medicalized (read: problematized), thus enlarging the market base with an increasing number of female consumers (see Chapter 5 of Loe (2004) for a comprehensive discussion of the female Viagra phenomenon.)

[6] The presidential candidate and war veteran, Bob Dole, was Viagra's first famous spokesperson whose late-middle-aged, courageous, mainstream persona helped to sanitize the 'seedier' side of the product, thus legitimating its use among mature heterosexual couples (see, e.g., Marshall and Katz (2002: 45) for a historical study of beliefs and attitudes toward ageing and male sexuality and an explanation of 'the ascendancy of the status of sexual functionality and potency apart from conventional affiliations with procreation').

[7] Elliott (2002) offers a succinct summary of the Freudian position: 'The denial of feelings, the structuring of sexuality into narrow paths of monogamy and marital legitimacy, the rigid (male) insistence upon genital monosexuality: these are, Freud argues, the oppressive emotional repressions inflicted upon human subjects' (p. 42).

[8] This is not to say, however, that members of alternative sexual categories may not still be playing out the same fantasies of power, domination, penetration, and the same biases on active and passive roles as heterosexual individuals, but that they're challenging a type of heteronormative regulation (to choose other sex) (Robert Mochain, personal communication, May 10 2006).

References

Bordo, S. 1999. *The male body: A new look at men in public and private.* New York: Farrar, Straus and Giroux.

Bucholtz, M., A.C. Liang and L.A. Sutton, eds. 1999. *Reinventing identities: The gendered self in discourse.* Oxford: Oxford University Press.

Butler, J. 1990. *Gender trouble: Feminism and the subversion of identity.* New York: Routledge.

Cameron, D. and D. Kulick. 2003a. *Language and sexuality.* Cambridge: Cambridge University Press.

Cameron, D. and D. Kulick. 2003b. "Introduction: Language and desire in theory and practice." *Language & Communication* 23: 93-105.

Coupland, J. 2003. "Ageist ideology and discourses of control in skincare product marketing." In *Discourse, the body, and identity.* Ed. J. Coupland and R. Gwyn. New York: Palgrave Macmillan, 127-150.

Elliott, A. 2002 *Psychoanalytic theory: An introduction.* Durham, NC: Duke University Press.

Fairclough, N. 1989. *Language and power.* New York: Longman, Inc.

—. 1995. *Critical discourse analysis: The critical study of language.* New York: Longman Publishing.

Fausto-Sterling, A. 2000. *Sexing the body: Gender politics and the construction of sexuality.* New York: Basic Books.

Foucault, M. 1975. *The birth of the clinic: An archaeology of medical perception.* New York: Vintage books.

—. 1978. *The history of sexuality: Volume I: An introduction.* New York: Random House.

Freud, S. 1905/1981. *Three essays on the theory of sexuality.* Pelican Freud Library, Vol. 7, Harmondsworth, UK: Penguin.

Goffman, Erving (1976) *Gender Advertisements.* Cambridge, MA: Harvard University Press.

Gramsci, A. 1971. *Selections from the prison notebooks.* Ed. and transl. by Q. Hoare & G. Nowell Smith. New York: International Publishers.

Kirby M. and B. Costello. 2004. "Displaying the phallus: Masculinity and the performance of sexuality on the Internet." In *Feminism and masculinities.* Ed. P. Murphy. Oxford: Oxford University Press, 214-227.

Loe, M. 2004. *The rise of Viagra: How the little blue pill changed sex in America.* New York: New York University Press.

Mamo, L. and J.R. Fishman. 2001. "Potency in all the right places: Viagra as a technology of the gendered body." *Body & Society* 7(4): 12-35.

Marshall, B. 2002. "Hard science: Gendered constructions of sexual dysfunction in the Viagra age." *Sexualities* 5(2): 131-158.

Marshall, B. and S. Katz. 2002. "Forever functional: Sexual fitness and the ageing male body." *Body & Society* 8: 43-70.

Potts, A. 2000. "The essence of the hard on: Hegemonic masculinity and the cultural construction of erectile dysfunction." *Men and Masculinities* 3(1): 85-103.

Rich, A. 1980. "Compulsory heterosexuality and lesbian existence." *Signs* 5: 631-661.

With a wink and a nudge, Viagra joins its racier rivals (2004, August 17) *The New York Times*, p. 10.

CHAPTER THREE

MASCULINITY AS PUBLIC PERFORMANCE: GENDERED LANGUAGE PATTERNS AND RELIGIOUS IDENTITY IN A COLLEGE CLASSROOM

ALLYSON JULE, TRINITY WESTERN UNIVERSITY, CANADA

Abstract: This paper reflects on the male-dominated teaching discourse (lecturing) as used at a religious post-graduate college in Canada and the linguistic demands such a method seems to create among male participants. Lacan's (1968) theory of intersubjectivity is uniquely helpful in understanding the position of men as male/masculine linguistic participants. The study suggests that lecturing is a powerful tool of gender performance and that it is of particular power in propelling male learners into masculine performance of public speech. Lecturing is understood as a specific speech act, creating a stylized celebrative occasion of knowledge and knowing. In this study, the gendered speech performances set up a hegemonic masculinity (Connell 1995; Swain 2003). Because there is a transference relationship that lecturing presupposes, the silence of female students and the speech of male students affirms the possibility that within 'God-talk' (Ruether 1996) in particular, participants perform devout behaviour in gendered ways. This college study explores the participation of the students in an evangelical theology classroom. The clash of conservative/spiritual masculinity with pro-feminist/social justice masculinity in pedagogy is seen as in tension in this context and as provoking questions of gender speech performances alongside religious identity (Clatterbaugh 1990, Skelton 2001).
Key words: *Masculinity, Linguistic Space, Religious Identity.*

1. Introduction

The feminist social critic, Camille Paglia (1992) discusses the power of American-style evangelical[1] Christianity in her essay, 'The joy of Presbyterian sex,' saying there are 'Protestant looks, Protestant manners, Protestant values' central in American society today, and that being a Protestant evangelical Christian is about being in and of a specific 'tribe' with a specific, strict code of behavior, behavior which includes particular language habits and patterns (p. 29). She goes on to suggest that all societies, including America, continue to need organized religions precisely because of the 'austere, enduring legacy' of them (p. 37); in fact, she sees it as a mistake for today's American-style evangelical Christian 'tribe' to attempt to be anything other than strict because the demands of belonging and the rules of exclusion and inclusion are precisely why people, and women in particular, continue to choose it. That is, Paglia, a radical liberal feminist, believes the very austerity of religion is part of what drives many women to current expressions of evangelical Christianity. Because of the continual and rising popularity of evangelical Christianity in American public life, this paper explores one specific setting within it: life at an evangelical theology college.

Laurie Goodstein (2004) of *The New York Times* reports that religion has edged its way into the forefront of American life in the last twenty years in particular. Though American history has been woven with religious issues from its inception, the interest in religion and national concerns since the 1980s has risen to now hold at 53% of Americans citing religion as the key to how they vote (up from 22% in 1984—an all-time high at that point). It is now 'a normal thing' to discuss the role of religion in American society (Goodstein 2004: 2). Because of Canada's proximity to the States and the vast influence America has in the world in general, such sociological influences also impact on modern Canadian society (Stackhouse 2002).

It is within this highly religiously-charged American era that I went looking for intersections of religion, gender, and language habits, specifically within the evangelical Christian community and women's use of linguistic space as indicative of their role and place in a Christian community. My specific concern here is lecturing –the daily lecturing as happens in university courses. I locate my research in a Canadian evangelical theological graduate college because it allows for a discussion of religious identity and lived practice to bear on women's silence in this setting and as part of currently experienced 'Protestant manners, Protestant values'.

2. The Study

One of the most observable influences of feminism on North American Christianity is the increase of women in theological education (Mutch 2003). However, their presence in co-educational lectures, such as the context examined here, reveals power discrepancies, even amidst these modern egalitarian times. Ways of being female include quietness as specifically demonstrative of morality. Historically, and until relatively recently, theology schools were the domain of men so that women in theological education have an unusual set of conditions if compared to those in the university experience in general where women's place and equality are perhaps more solidly assumed.

Little more than a century ago women were not allowed into most college classrooms, let alone theology. When protesting in 1910 on the admission of women to the University of Michigan, the college president said, "We shall have a community of de-feminated women and de-masculated men. When we attempt to disturb God's order, we produce monstrosities" (in Frazier & Sadker 1973: 144). Gender and religion are connected, and much of 'God's order' is seen in the preservation of traditional masculine/feminine roles. Any variation of 'God's order' is viewed as a 'monstrosity'. As such, taking sociolinguist scholarship into a theology college appeared to me an important place to explore how religion and issues of religious identity influence gendered language practices today.

Women enter theological training en route to ordination' that is, en route to becoming ministers or pastors. However, many of today's evangelicals see ordination as something still reserved for men, with women limited to supportive roles (Grenz & Kjesbo 1995). The debates within evangelical Christianity concerning the ordination of women are vigorous and dynamic (Grenz & Kjesbo 1995, are among a host of academics writing on the subject). Yet, in spite of these continuing debates, it is interesting to find more and more women pursuing theological graduate degrees. Regardless of the range of views on women's roles at home or in the church, women today enroll and complete theological education and go on to careers in evangelical churches (Grenz & Kjesbo 1995; Busse 1998; Mutch 2003; Hancock 2003). There is also growing feminist thought within modern evangelicalism in spite of strong lobby groups on the religious right, such as Focus on the Family or Concerned Women for America, which promote and push 'traditional values' as central to being Christian (Coontz 2003).

For one year, I worked on a research project at this post-graduate college. My project was to focus on the views of feminism among devout Christians living in the area. The results of the interview study are discussed elsewhere (Jule 2004c, 2004d). However, as one trained in ethnographic methods and feminist linguistics, the year took on a slightly different focus for me, one that worked alongside the interview study. As a visiting scholar, I was able to sit in on any class of interest, either as a regular attendee or as a drop-in/on-off visitor. As such, what emerged was an ethnographic experience, one where I became a participant observer. What emerged quickly for me as a curiosity was the most used style of teaching at the theology college: lecturing.

3. Lecturing as Teaching Method

Lecturing is a major part of university teaching. My need to appraise the method emerged from my general interest in silence in classrooms and in silence as something uniquely and most often experienced by those born female. My previous work focused on a primary classroom and explored which speech acts teachers use to propel boys to speak up more than the girls during formal-classroom language lessons (2004a and 2004b). I identify this amount of talk as 'use of linguistic space' and highlight certain classroom teaching methods as legitimating participation of boys while serving to maintain silence among the girls.

Much research concerned with gender and its role in affecting classroom experience points to males as significant classroom participants and females as less so. Research, such as Walkerdine's (1990), Bailey's (1993), Corson's (1993), Thornborrow's (2002), and Sunderland's (2004), settles on teachers' lack of awareness of this linguistic space and of how teachers themselves overtalk in the education process and, in general, give more attention to their male students (Mahony 1985; Sadker & Sadker 1990; Jule 2004). Girls in particular are seen as often 'passive, background observers to boys' active learning' (Spender & Sarah 1980: 27). Other feminist sociolinguistic work suggests that the linguistic space used by male learners signifies and creates important social power and legitimacy (Holmes 1998; Baxter 1999, 2004). That is, who speaks tells us something about who matters inside the classroom. That men at this college participate more in question-answer time while their female classmates largely serve in the role of audience members suggests larger expectations of the community around them. That is, men contribute; women support the contributions.

Teachers and college professors talk more to their male students, beginning in the first years of schooling and on into post-graduate work. In general, women are rarely called upon to contribute and often find it difficult to interact with their professors. Sadker & Sadker (1990) suggested that female college students are the invisible members of the class. They suggest that one of the ways this invisibility is reinforced is through male domination of speech and through continual female silence. Kramarae & Treichter (1990) suggested that the reason women experience a 'chilly climate' in most academic settings (the college/university setting in particular) is male control of the linguistic space. Women in many college classrooms are marginalized from discourse and their silent position demonstrates and reinforces their lack of significance. That women in theology may be further silenced because of belonging to a particular religious identity tells us something else, something more, about the relationship of religion and gender and the influence of religious views on gender performance —the manners and the values.

Lecturing is a common teaching method at the college level. However, lecturing is often used in non-university settings as well, such as public lectures held in neighbourhood libraries or art galleries. In any circumstance, lecturing is a formal method of delivering knowledge: an expert prepares the lecture well in advance, allowing for considerable research, study, and rumination as well as carefully thought –through ideas and organization. People attend such public lectures for a sense of shared experience —one shared with the expert-lecturer as well as one shared with others in the audience. Lectures in such places are called 'celebrative occasions' by Goffman (1981). Frank (1995) articulates his amazement that people will disrupt their daily lives to come and hear such a lecture because they have 'self-consciously defined themselves as having emotional or practical needs; they arrive already prepared to be affected in certain ways' (p. 28).

However, university lectures are part of people's daily schedules; both the lecturer and the students are usually present for obligatory reasons. The lectures are meant to disseminate knowledge for the set purposes of fulfilling the requirements of a given course. Depending on the nature of the course material, whether the course is mandatory or optional, and the size of the student group, lectures may well constitute up to thirty hours of a given course in one semester (up to three hours per week for ten weeks of an undergraduate mandatory course —in most institutions). Such lectures occur with such frequency that much emotional involvement is limited and not often experienced as a 'celebrative occasion' but as a necessary practice in the university experience.

Roland Barthes (1971) considered the university lecture in terms of politics, belonging, and a location to rehearse performance discourse. While the lecturer is lecturing, the students are often silently attending to the ideas and often writing notes on specific new vocabulary or content pertaining to the lesson material. The ideas expressed are in the hands of the lecturer. Much freedom is allowed concerning his or her politics, his or her power/ego issues, and his or her ability at discursive performance. As such, the lecturer has enormous control over the mood and the dynamics of the room, as well as the significance placed on the material discussed. Lecturing as teaching method works by conveying information through summary and through elaboration –both at the discretion of the lecturer. The lecture is a gesture which presents the effect of universal truth. In these ways, it remains a 'celebrative occasion'. During question-answer time, students have opportunity to publicly interact with the professor, briefly taking on the role of performer themselves by signaling investment, interest, and involvement.

Goffman's (1981) ideas on the lecture differentiated between 'aloud reading', which is often perceived as more scholarly, and 'fresh talk', which is often perceived as more informal though not necessarily more engaging. Barthes (1977), Goffman (1981) and Frank (1995) all recognized the lecture as a multi-layered performance. Of course, students reading the lecture material would be faster, more time efficient than attending class and listening to a fully performed lecture. (Perhaps listening to a cassette of the lecture while driving or cleaning the house would also be more time efficient). Nevertheless, the university lecture persists as a marker of scholastic participation —both attending lectures and performing lectures are parts of the academic experience. Spoken delivery is also taken as candid and dynamic, more 'real' than listening to a lecture on tape or reading the notes of a lecture silently at home. Reading *A Room of One's Own* is one type of experience; sitting in Girton College's lecture hall in 1928 and listening and watching Virginia Woolf present it would be quite another. A valuable academic lecturer is certainly one to be encountered if at all possible. As a result, the pedagogy of the lecture is 'intensely personal', even if it is personal in precisely impersonal, academic ways (Frank 1995: 30).

4. Lecturing as Power

A lecture presents a text which somehow appears to be independent of the lecturer but instead reveals the value of the lecturer's personal presence; it is a mark of the lecturer's authority. What fascinates me is the way the participants themselves also play the role of performers as well as the role of audience members. This performance is briefly seen during the question-answer time of the lecture —a time students pose questions to the lecturer. Lacan (1968) and his work on 'the other' as the one observed with 'the subject' as the observer influence my understanding of power relations in classrooms. His ideas propel these questions: Who is observing? Who is being observed? Which action signals and evokes power? Feminism offers various responses to these questions but it may be fair to say, in light of the vast feminist scholarship concerning pedagogy, that power largely lies in the teacher's hands. The teacher observes and the teacher speaks; both signal power. Holding the floor is the teacher's prerogative and is something which demonstrates the room's point of reference; that is, power is revealed in and created through the language practices of the lecturer. The lecturer is the subject or, for Lacan, the lecturer is the 'presumed-to-know'. The lecturer is perceived as knowing and the audience members are the ones seeking the knowledge; they are the observed. What is said in lectures implicitly and explicitly hints at the personal: the lecturer's views, the lecturer's opinions on a host of issues, the lecturer's personal life and choices, including religious and moral ones.

Lecturers in a theology college also reveal the particular context. I here suggest that lecturing, followed by question-answer periods, as is the pattern in this college, alienate the female students at this college because the feminine/masculine tendencies in classroom settings are validated and condoned by feminine/masculine patterns of behavior within evangelical Christianity itself. With the steady increase of female theology students, it seems worthwhile to reflect on the continued high prevalence of lecturing as common teaching method in a theology college and position it as a masculinist pedagogical tool, one that rehearses female students in feminine patterns of silence. At the same time, lecturing rehearses male theology students in masculine tendencies to dominate linguistic space. That is, the use of lectures in this theology college works to reinforce hegemonic masculinity (Connell 1995; Swain 2003); a masculinity which insists on feminine subservience and 'reverent awe' (Gallop 1995). Because of the transference of information/knowledge that lecturing presupposes, the silence of female students during question-answer time (a time they could speak) affirms the possibility that women behave quietly as a way of performing a specific and understood role of feminine devout behavior: women are quiet in such a setting because their religion values their silence.

5. Morality as Gendered

In 1982, Carol Gilligan wrote *In a different voice* which explored various ideas of gendered language patterns: a woman's place in society, gendered patterns in dealing with crisis and intimacy, as well as gendered patterns of expressing morality. To Gilligan, morality is closely if not entirely connected with one's sense of obligation and views of personal sacrifice. She goes on to suggest that masculine morality is concerned with the public world of social influence, while feminine morality is concerned with the private and personal world. As a result, the moral judgments and expressions of women tend to differ from those of men. In light of Gilligan's ideas, it may be reasonable to suggest that students of theology invite the suggestion that masculine behavior is particularly connected to public displays of influence with feminine behavior not concerning itself with public displays of participation, such as use of linguistic space. Women are rehearsed into silence for moral reasons; their silence demonstrates to others and to themselves their devoutness to God: their silence is their way of being good. Out of respect for others and for God, women are quiet.

The current increased presence of women, the rise in feminist theology, and the growth of women's ordination have significantly changed the nature of theological education. Recent research into the lives of evangelical women who chose theological education indicates that the lived experiences of these women are often painful and confusing ones (Gallagher 2003; Ingersoll 2003; and Mutch 2003). With various other religious experiences possible, some women remain in their evangelical subculture because they also experience support and solace in their church involvement. Women who study theology say they are often dismissed as feminist for pursuing theology and are marginalized as a result. Others feel marginalized and limited and nervous about their possible or future contributions; they anticipate problems though have no experience yet (Mutch 2003). Canadian women in theological education largely report that being a woman in ministry requires 'commitment of conviction' which is carried out within the 'context of challenge' (Busse 1998). Most cite loneliness and stress as part of their career choice and part of their theological education experiences. Nevertheless, women continue to enroll and to graduate and to go on to seek ordination in various evangelical denominations.

Much debate in theology education settles on how or if a woman can represent God or Christ to the church as some see the role of minister or pastor to be: to represent Christ. As such, women who choose to enter theological training at an evangelical college do so with a burden of explanation. Unlike their male classmates, they will have had to grapple with the possibility that their sex (being born female) will be a distraction at best or a continual controversy and challenge at worst.

6. The Theology College

This particular theology college is located on the University of British Columbia's large campus in Vancouver, Canada[2]. The college advertises itself as 'an international graduate school of Christian studies' (school website). It also advertises itself as a 'transdenominational graduate school', not affiliated with a specific Christian denomination, though it clearly articulates evangelical Christian ideas (such as 'to live and work as servant leaders in vocations within the home, the marketplace, and the church').

Forty percent of the student body is Canadian with an equal number (40%) from the United States; the remaining twenty percent are from other areas including Britain and Australia as well as some who travel from parts of Asia, Africa, and Latin America. There are 350 full-time students and approximately 350 part-time students. Because the college is for graduate students, most are over the age of twenty-five and all have one degree behind them. This degree need not be theology; students come from a variety of fields (including education, medicine, law, arts, sciences). There are roughly 40% female to 60% male students. There are no student residences set aside for this college. Students are encouraged to find their own accommodations through the university's housing office or to live off campus. The students I spoke to all lived off campus and independently.

Students choose from a variety of Master's programmes, including a Masters of Divinity (the degree needed for ordination in most evangelical churches). There are no doctoral programmes offered, though some students continue on to Doctor of Theology at larger theology colleges, such as those at Oxford, Harvard, Yale, or Princeton. Most, however, enter theology college to eventually gain ordination to serve as clergy in the evangelical church. This they can do with a Masters degree.

The college employs nineteen faculty members: seventeen are male, two are female. The first woman was hired in 1991 and still holds the post. The other was hired in 2000. The imbalance of male to female faculty members, particularly in light of the male: female ratio represented in the student body, was my first clue to particular gender issues in such a setting. It is my suggestion that the religious views of this community have greatly influenced the low numbers of females in faculty positions as well as their lack of linguistic space in the classrooms.

7. The Classes

In light of the specifics of this evangelical community, the college is a unique location for sociolinguistic gender research. I spent eight months (one academic year) at this college as a visiting scholar. The college provided me with office space as well as access to all classes. Fifty-five classes are offered every twelve weeks (Fall term, Spring term, Summer term). The mandatory core classes are held in lecture halls which fill at two hundred students; however, some elective courses fill at ten or twelve and some classes run with forty to sixty students.

I sat in on two of the large lectures, both consisting of approximately two hundred students, both core courses. Both courses were held once a week during the Fall term. Both classes ran for three hours with one or two breaks. Both lecturers were male; the large lecture classes at the college were all taught by male faculty. The courses taught by the two women were smaller grouped classes and were not core requirements.

The male lecturers were known as senior scholars in their fields; both were well published and well known in evangelical circles. All lectures in the core courses held in the main lecture hall (such as two in focus here) are also taped onto audiocassettes and sold in the college bookstore; hence, classroom lectures in this college serve the purpose of instruction as well as supplementary income for and promotion of the lecturer and the college.

It was clear that both lecturers, Dr. Smith and Dr. Jones[3], had lectured on their material before, perhaps for years. Dr. Smith was over fifty years old; Dr. Jones was in his late forties. Both were of British extraction and their accents identified their ethnic background and their training. Both lectured from prepared agendas given to students. These two classes were chosen because of the similarities in class size and in their use of lecture-style, but mainly because both classes represented the 40:60 ratio of female students to male students as seen in the college more generally.

Dr. Smith began each class with approximately five minutes of announcements, such as where to collect marked assignments. Dr. Smith had three tutorial assistants who marked weekly essay submissions. Sometimes one of the tutorial assistants (all of whom were male) would speak to these details before Dr. Smith would ascend the podium. A microphone was usually clipped onto the lapel of Dr. Smith's suit by a sound technician so as to record the lecture as well as to allow the entire lecture hall to hear adequately. The lecture would then begin with a two or three minute prayer by Dr. Smith. Dr. Smith would speak without visible notes, though students followed along in the student packs where each lecture was provided in outline form –something purchased at the beginning of term. Most students appeared to use the lecture outlines to follow along and write steady notes throughout, filling in each section of the page. At the end of the three hours (including one half-hour break), twenty minutes would be given over to questions from the students. For the twelve weeks of lectures in Dr. Smith's class not one woman asked a question. Three to five male students would ask suitable questions, all higher order questions spoken into standing microphones. Each week, different male students would ask questions. No female students spoke the entire term.

Dr. Jones' class appeared less formal than Dr. Smith's. Dr. Jones did not wear a suit and often arrived late and with scattered papers. Nevertheless, Dr. Jones also had the aid of three tutorial assistants who often started off the class on time for him with announcements of assignments or sometimes reminders of college activities (such as the Christmas banquet ticket sales). Dr. Jones usually began his lectures with a joke or humorous anecdote from his family life. Eventually an opening quick prayer was said, and Dr. Jones would begin his lecture. Dr. Jones used PowerPoint images which would include particular Bible passages under examination in the lecture or photographs of Biblical sites or maps. Students took copious notes; only a course outline indicated the general lecture topic per week. Dr. Jones gave a very long break, sometimes one hour. During the hour, Dr. Jones would retreat to his office. Dr. Jones also gave time for questions, often as long as ten minutes but averaging seven minutes most weeks. In the twelve weeks spent sitting in on Dr. Jones's lectures, one woman asked a question once. It was brief and answered quickly, but it stood out to me as indication of some accessibility for women in the less celebratory occasion.

In my opinion, Dr. Jones was the more engaging of the two lecturers, though in my casual conversations with students, they noted very little difference. The content of each course seemed of more significance to the students than the personality of the professors, even though all students were aware of the distinguished academics in their midst and mentioned this often to me. When I asked both lecturers (casually and privately) if they noticed that only men asked questions during question time, Dr. Smith said he had not noticed this; Dr. Jones said he had noticed this 'years ago'. He also said, "Women don't like to ask questions in public."

To highlight the discrepancy of linguistic space, Dr. Smith's and Dr. Jones's classrooms are represented in pie-chart form.

8. Discussion

Both Dr. Smith and Dr. Jones use most of the linguistic space during their lectures. This is not surprising, considering the method of instruction. However, of the remaining linguistic space, men used disproportionately more. In Dr. Smith's lectures, the male students used all of the student linguistic space: 100%. In Dr. Jones's room, the male students used much more than 60% to 40%, as is the population ratio. Instead, the male students speak over 90%.

Given the prominence of evangelical voices in current North American life, it is not surprising that social scientists like me have interest in exploring the intersection of religion, gender, and language. Many other researchers have undertaken numerous studies on the relationship of evangelical faith and femininity, most recently Gallagher (2003) and Ingersoll (2003). Both scholars offer robust research on gender and the evangelical sub-culture. Both suggest that evangelicalism appears a personally salient and robust religious experience to many, even with (or perhaps because of) high levels of participation and adherence to traditional Christian teachings concerning a woman's place in the home. Its ability to thrive in the midst of larger secularism and current religious pluralism is in part because it is a religious subculture that appears to accommodate cultural engagement along with theological orthodoxy (Smith *et al* 1998 in Gallagher 2003).

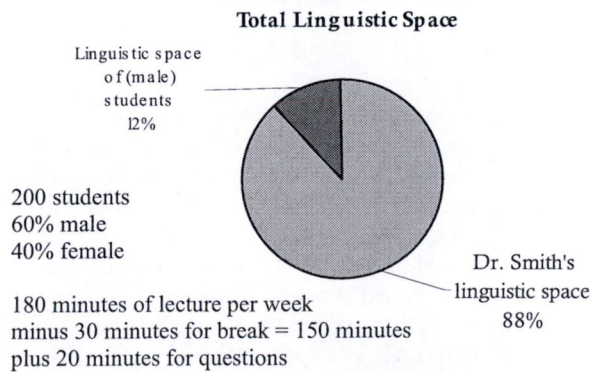

Fig. 3-1: Dr. Smith's lectures

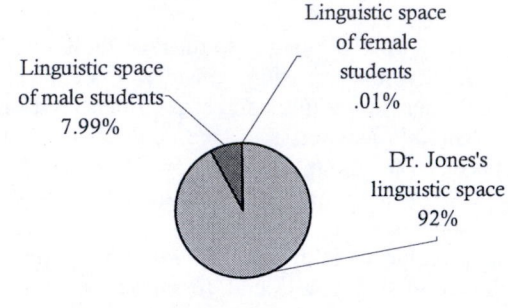

DR JONES's LECTURES
Total Linguistic Space

200 students
60% male
40% female

180 minutes of lecture per week
minus 30 minutes for break = 150 minutes
plus 20 minutes for questions

Fig. 3-2: Dr. Jones's lectures

Evangelicalism and evangelical theological education thrive not because they are effective in establishing a market niche (which they have done, Gallagher 2003) but because they are somehow relevant and useful to the people involved. The 1980s and 1990s in particular emerged as anti-feminist in American society as well as in evangelical circles (what is termed the 'backlash', Faludi 1993). In spite of earlier feminist claims made by many evangelical women, the Christian 'right' began to assert political pressure on issues concerning 'the family' and in opposition to gender issues. In short, evangelicals articulate a view of society that rejects modernity and relativism in favour of a preoccupation with certainty and control. Their views emerge from a belief that men serve as 'benign patriarchs' who insulate their families from the complexity of secular life (Gallagher 2003). As a result, both men and women achieve morality and peace of mind by behaving in stereotypically masculine and feminine ways (men to lead, women to submit to male leadership and significance).

It may well be that women choose evangelicalism precisely as a way to find meaningful communities and to reduce the stress of navigating more complex gender roles at work and with family (Busse 1998). Gallagher (2003), in her discussion of women in evangelicalism, suggests that evangelicals 'accommodate feminism but do so selectively' (p. 11). Gallagher suggests women remain in evangelicalism precisely because of the set roles for women. Such women find the clarity 'empowering'. She says that the rhetoric of masculine Christianity appeals to men as well as many women. Even organizations within evangelicalism which support and promote female ordination do so within the set dogma, offering differing interpretations of key scriptures concerning the role of women but not differing interpretations of gendered behaviour; men are still to lead (never to submit), women are still to support male 'headship' (even if ordained).

These complexities within evangelical circles, specifically that one could be a female ordained minister and still remain a woman committed to submission as a key moral and gendered behaviour, suggest that women in this college manage the contradiction with these ideas. These women have proceeded to pursue theological education, not for reasons of liberation or female emancipation from male domination in the church, but as a way to serve. Though some women may have difficulty remaining in such a context, many appear to remain and further invest themselves precisely because of a sense of clarity. They remain in their 'context of challenge' because of their 'commitment of conviction' (Busse 1998). They work out their gender roles within a larger framework of male leadership and domination. Even if ordained, women see their roles as supportive and not leadership-driven.

That lecturing is used in such old-fashioned ways within this theology college (and my guess is in many others as well) suggests a clash of conservative/spiritual masculinity with pro-feminist/social justice masculinity within university education (Clatterbaugh 1990; Skelton 2001). In fact, such a domination of linguistic space is what Skelton calls 'the school and machismo': that the ways males experience or exploit educational opportunities are 'skills' which males in society 'learn to develop' (p. 93).

9. Conclusion

I agree with Camille Paglia (1992) in that there are 'Protestant looks, Protestant manners, Protestant values' and that the codes of belonging to evangelical Christianity are attractive to many women. That women choose to belong and to support a religion which sees stereotypically gendered behavior as desirable might explain their alarming silence throughout the courses I observed at two theology courses. The women remained silent all term. Such specific manners and values are part of being specifically devout.

Women's roles, even if appearing to reach for the top levels of church governance by enrolling in Masters of Divinity programmes, are supportive roles. The 'Protestant looks, manners, and values' seem to include feminine silence. Though the evangelical world has competing debates within it concerning the role of women in the home, in society, and in the church, it appears to be the case at this college that female presence has not meant an upset in 'God's order' and that women serve as supportive listeners to the larger male-dominated linguistic space of the lectures.

If there had been a fear that women in theological education would 'de-feminate women and de-masculate men' this fear appears an unnecessary worry because, even when present, women continue to behave in quiet, submissive ways in these college classrooms. A masculine style of seeking influence as a way to be moral seems also at work at this college; the men acted the part of knowing and belonging to power, while women served the part of audience. These patterns are so commonly seen in other pedagogical research that the findings are not surprising. What this research does point to is cultural and historical threads which have appeared as patriarchal but which may reveal women consciously colluding in such patterns.

Many women remain in evangelical Christianity; women participate in theological education; women continue to serve well as audience members in their own educational experiences; and lecturing as pedagogical tool remains a popular teaching method at this college. These are the Protestant manner and values at work in American society. The lecturer as performer is well-received and well-supported by college life in general. The male privileging of the style is one not well-interrupted and my guess now would be that both the men and women who belong to such groups would defend it as 'God's order'. The popularity of evangelism, particularly in America, gives rise to feminist scholarship in a search for women's experiences in public life.

Notes

[1] The term 'evangelical' will be used to refer to those of Protestant faith who are Pentecostal, fundamentalist, or mainline liberal—terms articulated by Gallagher 2003. She also suggests evangelicals are generally anti-feminist and anti-big government; they hold these views because of their perceptions of what 'the Bible says' and they promote the 'Good News' to convince others.

[2] There are several theology colleges on the University of British Columbia's campus. The one examined here will remain nameless for reasons of anonymity.

[3] The names are fabricated to protect anonymity. Also, 'Doctor' is the title used for professors in Canada, indicating a PhD as well as professor status. To be called 'Professor' indicates no PhD and, hence, fewer credentials.

References

Bailey, K. 1993. *The girls are the ones with the pointy nails.* London, Canada: Athouse Press.

Barthes, R. 1977. "Writers, intellectuals, teachers." In *Image-Music-Text.* trans. Stephen Heath. New York: Hill, 190-215.

Busse, C. 1998. *Evangelical women in the 1990s: Examining internal dynamics.* MA thesis. Briercrest Bible Seminary, Caronport, Saskatchewan.

Clatterbaugh, K. 1990. *Contemporary perspectives on masculinity: men, women and politics in modern society.* Washington, DC: Westview Press.

Coates, J. 1993. *Women, men and language.* 2nd ed. New York: Longman.

—. 2003. *Men talk.* Oxford: Blackwell.

Connell, R. 1995. *Masculinities.* Cambridge: Polity Press.

Coontz, S. 2000. *The way we never were: American families and the nostalgia trap.* New York: Basic Books.

Corson, D. 1993. *Language, minority education and gender.* Clevedon, UK: Multicultural Education.

Daly, M. 1968. *The church and the second sex.* New York: Harper and Row.

Doriani, D. 2003. *Women and ministry.* Wheaton, USA: Crossway Books.

Eckert, P. and S. McConnell-Ginet. 2003. *Language and gender.* Cambridge, UK: Cambridge University Press.

Edelsky, C. 1981. "Who's got the floor?" *Language in society* 10.3: 383-422.

Frank, A.W. 1995. "Lecturing and transference: the undercover work of pedagogy." In *Pedagogy: the question of impersonation.* Ed. J. Gallop. Bloomington, USA: Indiana University Press.

Frazier, N. And M. Sadker. 1973. *Sexism in school and society.* New York: Harper.

Gal, S. 1991. "Between speech and silence: the problematics of research on language and gender." *Papers in Pragmatics* 3.1: 1-38.

—. 1995. "Language, gender, and power: an anthropological review." In *Gender articulated.* Eds. K. Hall and M. Bucholtz. New York: Routledge, 169-182.

Gallagher, S.K. 2003. *Evangelical identity and gendered family life.* London, UK: Rutgers University Press.

Gilligan, C. 1982/1993. *In a different voice.* Cambridge, USA: Harvard University Press.

Goffman, E. 1981. "The lecture." In *Forms of talk.* Philadelphia: University of Pennsylvania Press, 160-196.

Goodstein, L. 2004. "Politicians talk more about religion, and people expect them to." *The New York Times*, 4 July 2004. p. 2.

Grenz, S. And D.M. Kjesbo. 1995. *Women in the church.* Downers Grove, Ill., USA: Intervarsity Press.

Griffith, R.M. 1997. *God's daughters: Evangelical women and the power of submission.* Berkeley: University of California Press.

Hammersley, M. 1990. *Classroom ethnography.* Buckingham, UK: Open University Press.

Hancock, M., ed. 2003. *Christian perspectives on gender, sexuality, and community.* Vancouver, BC: Regent College Publishing.

Ingersoll, J. 2003. *Evangelical Christian women: war stories in the gender battles.* New York: New York University Press.

Jaworski, A. 1993. *The power of silence.* London, UK: Sage.

Jule, A. 2004a. *Gender, participation and silence in the language classroom: sh-shushing the girls.* Basingstoke, UK: Palgrave Macmillan.

—. 2004b. "Speaking in silence: A case study of a Canadian Punjabi girl." In *Gender and English Language Learners.* Eds. B. Norton and A. Pavlenko. Virginia, USA: TESOL Press, 69-78.

—. 2004c. "Gender and religion: Christian feminism." Paper presented at the Religion and Society Conference, Point Loma University, San Diego, California (March 23-26).

—. 2004d. "God's daughters? Evangelical women speak for themselves on feminism." Poster presented at IGALA3, Cornell University, Ithaca, NY (June 5-7).

Kramarae, C. 1980. "Gender: How she speaks." In *Attitudes towards language variation.* Eds. E.B. Ryan and H. Giles. London: Edward Arnold, 84-98.

Kramarae, C. and P. Treichler. 1990. "Power relationships in the classroom." In *Gender in the classroom: power and pedagogy.* Eds. S. Gabriel and I. Smithson. Chicago: University of Illinois Press, 41-59.

Lacan, J. 1968. *The language of the self: the function of language in psychoanalysis* (trans. Anthony Wilden). Baltimore: Johns Hopkins University Press.

Matthews, W. 1991. *World religions.* St. Paul, USA: West Publishing Company.

Mutch, B.H. 2003. "Women in the church: a North American Perspective." In *Christian perspectives on gender, sexuality, and community.* Ed. M. Hancock. Vancouver: Regent College Press, 181-193.

Paglia, C. 1992. "The joy of presbyterian sex." In *Sex, art, and American culture: essays.* New York: Vintage Books, 26-37.

Porter, F. 2002. *Changing women, changing worlds: Evangelical women in church, community and politics.* Belfast, UK: The Blackstaff Press.

Ruether, R.R. 1998. *Introducing redemption in Christian feminism.* Sheffield, UK: Sheffield Academic Press.

Sadker, M. And D. Sadker. 1990. "Confronting sexism in the college classroom." In *Gender in the classroom: power and pedagogy.* Eds. S. Gabriel and I. Smithson. Chicago: University of Illinois Press, 176-187.

Scanzoni, Letha Dawson. 1966. "Women's place: silence or service?" *Eternity* 17 (February): 14-16.

Skelton, C. 2001. *Schooling the boys: masculinities and primary education.* Buckingham, UK: Open University Press.

Spender, D. And E. Sarah, eds. 1980. *Learning to lose: sexism and education.* London, UK: The Women's Press.

Stackhouse, John G. 2002. *Evangelical landscapes.* Grand Rapids, MI, USA: Baker Book House Company.

Storkey, E. 2001. *Origins of difference: The gender debate revisited.* Grand Rapids, Michigan: Baker.

Sunderland, J. 1998. "Girls being quiet: a problem for foreign language classrooms." *Language Teaching Research* 2.

Thornborrow, J. 2002. *Power talk.* London, UK: Longman.

Walkerdine, V. 1990. *Schoolgirl fictions.* London: Verso.

Chapter Four

The *Missus*, the *Cohabitee* and the *Real Babe*: Heteronormativity in Swedish Conversations

Stina Ericsson, Växjö University

Abstract: Heterosexuality's position as the "natural", unmarked and default sexual identity, and the fact that it has remained unstudied in comparison with other sexual identities, have been given increasing attention in recent years. Based on a social constructivist view of sexual identity as recreated and maintained in social interaction, of which conversation is an important part, the paper investigates some ways in which heterosexuality is performed as the norm in Swedish conversational data. Three groups of examples are analysed, based on the types of communicative activity involved, and the types of phenomenon uncovered. The first set of examples makes use of earlier research on non-recognitional person reference forms, the second set concerns the Swedish term "sambo" ("cohabitee"), and the third set of examples investigates interviews involving pre-adolescents and young adolescents. Together, the examples show how heteronormativity is maintained in conversation, rendering a view of heterosexual identity as desirable and unproblematic.
Keywords: *heteronormativity, conversation, Swedish.*

1. Introduction

A few years ago I was present when a group of women, all with small children and in heterosexual relationships, gathered for lunch. One of the women was on maternity leave, and had brought her young son, a few months old, with her to the lunch. The boy had big beautiful eyes and a striking face, and one of the women commented on this by saying:

(1)   Han kommer bli farlig för tjejerna
Eng. *He'll be dangerous to the girls*

With this utterance, the very young boy's physical beauty is encoded as heterosexual attractiveness. The effortlessness of the production of the utterance and the unproblematic acceptance of it by the other women in the conversation, in addition to the content of the utterance, shows heterosexuality being displayed as the norm in this conversation. Over the years I have encountered many similar utterances, addressed to adults as well as children.

Rich (1980), Cameron & Kulick (2003) and others point out that heterosexuality has a very special status in relation to other sexual identities, in that it is "compulsory", normative, and often seen as natural. It is in many contexts unmarked and the assumed sexuality. As such it has also to a large extent remained unstudied in comparison with other sexual identities. Yet at the same time as heterosexuality is unmarked and considered natural, its unmarkedness and naturalness comes about only through a great deal of effort – a great deal of propaganda – in a number of different aspects of society.

On the social constructivist assumption that much of the human world is created and continually recreated by the human members themselves, and this through social interaction where conversation plays an important role, identities concerning gender, age, social status, and so on, are recreated and maintained interactionally. That is, identities are not already "out there", but rather maintained and transformed during human encounters. This idea is expressed within ethnomethodology (Garfinkel 1967, 1972), which has influenced work on human interaction in the Conversation Analysis (CA) framework. The idea can also be seen in the 'performativity' of gender as discussed by Butler (1990).

This (re)creation of identities through social interaction extends to sexual identities. This means that heterosexual identities are also maintained and recreated during, for instance, social interaction in the form of conversations. Leaving the construction of heterosexual identities in social interactions unstudied, may therefore help foster a view of heterosexuality as a neutral, natural, unchanging and unchangeable sexual identity, as opposed to other sexual identities. It is therefore essential that its linguistic performance be scrutinised, to investigate and show just how heterosexual identity is a social construction. Another aspect of this is that the view of heterosexuality as the norm has interactional costs for non-heterosexual participants in conversations, as can be seen through the need for correction (Land and Kitzinger 2005, further discussed below).

Cameron and Kulick point out that heterosexual identity, although "default" and "unmarked" does not necessarily go unmarked in discourse. That is, it is clearly possible to study the way linguistic means are used to construct heterosexual identity. I have chosen to do so here using recordings of conversations, as such interactions play a daily role in many people's lives and thus constitute an important arena for the construction of identities. In addition, many conversations are often not explicitly about sexual identity, and the construction of heterosexual identities in such contexts is particularly interesting. The overall question that I address below is therefore how heterosexuality is performed as the norm using communicative means in conversations, with a particular focus on Swedish conversational data. To some extent I also address the issue of how different kinds of communicative activity influence this performance of heterosexuality.

I address the issue of heterosexuality as the norm using the term 'heteronormativity', by which I mean a system whereby heterosexuality is considered normal, natural, and desirable, marginalising and stigmatising other sexual identities (see e.g., Cameron and Kulick (2006)).

I begin by introducing the data that is used in this study, and by outlining relevant recent work on heterosexuality in conversations. I then turn to a qualitative analysis of a few different conversations, grouped into three different kinds based on the types of communicative activity involved, and the types of examples uncovered.

2. Background

This section introduces the data that is used in the study, and outlines a recent study of heteronormativity in ordinary conversations. As a brief background to heteronormativity in Sweden, homosexuality was considered a crime until 1944 and an illness until 1979. A 1995 law gave homosexual couples the right to register as legal partners, but same-sex marriage is still not legal. Lesbians were given the right to insemination in 2005. Hate crimes against LGBTQI people occur all over Sweden, in particular in the larger cities, and even seem to have increased in recent years according to official statistics.

2.1. Corpus material

The main source of empirical data for the present study is data in the form of conversations in the Göteborg Spoken Language Corpus (GSLC), collected and transcribed at the Department of linguistics, Göteborg

University, as described by Allwood (1999) and Allwood, Björnberg, Grönqvist, Ahlsén & Ottesjö (2000). The GSLC is a continually growing corpus of spoken Swedish, currently comprising 371 recordings of varying lengths. One aim of the corpus is to include spoken language from several different social activities, as spoken language varies in different activities with regard to different linguistic levels such as vocabulary and grammar. Activities also differ in terms of participant roles, aims of the activity, and so on, all of which may also influence the communication in the activity. This view of activity-dependent spoken language is also one that I adhere to in the study presented below.

Activities in the GSLC include consultation, discussion, formal meeting, informal conversation, interview, phone, and shop, among many others. Activities may also be divided into subtypes. For my study I have chosen a subset of the activities and conversations in the GSLC. For the analysis in section 3.1 I have chosen the 15 doctor-patient conversations in the corpus, doctor-patient being a subtype of the consultation activity. I have chosen these partly because doctor-patient interaction is an already well-known area for linguistic inquiry, such as for power relations, see for instance Treichler, Frankel, Kramarae, Zoppi & Beckman (1984), and West (1984). I have also chosen this (sub)activity because the interaction here provides a suitable kind of activity for a phenomenon that I am particularly interested in, non-recognitional person reference forms, as will be explained in the next section.

The analysis in section 3.2 starts from a field example of my own, and this example will be introduced in detail in that section. It also contains an automatic search of the whole GSLC. The search was performed using the Corpus Browser, an on-line search tool that provides a web interface to the GSLC.

The third and final analysis in section 3.3 is based on the three GSLC recordings of school boys' and school girls' interviews, a subtype of the interview activity. I have included these conversations to get non-adult data, and these conversations are some of very few examples of such data in the GSLC. The participants in the conversations are pre-adolescents and young adolescents, and they interview each other using questions concerning school life, their interests, their dreams for the future, and the like.

2.2. Heterosexuality as the norm in everyday conversations

One of few studies taking a linguistic perspective on heteronormativity in everyday conversations is given by Kitzinger (2005b). Using CA and

CA data sets from the 1960s to the 1980s, she reanalyses these data sets in a perspective not originally used within CA: she investigates how these interactions display heterosexuality as a taken-for-granted background that can unproblematically be referred to, both in conversations between people who know each other and between strangers. The data sets consist of recordings of British and American conversations, mainly over the phone, and previously used in classic CA studies.

Kitzinger highlights some examples of explicit heterosexual topics in the data –such as sexual joking, heterosexual activity, and various aspects of heterosexual relationships– but otherwise focuses on conversations and parts of conversations where heterosexuality is *not* the topic, or under discussion in any way. For this, she chooses to investigate the use of non-recognitional person reference forms in the data, as references to other people such as partners are a very common way of displaying a speaker's or someone else's sexual identity. Non-recognitional person reference forms are discussed by Schegloff (1996), who categorises referring expressions based on (the speaker's view of) their relationship to the recipient: "[r]ecognitional reference forms are such forms as convey to the recipient that the one being referred to is someone that they know (about)" (Schegloff 1996, p. 459), and non-recognitional forms then signal to the recipient that the referent is someone they do not know (about). Examples of the former include personal names, and the latter expressions such as "someone" and "this woman".

Kitzinger identifies five types of non-recognitional person reference forms in the data that involve references to roles in the heterosexual family system, thereby displaying the heterosexuality of the speaker or the assumed heterosexuality of someone talked to or talked of. The first of these types is the reference form that locates someone within a heterosexual marital unit, such as "my wife" or "my husband" (note that all the conversations studied by Kitzinger were recorded no later than the 1980s, thus before any country recognised same-sex marriages). One example that Kitzinger discusses here is the following, originally from Sacks (1972):

(2)   A: Has there been some personal problem or difficulty that you're experiencing?
       B: Yes. I just lost my wife and I feel awfully depressed.

Person *A* is here working for a suicide prevention centre, and is counselling person *B* over the phone. Person *B* uses the non-recognitional reference form "my wife" while giving the reasons for his suicidality, thus displaying his heterosexuality without the conversation being concerned with sexual identity, and without the conversation turning to a focus on this identity *per se* in subsequent turns.

The other four types of non-recognitional person reference forms identified by Kitzinger in the data are in-law terms (e.g., "my mother in law", "my son in law"); expressions identifying someone through reference to their spouse (e.g., "Mister Quinn's wife", "Mittie's husband"); reference to heterosexual couples (e.g., "the Grahams", "Bill'n Gladys", "Liz en uhr husb'n"); and pronouns being used as the first reference to someone (e.g., "he" to refer to a husband not previously mentioned in the conversation nor physically present). Using non-CA terminology, the non-recognitional reference forms identified by Kitzinger are all existentially presuppositional expressions for which the recipient is expected to accommodate a referent.

Kitzinger argues that all these examples show how heterosexual identity can be referred to unproblematically in ordinary conversations without the topic of discussion being sexual identity. It is the unmarked nature of the reference forms and their use that shows heteronormativity in play. Kitzinger specifically points to two aspects for the reflection and construction of heteronormativity in her data: the "inattentiveness to heterosexuality as a possible identity category", and "the ease with which interactants make heterosexuality apparent without being heard as 'talking about' heterosexuality" (Kitzinger 2005b, p. 223).

Using doctor-patient conversations, Kitzinger (2005a) similarly investigates heteronormativity, in the form of heterosexual references and inferences that are drawn from these. Land and Kitzinger (2005) include an investigation of institutional telephone calls in lesbian households, showing how heteronormative presumptions force non-heterosexuals either to play along with heteronormativity or to initiate corrective sequences in the conversation. An example is an insurance salesman assuming that a partner that is referred to is a husband, and the lesbian having to initiate a correction sequence before the conversation can return to the matter of insurance.

3. Analysis and discussion

Having introduced the conversational data in the form of the GSLC and the study of non-recognitional person reference forms as one way of analysing heteronormativity in ordinary conversations, I now turn to my analysis of heteronormativity in Swedish conversations.

3.1. The *missus*: doctor-patient conversations in the GSLC

Turning first to non-recognitional person reference forms, doctor-patient conversations form an activity where, at least in some cases, the doctor and the patient are strangers, providing a setting where one or the other may choose to talk about, for instance, a spouse the existence of which needs to be accommodated by the other, thus giving an opportunity for non-recognitional person reference forms. Of the 15 conversations, most show no reference to sexual identity, either directly or indirectly. Among those that do, there seem to be examples of non-recognitional person reference forms, used in a way that parallels the examples found by Kitzinger. One instance involves an older male patient (*P*) and a male doctor (*D*). The conversation concerns the medication that the patient is taking, and its effects and side-effects. The transcription of this and other extracts from the GSLC have been edited slightly, omitting details not relevant to present discussions. An explanation of transcription conventions can be found as an appendix. Translations into English are given as approximate paraphrases rather than literal translations. The extract containing the person reference form of interest (marked in boldface) in the conversation between the doctor and the older male patient is given in (3):

(3) D: m / märker du några skillnader det här att dom dagar du äter dina
urindrivare tabletter å dom dagar du inte [19 äter (...)]19
D: m / do you notice any differences here that those days when
you take your diuretic and those days that you don't [19 take (...)
]19
P: [19 nä]19 ingen [20 skillnad]20
P: [19 no]19 no [20 difference]20
D: [20 ingen]20 skillnad
D: [20 no]20 difference
P: nä
P: no
D: okej
D: okay
P: det e bara **frugan** som säger nu får du ta dom [21 idag]21 å då
[22 tar jag] 22 dom < > ja nä inte nu [23 säger jag]23 för < jag ska
nu bort till något > sammanträde
*P: it's just **the missus** who says that now you have to take them*
[21 today] 21 'n then [22 I take]22 them < > yes no not now
[23 I say]23 because < I'm going to some > meeting
@ <laughter>
@ <laughing>
D: [21 ja]21

> D: *[21 yes]21*
> D: [22 ja]22
> D: [23 ja ja]23
> D: ja [24 hör du]24
> > D: *yes [24 can you hear]24*
> P: [24 enda]24 som krånglar ibland så jag tycker jag HÖR // lite
> > P: *[24 the only thing]24 that troubles me sometimes I think I HEAR // a little*
> D: ja
> > D: *yes*
> P: jag HÖR HÖR ju men inte så att / jag hör som man [25 SKA]25 göra men [26   herregud]26 när man är såpass gammal så så < [27 börjar]27 >
> > P: *I can HEAR HEAR but not so that / I hear as you [25 SHOULD]25 do but [26 goodness]26 when you're this old so so < [27 you start]27 >*
> @ <laughing>
> D: [25 ja]25
> D: [26 m m]26
> D: [27 m]27 ja / har du tagit urindrivande tablett idag
> > D: *[27 m]27 yes / have you taken your diuretic today*
>
> (GSLC recording A5002011)

In the patient's third utterance in example (3) he refers to his wife using the expression "frugan" ("the missus"). This is a person reference form of the first type identified by Kitzinger, reference forms giving a person's location in a marital unit.

The conversation does not concern the patient's sexual identity, and the patient makes his sexual identity known while the topic is his intake of the medication in question. The patient's mention of his wife is not linguistically marked in any way, and there is nothing in the conversation that indicates that the doctor and the patient pay any specific attention to the patient's mention of his wife and the implication for his sexual identity. The doctor acknowledges what the patient is saying, and after a while brings the conversation back to the diuretics. This example then clearly parallels Kitzinger's examples – and also the doctor-patient conversations investigated by Kitzinger (2005a) – for which she argues that heterosexuality is a taken-for-granted resource that can be made use of in an unproblematic way in ordinary conversations.

A second GSLC example shows a person reference form not identified by Kitzinger (2005b) in her data: an expression used to identify the other parent of a child. The conversation in question involves a younger female patient and a male doctor. As part of charting the patient's symptoms, the doctor tries to establish her general situation. The patient's young daughter is also present during the consultation.

(4) D: vad är det som händer som (...)
        D: what's going on that (...)
     P: jaa det är mycket / < / > jag har jobbigt med **hennes pappa** då för
     vi skilde oss för två år sen men // det är jättejobbigt hela tiden
        *P: uhm it's a lot / < / > I have a hard time with **her dad** because*
        we got divorced two years ago but // it's really hard all the time
     @ <laughter>
     D: jaa
        D: yees
     P: det är rättegångar å det är underhåll å det är allt möjligt så han är
     en riktig bråkstake då
        P: it's court proceedings and it's alimony and it's everything so
        he's a real troublemaker
     D: ja
     P: så det är liksom man får aldrig lugn å ro heller då å så det är det
     jobbigt då ibland på jobbet många är sjuka å man får stressa å stressa
     å det är så där
        P: so it's like you never get peace 'n quiet either then so that's
        the way it is sometimes at work lots of people are out sick and
        it's stress 'n stress 'n that way
     D: jaa /

                                        (GSLC recording A5006021)

In this conversation, a person not present and not previously mentioned in the conversation, is referred to by the expression "her dad". The possessor in this genitive construction is quite clearly the daughter. This in itself is not enough to convey heterosexuality, and the sexual identity of the patient is made clear in the remainder of the turn speaking of the patient's divorce from the person referred to as "her dad". Thus the referential expression is coupled with information about location in a marital unit.

In a third GSLC example, the conversation is between a male doctor and a patient described as an older female. The conversation concerns the patient's symptoms, followed by talk about medication, physical exercise, and weight. The doctor then asks the patient "Är du gift eller hur har du det?" ("Are you married or what is your situation?"), to which the patient answers with the one-word utterance "Änka" ("Widow"). The patient's utterance here involves the heterosexual marital unit, as a widow is someone who has been part of a heterosexual marriage. Of particular interest in this conversation, however, is the doctor's question. This explicitly refers to heterosexuality through asking about marriage, and it may be argued that the doctor's utterance shows a heterosexual bias. A less normative question might be one asking whether the patient lives alone or together with someone.

Thus, person reference forms similar to those in Kitzinger's data, can indeed be found in the GSLC doctor-patient conversations. When these reference forms are used, the topic of the conversation is not sexual identity in any way. The expressions are unmarked in the conversations, no attention is drawn to heterosexuality as a category, and with Kitzinger one may argue that these examples show the use of heterosexuality as a taken-for-granted background resource. However, at this point I need to introduce a caveat. Very little background information is included in the GSLC corpus, and from the conversations themselves it cannot be excluded that the doctors in examples (3) and (4) have access to information about the patients' marital status. If that is the case, the reference forms will not be non-recognitional. Thus, it may be argued that I cannot conclude with absolute certainty that these are indeed non-recognitional person reference forms, and that the most I can say is that the GSLC conversations studied here show unproblematic references to heterosexuality (and no references to non-heterosexuality).

In terms of the type of activity involved, the (possibly non-recognitional) person reference forms are all used by patients, and to refer to their present or former spouse. The spouse is referred to as part of the patients' motivating their medical condition or to elaborate on some aspect of their ailment or medication. Although the number of conversations investigated here is small, a tentative conclusion is that participant roles in an activity is a factor in how heterosexuality is displayed as a norm in conversations. Patients may use (non-recognitional) person reference forms to refer to their own spouse, whereas this is less likely for the doctor. The doctor, on the other hand, may use other means of recreating heteronormativity in their questions to the patient. Most of the GSLC doctor-patient conversations show no reference to sexual identity at all, which may also be a reflection of the activity.

3.2 The *cohabitee*: a field example

The "refugee guide project" in Gothenburg, Sweden is a cultural, social, and language exchange programme for integration, based on individual voluntary participation. Newly arrived immigrants and refugees are matched with Gothenburgians, who then meet regularly for various activities, with the Gothenburgian acting as a "guide". The match between a refugee or immigrant and a Gothenburgian is based on factors such as sex, age, interests, and education/profession, as determined by a questionnaire and an interview.

The field example below is taken from one of these interviews. The interviewer (*A*) has just asked about the interviewee's (*B*) civil status. *B* has replied using the word "sambo" ("cohabitee"). The interviewer then asks:

(5)   A: Vad gör din ö:h < sambo > ?
          A: What does your e:h < cohabitee > do (for a living)?
       @ < gaze, smile >

The term 'sambo' for someone you are living with but are not married to, is a commonly used term in Swedish. It is a gender neutral term, but does not carry any implications that the relationship is non-heterosexual. In this respect it is similar to the term 'partner' as used in British English, but may contrast with the use of 'partner' in an American English context.

In the field example in (5) the interviewer repeats the interviewee's "sambo" rather than using a subsequent reference form such as "hon", *she*, or "han", *he* (as is unmarked or normative in this context, e.g., Schegloff (1996)). This departure from unmarked referring avoids assuming anything about the sex of the cohabitee in question, thereby avoiding the reinforcement and reproduction of heteronormativity and the kinds of error displayed by Land and Kitzinger (2005).

Now, in addition to "sambo" being a marked reference form in the example, as opposed to a pronoun in the same position, the example is particularly interesting by being highly marked in other ways as well. There is a hesitation marker before "sambo", and during the utterance of "sambo" the interviewer looks at the interviewee and smiles in a self-conscious way. This creates an even more marked situation with "sambo" as the centre of this markedness. It can be contrasted with the patient's production of "the missus" above, and the use of non-recognitional person reference forms in Kitzinger's data, which are not accompanied by similar linguistic markedness.

I want to suggest that the markedness of "sambo" in example (5) can be interpreted as creating a situation in which heteronormativity is still upheld, in spite of the interviewer's possible attempt at not making heterosexuality the norm. Clearly, linguistic markedness itself is not enough for this inference, as markedness may go together with a number of different reasons. However, if the example is recognised as the interviewer explicitly choosing a gender-neutral term, which has explicit consequences for assumed sexual identity here, and the markedness can be connected to this very choice, then the markedness can be seen as concerning sexual identity. The interviewer avoids making any assumptions about sexual identity, but the very avoidance is marked, implying that an unmarked situation would have involved an assumption of the default sexual identity, that is, (in this context as in many others) presumably heterosexuality.

An automatic search for the word "sambo" in all conversations in the GSLC gives six relevant instances of this word, two of which are from the same conversation. None of these instances of "sambo" are linguistically marked as in example (5) above, which may be taken as an indication that there is nothing about the term 'sambo' in itself that prompts markedness. In four of the GSLC examples "sambo" is used referentially for an actual person, and for all of these four examples the sex of the cohabitee is also explicitly made known in the conversation, either because the person is referred to as "han", *he*, or "hon", *she*, later in the same utterance, or because the person in question has already been referred to in the conversation in a gendered way. In all these four examples "sambo" is used for a heterosexual cohabitee.

One of these four instances of "sambo" is a non-recognitional person reference. Person *A* is calling *G*, the latter representing a telephone-based yellow pages information service. Both participants are male. *A* wants information about insurance companies, and after a discussion of *A*'s needs, *G* suggests that *A* should contact a large insurance company as opposed to a small specialised one. *A*'s reply to this suggestion is as in (6), where Folksam and Trygghansa are (large) insurance companies:

(6) A: ja det äh stämmer nog (...) / ja / öh jag har ju redan folksam å å och **min sambo** hon har trygghansa så att äh / det kanska e bra å ta numret till dom först å höra vad dom kan erbjuda då
   *A: yes that eh is probably right (...) / yes / eh I already have folksam 'n 'n and **my cohabitee** she has trygghansa so that eh / it might be a good idea to take the number for those first and hear what they have to offer*
   G: jaa där kan du säkert / teckna dom försäkringarna du nämnde där
   G: yes you can surely / take out the insurances that you mentioned there

(GSLC recording A8102091)

The expression "min sambo" ("my cohabitee") is immediately followed by a gendered pronoun showing the sex of the cohabitee, "min sambo" and the pronoun together showing the sexual identity of the male caller *A*. This is then an example of a non-recognitional person reference form not directly discussed by Kitzinger (2005b): an expression that locates someone in a relationship that does not involve marriage. However, Kitzinger (2005a) includes "girlfriend", and Land and Kitzinger (2005) investigate lesbian relationships. The construction nominal phrase + pronoun + verb phrase, as in "min sambo hon har ..." ("my cohabitee she has ...") in example (6), is a common construction in spoken and informal Swedish, but the pronoun is not required to be present.

The expression "min sambo" is also found in another one of the four conversations with "sambo" in a referring expression. This is an interview where the interviewee, a female, refers to her cohabitee, and later in the same turn also refers to this cohabitee as "he" (GSLC recording V0255011). In this conversation, however, it appears that the participants knew each other beforehand, which may mean that the interviewer may already know or know of the interviewee's cohabitee, that is, the interviewee's "min sambo" is presumably not a non-recognitional reference.

In the remaining two examples of "sambo" in the GSLC, the term is not used referentially for an actual person, but rather to ask a question about a hypothetical situation (roughly "And you wouldn't do all the household work for your cohabitee or husband?" addressed to a woman, GSLC recording V0643011), or to ask about consequences of someone not having a cohabitee (roughly "And you have no cohabitee, so you're not economically responsible for someone else?" addressed to a man, GSLC recording A8405011).

3.3 A *real babe*: school children's interviews in the GSLC

The three GSLC recordings containing interviews by and of pre-adolescents and early adolescents contain no instances of non-recognitional person reference forms implying sexual identities. As very many of Kitzinger's examples refer to spouses and others related by marriage, for speakers and their friends and acquaintances, it is perhaps not surprising that such reference forms are missing from these conversations.

In the school children's interviews, there is one instance of heterosexuality displayed explicitly. This is from an interview between two boys, Clark (*C*) and Daniel (*D*), who are friends or at least know each other beforehand. The following utterances are the opening utterances in the interview (*B* is an adult male seemingly in charge of the recording):

(7)   C: ska jag börja ställa fråga (åt) han
           C: will I start asking him questions
       B: ja
           B: yes
       C: e:h vad vill du: helst ha i hela världen
           C: e:h what do you: want most of all in the whole world
       D: < e:h > en pangbrud å en god bil
           D: < e:h > a real babe and a nice car

@ < laughing>
C: jaha / ha vad är du intresserad i förutom sport då
   C: u-huh / huh what are you interested in besides sports
(GSLC recording A3501021)

Daniel here makes an explicit reference to his heterosexuality, by identifying a sexually attractive woman as one of the two things he wants the most.

Kiesling (2002) investigates heterosexuality in conversations among American male university students, and argues that narratives of heterosexuality is an important part of performing relationships for these young men. He also suggests that displays of heterosexuality through speech in men-only groups is a way of creating status in the group. Conceivably, Daniel's uttering "a real babe" in the extract above is an attempt at acquiring status, in the eyes of his friend Clark, and possibly also in the eyes of the adult male present, *B*, and anyone who is going to listen to the recording.

Daniel's utterance may also be an attempt at showing maturity. Cameron and Kulick (2003) discuss research by Penelope Eckert involving adolescents and pre-adolescents, including how displays of knowledge about adult heterosexual practice is a required part of these young people's behaviour. Cameron and Kulick cite the following utterance from one of the boys in Eckert's material during a conversation about cruise control in cars:

> When you're going at 60 miles per hour like in a James Bond movie and you press auto control and then you go make out with a woman in the back then you put it on cruise control and you stay at the same speed. (Cameron and Kulick 2003: 71)

This utterance shows knowledge about adult heterosexual masculinity, and Daniel's utterance in example (7) may work in the same way. Interestingly, the quote from Eckert's material and Daniel's utterance in the GSLC conversation also both connect desirable women as well as cars to displays of heterosexuality and masculinity.

Daniel's utterance in (7) can be seen as containing markedness: in contrast with the production of "the missus" in example (3), but similar to the production of "your cohabitee" in example (5), Daniel's utterance contains a hesitation marker, "eh", and laughter. This is further evidence that (un)markedness alone is not enough to warrant a conclusion of a particular sexual identity being displayed. Rather, in example (7) the markedness of Daniel's utterance may go together with his aim for adult heterosexual masculinity and his attempt at acquiring status.

4. Conclusion

In this paper I have begun to explore heteronormativity in Swedish conversations in a few different activities. I have looked both at person reference forms –non-recognitional to various degrees– following Kitzinger (2005b), and more explicit displays of heterosexuality.

The heteronormative aspect of the person reference forms is given by their use in frequent and, importantly, unproblematic references to the heterosexual kinship system. The person reference forms found in the Swedish data have mainly involved locations within the marital unit, as well as expressions of the form "min sambo" ("my cohabitee"), which is a common term in Swedish for someone you are living with but not married to. Correspondences to other types of non-recognitional person reference forms identified by Kitzinger in her material, such as expressions using in-law terminology, could be identified in the Swedish data through an automatic search: the interface to the corpus enables a quick search through the whole corpus for any expression, such as "svärmor" ("mother-in-law"), and so on. This could also be complemented by a more qualitative analysis of the conversations for the identification of any other reference forms. As it is sometimes uncertain that person reference forms in the GSLC are indeed non-recognitional, the analysis of this corpus may also be complemented by other recordings where no such uncertainty exists.

More explicit references to heterosexuality have notably been included in the form of a young adolescent's display of normative adult heterosexual masculinity. A more subtle heteronormativity in play could also be seen in the field example involving the expression "din sambo" ("your cohabitee"), where I argued that an attempt at avoiding heteronormativity was carried out using a linguistically marked utterance, and the marked avoidance implied a default sexuality as the underlying norm.

The relation between heteronormativity and different activities has been a secondary focus of the research presented here. Even though the number of conversations and activities in the study is fairly small, there are indications that activity type does play a role. The school children's interviews contain no non-recognitional person reference forms, which is to be expected if these reference forms are limited to the marital system, but may perhaps be found in other such material in the form of expressions involving "boyfriend" and "girlfriend". In contrast, doctor-patient conversations contain person reference forms that may be non-recognitional, and these are all produced by the patients as part of their relating background factors for their symptoms or medical treatment. An interesting indication in the doctor-patient conversations is that not only activity type but also participant roles are important to the display of heterosexuality: patients may refer to their spouses, but this would presumably not be expected of the doctor. However, doctors may display heteronormativity in their questions to and assumptions about the patient, as indicated by one of the questions in the doctor-patient material. A natural extension of this line of research is the investigation of several more activity types, as well as a more principled approach to the description of participant roles and other activity-dependent aspects.

In terms of heterosexual identity as a social construction, I have taken some steps towards investigating the recreation of heteronormativity in Swedish conversations. The school boy Daniel clearly makes an attempt at assuming a normative adult heterosexual identity, which shows the desirability of such an identity and gives a view of its transmission to another generation. Person reference forms in other conversations indicate unproblematic references to heterosexuality, and these may help construct heterosexuality as unproblematic and normal. This is perhaps particularly seen in relation to the data from lesbian households investigated by Land and Kitzinger (2005). The field example involving "sambo" ("cohabitee"), finally, shows how non-lexical communicative clues help maintain heteronormativity even when a non-normative approach is sought.

Acknowledgement

The author wishes to thank the audience at IGALA4 for helpful comments and suggestions that have improved this paper. The author is also greatly indebted to Gunilla Byrman and Celia Kitzinger for helpful feedback on a first version.

Transcription conventions

/	short pause
//	pause
[19]19	overlapped speech
(…)	inaudible
< text >	*in an utterance line*: 'text' has a comment on comment line below utterance
< text >	*in a comment line*: 'text' is the comment to corresponding part in utterance above

@   comment line
TEXT   emphatic stress

References

Allwood, J. 1999. "The Swedish spoken language corpus at Göteborg University." In *Fonetik'99: Proceedings from the Twelfth Swedish Phonetics Conference 5-9*.

Allwood, J., M. Björnberg, L. Grönqvist, E. Ahlsén and C. Ottesjö. 2000. "The spoken language corpus at the Linguistics Department, Göteborg University." *Forum: Qualitative Social Research [Online Journal]* 1.3. Available at http://www.qualitative-research.net/fqs-texte/3-00/3-00allwoodetal-e.htm

Butler, J. 1990. *Gender trouble: Feminism and the subversion of identity*. New York: Routledge.

Cameron, D. and D. Kulick. 2003. *Language and Sexuality Reader*. Cambridge: Cambridge University Press.

Cameron, D. and D. Kulick. 2006. "General Introduction." In *The Language and Sexuality Reader*. Eds. D. Cameron and D. Kulick. London and New York: Routledge, 1-12.

Garfinkel, H. 1967. *Studies in Ethnomethodology*. Englewood Cliffs.

—. 1972. "Remarks on Ethnomethodology." In *Directions in sociolinguistics: The ethnography of communication*. Eds. J. Gumperz and D. Hymes. New York: Holt, Rinehart and Winston, 310-324.

Kiesling, S.F. 2002. "Playing the straight man: Displaying and maintaining male heterosexuality in discourse." In *Language and Sexuality: Contesting Meaning in Theory and Practice*. Eds. K. Campbell-Kibler, R. Podesva, S.J. Roberts and A. Wong. Stanford, CA: CSLI Publications.

Kitzinger, C. 2005a. "Heteronormativity in action: Reproducing the heterosexual nuclear family in after-hours medical calls. *Social Problems* 52.4: 477-498.

—. 2005b. "Speaking as a heterosexual": (How) does sexuality matter for talk-in-interaction? *Research on Language and Social Interaction* 38.3: 221-265.

Land, V. and C. Kitzinger. 2005. "Speaking as a lesbian: Correcting the heterosexist presumption." *Research on Language and Social Interaction* 38.4: 371-416.

Rich, A. 1980. "Compulsory heterosexuality and lesbian existence." *Signs* 5: 631-661.

Sacks, H. 1972. "An initial investigation of the usability of conversational data for doing sociology." In *Studies in Social Interaction*. Ed. D. Sudnow. New York: Free Press, 31-74.

Schegloff, E.A. 1996. "Some practices for referring to persons in talk-in-interaction." In *Studies in Anaphora*. Ed. B.A. Fox. Amsterdam: Benjamins, 437-485.

Treichler, P.A., R.M. Frankel, C. Kramarae, K. Zoppi and H.B. Beckman (1984) "Problems and *prob*lems: power relationships in medical encounter." In *Language and Power*. Eds. C. Kramarae, M. Schulz and W.M. O'Barr. New York: Sage.

West, C. (1984) "When the doctor is a "lady": power, status and gender in physician-patient encounters." *Symbolic Interaction* 7: 87-106.

Chapter Five

Gender Stereotypes and Globalised Customer Service Communication in Poland

Agnieszka Kiełkiewicz-Janowiak and Joanna Pawelczyk, Adam Mickiewicz University, Poznań

Abstract: Over the last few years call centres have become a new and rapidly expanding arena for communication between customers and companies. The prescribed procedures for this type of interaction have followed international corporate norms. It has been claimed (notably by Cameron 2000) that the prescribed communicative strategies for interaction with the customer in call centres resemble what is commonly referred to as feminine discourse. Therefore, as far as professional desirability is concerned, women may be expected to be 'naturally' suited to the work of call centre operators.

Customer service work entails the management of emotional states and involves attending not only to others' but also to one's own feelings and emotions (Hochschild 1983, Taylor and Tyler 2000). In general, modern psychologists make claims about *caring* being an essentially feminine domain (Paoletti 2002, Graham 1983).

This paper applies the concepts of customer service, emotional labour and feminine discourse to the analysis of call centre communication in the local Polish context. Specifically, it is considered whether in view of the gender relations following the recent political, economic and social transformations in Poland (Fodor 1997) the patterns imposed by the global customer care standards overlap with stereotypically feminine interactive skills (cf. Kiełkiewicz-Janowiak and Pawelczyk 2006).

For this purpose three types of data have been investigated: (1) written descriptions of call centre procedures, (2) interviews with call centre trainers, supervisors and operators, (3) recordings of customer-operator exchanges.

The communicative style preferable in the context of CC service can be described as a 'both…and' style: an ideal CC worker possesses a mixture of communicative features stereotyped in Poland as feminine and masculine. Importantly, feminine and masculine features become salient (and indispensable) depending on the type of task to be tackled and the personality of the customer. Although the communicative behaviours which are stereotypically feminine feature as core prescriptions for CC performance (thus they are valorised), CC operators have been found to fail in applying them in their interactions with customers.

Keywords: *call centre, feminine discourse, globalisation, Poland.*

1. Introduction

Over the last few years call centres have become a new and rapidly expanding arena for communication between customers and companies. The prescribed procedures for this type of interaction have followed international corporate norms.

It has been claimed that the prescribed communicative strategies for interaction with the customer in call centres resemble what is commonly referred to as feminine discourse. Furthermore, as far as professional desirability is concerned, females are described as "naturally" suited to the work of a call centre operator. According to Cameron the preferred communication strategies at call centres largely overlap with "ways of speaking that are symbolically coded as 'feminine' (and that in some cases are also associated with women speakers)" (Cameron 2000a: 333)

Indeed, *effective* customer service provides *care* which is a typically feminine domain: women's most important role in most societies has for long been the care for others (cf. the traditional and historical roles ascribed to women and imposed on them in the process of socialisation). At the same time, however, it also calls for a fairly *powerful management* of discourse; *taking control* in conversation is in many cultures perceived as a typically masculine skill.

We have looked into the practice of call centre work in Poland to see how the tasks assigned to operators are tackled in stereotypically feminine and stereotypically masculine ways. The present paper considers whether Cameron's (2000a) claim applies to the local Polish context. Therefore, two elements of the local context will first be presented: gendered social roles and CC communication.

1.1. Women in Poland

One dominating source of influence on the social roles of women in Poland has been the knight-and-his-lady tradition, especially strong because of the country's history. Secondly, the Catholic Church has glorified the role of the woman as 'Polish mother' – patriotic and caring. After the Second World War, both the communist regime and the unceasingly strong authority of the Church preserved the traditional gender roles: for men to struggle for the country and support the family, and for women to care for the(ir) men and the family (cf. Walczewska 1999). In fact, the period of state socialism brought about women's even stronger identification with the private sphere (home, family, religion) as a safe haven from the communist-oppressed public sphere (Graff 2003, referring to Sidorenko). In return they were societally appreciated as brave and resourceful in the face of everyday economic hardships. It is a debated question whether after 1989 the self-sacrificing Polish woman has given way to the self-investing professional (Marody and Poleszczuk 2000).

1.2. Stereotypical Polish woman

The portrait of the contemporary Polish woman has been drawn by Kwiatkowska (1999), who pointed to three groups of values relevant to the stereotyping of men and, especially, women in Poland. They are related to (1) the history of the Polish gentry and their traditional ethos, (2) Polish Catholicism and, in particular, the cult of the Virgin Mary; (3) the 'egalitarian' ideology of communism. She referred to the stereotypical Polish woman as a 'lady', whose complex social perception is shown in the following table:

A 'Lady' according to women	A 'Lady' according to men
traditional – patriotic, Catholic, caring for others	
	privileged – respected, treated with special attention, admired
ambitious – aspiring, independent	

Table 5-1: The subtypes of the stereotype of a LADY (based on Kwiatkowska 1999)

Both women and men agree as to the stereotype of the 'traditional' Polish woman: gentle, nice, empathic, forgiving, dependent on the man, accepting the priority of the (patriotic and Catholic) family over any other matters in her life. However, the 'ambitious' subtype runs against the 'traditional' subtype, and, notably, it is favoured by women.[1] The stereotypes also reflect the nature of gender relations in Poland: women are disadvantaged and idealised at the same time (cf. men's stereotype of a 'privileged' woman). In fact, *benevolent sexism* (cf. Glick & Fiske 1997) seems to accurately describe Polish gender relations.

1.3. Women in the transitional labour market

Under state socialism Polish women were encouraged to participate in the paid labour force as well as work in the home and have (more) children. They were supported by the state's maternity benefits and its contributions to child rearing. The family-and-gender ideology were part of state policies: the working woman was a symbol often used by communist propaganda, showing off women's equality of opportunities under socialism[2]. However, the state's provisions dwindled dramatically after the political transformation following the year 1989. In comparison with other Eastern European countries (i.e. Hungary and Romania), the Polish state has most significantly restricted access to maternity benefits, thus forcing women out of the labour market. Nowadays, women in Poland are severely affected by job loss and their unemployment tends to last long (Fodor *et al* 2002). They are highly dependent on their spouses (and families), especially when they have young children because maternity and childcare policies force them to drop out of paid work[3].

For women's job opportunities in post-communist European economies the service sector is of special significance. Fodor's (1997) job segregation theory which posits that most jobs are segregated by sex to the disadvantage of women also argues that in a time of economic transition women's concentration in the service sector protects them from unemployment. Additionally, women's much better educational credentials, in particular their "fluency in languages, analytic skills, better self-presentation, and more flexible retraining possibilities" (Fodor 1997: 486) provide them with a kind of "cultural capital" and security in the job market. In 1988 and through the period of transition women have continued to dominate the service sector while men – industry. As the service sector has grown rapidly over the last 15 years, Glass and Kawachi (2002) suggest that "service sector experience still helps to keep women, but not men, out of unemployment".

However, as a consequence of the process of retraditionalisation and market discrimination, women who have young children are at a strong disadvantage (compared to men and compared to non-mothering women), i.e. they are more likely to become unemployed (Glass and Kawachi 2002).

2. Customer service in a transitional economy: From 'Customer is king' to 'Customer care'

Traditionally, service work was supposed to make the customer satisfied. One way of doing this was to suggest who was in power in a service encounter, as in the old slogan, "the customer is king". Modern marketing has additionally ascribed a new role to the service worker who is now to be *in control,* though the customer does not necessarily need to realise this. This change of attitude has been marked by a discursive shift from 'client' to 'customer' and from 'service' to 'care', with the new usage suggesting less formality, and more friendliness and warmth. 'Customer care' is what is practised and, on the whole, customers do not mind being cared for.

In the local context of Poland the slogan "(nasz) klient nasz pan" (a rough equivalent of "the customer is king") is a relic of the pre-war economy but it, interestingly, also proved attractive to communist leaders and survived through communist times. Hartman (2004) describes its quasi-official existence in a socialist economy as a manifestation of a game of pretend played by the producer/retailer and the customer in times of notorious shortages in the supply of almost any product or service. Later on, as a consequence of economic changes, a shift in power occurred: customers found themselves empowered and in a position to be served/cared for by service providers. The same master-servant metaphor created an antagonism, strengthened by the growing awareness of the customers of their being manipulated through advertising. Nowadays, the relationship should more accurately be described as a form of interdependence in which the fundamental notion is the interpersonal relation through which services are transacted (cf. 'relationship marketing' Varey 2002, Rogoziński 2003). In this dialectical tension between the two sides of the transaction what is noteworthy are the local circumstances of the customer's response to service as well as the behaviour of service people, in particular their willingness to subordinate themselves.

3. Call Centres in Poland

In Poland, getting commercial information or finalizing deals over the phone is still a relatively new practice, both to customers and to business people. Statistics show that it is the more educated customers who choose to turn to an infoline for product information or to use a bank hotline to make financial transactions (Datamonitor for 2005). Nevertheless, the area of customer service via telephone is growing popular and stronger.

Numbers differ, but it may be assumed that there are about 1000 call centres in Poland (Datamonitor for 2005). The majority of CC services in Poland (an estimated 60%) are outbound rather than inbound and their services are designed to provide customers with information, mostly in the areas of banking, the motor industry, insurance, telecommunications, publishing, cosmetics, pharmaceuticals, information technology, and advertising. They are either in-house or outsourced CCs[4].

3.1. CC operators

Requirements for call centre operators and telemarketers involve good management of stress and monotony, an ability to be assertive, good communication skills, in particular skills for conflict resolution. On the linguistic side, candidates are expected to have no speech disorders and to have a 'nice' voice quality. On the whole, most of the attributes of a good CC operator involve *understanding* the customer well (by intuiting his/her personality and current mood) and *taking good care* of his/her needs. Thus, there are two tasks to tackle: one centres around providing information or making transactions, the other is communicative and therapeutic[5]. *What* is to be done is closely bound to *how* it is to be achieved.

The prestige of the profession in Poland is relatively low. Most people doing the job have a high school education and they have to go through a specialized course preparing them for the job. The training is oriented towards the technicalities of providing service to the customer – how to input and retrieve information from the computer, and how to ask questions to find out exactly what the customer wants[6]. At the same time, however, trainers admit that one of the most difficult aspects of the job is *handling* customers, notably dealing with their stress and resolving conflict situations. Appropriate psychological training is rarely provided[7]. CC work is rather exhausting, which results in high levels of staff turnover.

On the whole, global norms have been taken over for training in Poland. As it turns out, Polish CC consultants find it difficult to master the strategies of conversation, with the customers performing most of the conversational work (Kiełkiewicz-Janowiak and Pawelczyk 2004).

3.2. Training CC operators

In the process of training, call centre workers are taught how to take on a constructed identity of a person who is genuinely interested, understanding and caring. This attitude is supposed to serve the purpose of commercial efficiency as well as be effective. The target behaviour of the operator is definable in terms of positive and negative face wants, as listed in Table 2.

POSITIVE FACE WANTS	NEGATIVE FACE WANTS
Get to like your customer: Gather up positive energy well before you start the conversation. Use 'positive' phrases. Try to match their communicative style.	**Don't impose on the customer:** Say 'I' rather than 'you'. Don't order people about. Don't interrupt the interlocutor. Don't rush them.
Work toward effective communication: Confirm understanding. Make sure you are understood.	
Focus on the customer and make them feel 'special': Make the impression that you have been waiting for this very customer's call. Smile to the customer.	

Table 5-2: Positive and negative face wants

Along with the requirement to mind the face wants of the interlocutor comes the necessity of being *in control*: in control of the voice quality, in control of (one's own and others') emotions, and ultimately in control of the conversation. The ideal CC operator is to be open and flexible, oriented towards the customer and able to influence him/her. To conclude, call centre operators are supposed to conform to the norm which is composed of a set of directives and guidelines, taught to the operators and published in call centre manuals[8].

Professional training also takes care of the candidate's voice quality and uses techniques which make one's voice nice and warm. Ideally, the effect of the so-called 'smiley voice' is obtained. Manipulating voice quality as well as intonation, rhythm and tempo in very unique ways provides an impression of the operator's friendliness, enthusiasm and competence.

4. Gender and call centre work

The question we wish to consider here is whether the speaker's gender may play a role in the communicative activity practised at a call centre. Specifically, we would like to question the claim that, in the Polish context, it is women who are stereotyped as better communicators and better service workers, and therefore better suited to work at CCs.

4.1. Women as (better?) communicators

Historically, in English speaking societies women have always been commented regarding their unique/special language use; this is documented in literature as well as in proverb lore. More importantly, there have been very explicitly articulated social expectations about women's communicative behaviour, phrased as prescriptions for taciturnity and consideration of others, listed in Table 3.

• Silence or taciturnity is a woman's virtue.
• Listening is a particularly desirable feminine quality.
• Women should be the guardians of linguistic propriety.
• It is desirable for a woman to be unimposing and considerate to others, i.e. she should listen rather than speak, understand rather than argue.
• When invited to speak, women were to display the virtue of 'sympathy'.
• Nineteenth century descriptions of an ideal woman conversationalist show her as being agreeable and useful, modestly knowledgeable and discreetly influential.
• Women's participation in debates was legitimised by their being particularly skilful as discussion mediators.

Table 5-3: Traditional prescriptions for women's communicative behaviour (cf. Donawerth 2002, Kiełkiewicz-Janowiak 2002)

This historical image of an ideal female speaker may be linked to the contemporary idea of woman as superior communicator. In a British Telecom booklet designed to encourage more telephone conversation feminine conversational habits and skills are extolled: women are presented as talkers more able (than men) to verbalise their emotional states (cf. Cameron 2000a; Talbot 2000).

Women are also believed to be very dedicated telephone talkers. The stereotype of a woman who would be happy to talk all day is very much alive (cf. historical and literary images of talkative women) and it is often taken for granted that for female call centre workers the job is pleasure rather than work. Sociologists Taylor and Tyler (2000) have presented the views of a call centre manager who claimed that women are 'naturally' better at chatting, interacting and building rapport and as they speak, "[i]t doesn't sound as forced" (Taylor and Tyler 2000: 84). If women have been considered better 'telephone communicators', it is frequently because of their voice quality: the preferred vocal signal is a 'girly' voice – high pitched, breathy, with 'swoopy' intonation (Cameron 2000c: 118). Finally, the emotional and attitudinal states projected by the operators, such as warmth, sincerity, excitement, friendliness, helpfulness, or any emotion other than anger, are culturally coded as 'feminine' rather than 'masculine' (Cameron 2000a).

4.2. Women as (better?) service workers

Another possible reason behind the suggestion that women may be 'naturally' suited to work at call centres is the general perception of women as better service workers. This again may be related to the historically enforced role of the woman as 'made for usefulness'[9]. Also modern psychologists make claims about caring being an essentially feminine domain: Paoletti (2002: 808) quotes Graham (1983:18) as follows: "'Caring' becomes the category through which one sex is differentiated from the other. Caring is 'given' to women: it becomes the defining characteristic of their self-identity and their life's work." At least in western culture women are made responsible for caring (Urgeson 1987, cf. 'compulsory altruism' Land and Rose 1985). It would thus seem that feminine social features perfectly fit the picture of a service person. In the minds of many people (including customers as well as employees) women are better suited to perform service to others – they (more easily than men) relate to others and are better at deducing other people's needs.

4.3. Polish women: useful, caring and communicative?

The historically perpetuated ideal of the "Polish mother" endowed women with the responsibility for caring for the country and for the family, often through self-sacrifice. As Hauser (1995) argues, "[i]n today's Poland the equation of Heavenly and Polish mother continues as a model of double service for women to follow. This double service entails service to her family and, through the family, to Poland. Fulfilling this double service guarantees the woman a 'double satisfaction' which she can obtain within the 'domestic' sphere (...)" (Hauser 1995: 89). Additionally, as part of the communist legacy, women have endorsed their work outside the home as their special virtue. Recent opinion poll results indicate that the majority of Polish women (60%) claim that general societal respect for professionally active women is greater than for those working 'only' in the home (CBOS for 2003).

As a consequence of the shift in power brought about by the transition to a capitalist economy, the current relations in the service encounters make the subordinate role of service workers particularly marked. This subordinate role has been traditionally associated with the roles and position of women in the family. Statistical data (for 2003) about the structure of the labour market in Poland testify to the predominance of women in jobs involving personalised care. Sectors of the Polish labour market with the highest participatrion of women are the following: education (76.1%), health care (80.6%), hotels and restaurants (64.6%), financial services (69.7%).

In the Polish context the universal (?) expectation of women to be 'naturally' caring is additionally strengthened by the Polish culture's preference for positive politeness (cf. Wierzbicka 1985)[10]. It is possible that the two sources of expectations combine to place a double burden on Polish women, i.e. a double responsibility for making others comfortable and saving their positive face.

4.4. Stereotypical feminine linguistic and communicative skills

In order to find out whether in Poland women are considered good communicators and service workers, we examined – in an earlier study – the (language-related) stereotypes of women in Poland (cf. Kiełkiewicz-Janowiak and Pawelczyk 2006).

The strongest stereotypes about gendered communication in Poland may be understood to project men – in relation to their interlocutor(s) – as authoritative, categorical and boastful. Polish women, on the other hand, are stereotypically believed to show high involvement in talking to others and show more understanding toward their listener(s). On the whole, the analysis of the differences shows women's greater emphasis on their own interlocutor-oriented behaviours (cf. "women are careful listeners").[11]

In order to map local gender stereotypes onto CC communication patterns, we have posed the following questions: (1) What are – in the minds of the respondents – these special communicative skills possessed by women? (2) Which of these skills are those of a perfect communicator? (3) Do either stereotypical women or men better overlap with the ideal of a good communicator? (4) Finally, which of the skills are useful in the CC context?

WOMEN (in comparison to men):
▪ often talk only for the sake of talking
▪ use diminutives more often than men
▪ speak more emotionally
▪ talk more
▪ ask more questions because they are nosy
▪ less often use vulgar and offensive words
▪ more often introduce new topics/themes into conversation
▪ are able to "read between the lines"
▪ use more adjectives to make their descriptions more vivid
▪ often talk simultaneously with other speakers
▪ are more oriented towards details
▪ show more understanding toward their listener

Table 5-4: Women's stereotypical communicative behaviour
(Kiełkiewicz-Janowiak & Pawelczyk 2006).

MEN (in comparison to women):
▪ are more fact-oriented
▪ are more matter-of-fact
▪ are more authoritative
▪ are more categorical
▪ are more brief
▪ tend not to use diminutives
▪ use vulgar words more often
▪ tend to stick to one topic in conversation
▪ like to show off

Table 5-5: Men's stereotypical communicative behaviour
(Kiełkiewicz-Janowiak & Pawelczyk 2006)

The global requirements for communicative skills of a CC operator could be grouped as overlapping with stereotypically feminine (1) and stereotypically masculine (2):

(1)
Sensitivity to interlocutor
Empathy
Flexibility
Relationship building

(2)
Matter-of-factness
Problem solving orientation
Decisiveness
Managing own and others'
emotions and handling stress

To conclude, a combination of Polish stereotypical feminine features and stereotypical masculine features overlap with global prescriptions for CC communication.

4.5. Are CCs gendered in the local Polish context?

It is estimated that the majority of CC operators (in Poland) are women. Most CC experts, when asked to explain this situation, state that the job has relatively low prestige and is relatively low paying. Secondly, in terms of social perception in Poland this is stereotypically "a woman's job" – that of a 'telephone operator'. Therefore, relatively few men choose to work at call centres. Even if call centre posts are advertised (as open to workers of either sex), men rarely apply. Opinions of trainers about the relevance of gender are diverse: some claim that female consultants are definitely better at inferring the customer's emotions and their mood, others consider this thinking stereotyped and unfounded.

Both groups of trainers insist that all the skills of successful operators may be taught and mastered through practice. However, some of the trainers express the reservation that communication skills desirable in CC interaction are learnable only to some extent and therefore it is the trainers' crucial role to select candidates with the right personality early on at the recruitment stage (cf. similar observations made by Cameron 2000c: 118).

We understand the process of training CC workers much as the process of imposing a constructed (i.e. inauthentic) identity on them, a process which Cameron (2000a) labels 'styling'. It is possible that women find it easier to cope with being 'styled', as they are socialised (to a greater extent than men) to 'please' and to be 'of use' to others. We predict at this stage that feminine discourse prevails in the performance of the service people (at call centres), yet we expect there to be a discrepancy between the CC preferred style and the actual performance of CC operators.

5. The Study

We have examined 92 inbound (i.e. customer initiated) CC exchanges on company hotlines representing banks, airlines, telecommunications, cosmetics and the chemical industry. We have also conducted numerous interviews with CC trainers, supervisors, and CC operators.

In the telephone exchanges examined for the purposes of this study, the operators tackled such tasks as problem diagnosing, managing a customer in despair, responding to 'requests for the impossible'. We have analysed the styles of CC interaction and described them in terms of masculine and feminine communicative styles as defined by local gender stereotypes. As a result we have recognized two styles: (Style 1) predominantly masculine (i.e. overlapping with stereotypically masculine features), and (Style 2) involving both masculine and feminine features.

Style 1 – masculine	Style 2 – masculine/feminine	
matter-of-fact	informational	empathic
categorical/authoritative	fact-oriented	caring
brief		involved
unemotional		
institutional		

Table 5-6: Style 1 (masculine) vs. Style 2 (masculine/feminine)

The salient discursive and communicative features of the first style found in the performance of the Polish CC operators will be exemplified with the selected excerpts of the exchanges characteristic of the whole corpus[12]. The discussion will point both to the features present in the extracts as well as indicate what aspects are missing in terms of the CC operator's desirable communicative style.

The exchange discussed below took place at a (well-known) paint manufacturer's call centre.

Excerpt 1 (PAINT COLOUR)
1   O: Good morning, [first name surname], how can I help you?
2   C: Good morning, I have a problem, I'd like to paint my apartment, well *actually* I'd like to redecorate
3   it but I'm not sure whether I should paint or tile it, you know tiles are always more expensive but I
4   wanted to paint the kitchen anyway but I have a problem with colour selection (3) because it seems
5   to me that the colour indicated on the label differs from the colour inside, maybe you could advise
6   me what to do?
7   O: Sir, I can't help you on the phone in colour selection, you need to visit one of our colour centres
8   located all over [country name], can you please tell me where you're calling from and I'll inform you
9   about your closest location.
10   C: Well, I'm calling from [city name] but maybe, you know, I was thinking that maybe I could get some
11   advice on the phone.

12   O: No, no, unfortunately it's difficult to advise on colour selection
      over the phone.
13   C: Ok, you know what, I think I'll have to go to that centre but the
      other thing is that my windows
14   face different directions and I have been wondering that the same
      shade may look different in a
15   different room, I don't know but is there any method
16   O: // that's   why   I
      recommend that you visit
17   one of our centres.

The customer in the first (long) turn presents his/her concerns as to
how his/her apartment should be redecorated. The uncertainty relates to
the choice of paint colour, hence the call to the centre is very much
justified (at least in the customer's view). There are a number of items in
the customer's first turn pointing to the advice-seeking character of the
call, e.g. *I have a problem* (used twice); *I'm not sure*; *it seems to me*. The
pause made by the customer in line 4 provides conversational space for the
operator to offer some feedback to the verbalized concerns. The
customer's first turn is completed with a question to the operator. The
qualifier *maybe* in the question attenuates its directness. This may point to
the fact that the operator in no way reacts to the customer's long
description of the problems, nor does the operator show any sensitivity
upon hearing the problem. In fact, the directly stated request for help
receives a very decisive negative answer (line 7) reinforced with an
imperative as to what the customer should do (lines 7-9). The operator's
lack of flexibility and empathy continues as the customer's plea for any
kind of advice is repeatedly rejected with forceful negation (double *no*,
line 12). The operator remains (consistently) solution-oriented yet not in
terms of responding to the customer's projected uncertainty. Rather the
aim is to send the customer off to another place. The customer, insisting
on finding out something during the call, draws on a marker of friendliness
and/or informality (*you know*, cf. Holmes 1998). This clearly begs for
some sensitivity and empathy which is – again – not offered (lines 16-17).
What is also significant is that the operator's authoritative stance manifests
itself in that he/she interrupts the customer (lines 16-17), which in fact
closes the interaction. Thus the operator is matter-of-fact and authoritative,
yet fails to respond to the customer's current needs. The exchange very
much resembles an institutional interaction characterized by a question-
answer sequence (cf. Drew and Heritage 1992). The operator's direct and
negative responses significantly contribute to the brief character of the
exchange. This is to say that while the customer's turns are longer and

more emotionally involved, the operator's contributions are short and uninvolved.

Excerpt 2 (GREASY HAIR)
1   C: Yes, I've been using this shampoo, but yes generally my hair gets greasy but I just don't know is it that
2   my hair is so hopeless or maybe this is how the shampoo works↑=
3   O: = It's difficult for me to explain it. You should check with a specialist. I don't know, have you
4   consulted a beautician or a hairdresser? and have you tried to find out whether it's just your
5   hair that tends to get greasy easily or <u>maybe</u> the type of work you do influences the condition of your
6   hair?

In excerpt 2 the operator receives a call from a desperate customer who would like to find out whether the shampoo he/she has been using makes his/her hair greasy. This is a very emotional call and the customer is in need of reassurance that his/her hair is manageable (*I just don't know, maybe*, rising intonation at the turn transition). The operator's response, however, fails to mirror the customer's emotional state, but instead intellectualises as to what may influence the customer's hair condition (providing a list of plausible reasons) and refers the customer to a specialist using a strong modal verb. In terms of evidentiality, however, the modality of the operator's response is quite doubtful (*I don't know; maybe*). There is a misattunement between the customer's emotionally charged inquiry and the operator's misaligned intellectual response. In fact, the operator attempts to deal with the confusion but does not really understand the customer's problem and, as a result, fails to be sensitive to the interlocutor and to build a relationship with him/her.

In excerpts 3 and 4 below illustrating similar problems), customers' inquiries receive unmitigated negative answers. If the operator's negative responses were in fact mitigated by, for example, *I am sorry to say that but...* or *I understand you but...*, these pre-answering phrases could point to some sensitivity and/or empathy on the operator's part.

Excerpt 3 (PHONE 1)
1   C: =Yes and I was wondering about changing my provider, well, I was considering you as one of the
2   options because you know, the main thing is that [company name] has really high rates and I would like to find
3   out first of all if I could become your client but keep my current telephone number.

4	O: No, there is no such possibility. Ok, I admit we now have a law
5	C: //
	exactly, that's what I'm talking
6	about=
7	O: =But we don't have any arrangements with [company name] yet.

In excerpt 3 the operator flatly rejects the customer's suggestion (*no, there is no...*) only to admit after a moment, in the same turn, that actually there exists a law to guarantee retaining the same number yet purely in theory. It seems that changing the order of the two clauses would contribute to being informational and/but at the same time projecting emphatic understanding of the customer's problem. It is interesting that the customer's interruption (lines 5-6) attempting to re-focus the operator's explanation is again discarded with a latched negative response (line 7).

Excerpt 4 (PHONE 2)

1	C: You know it would be very convenient for me to keep the same number because otherwise I would have
2	to let all my family and friends know about my new number and it is a bit of a hassle for me, right (4.0),
3	do you happen to know when it will be possible?
4	O: Unfortunately not.

In excerpt 4, the customer proffers reasons for keeping the same phone number. There is a strong appeal from the customer for the operator's understanding as manifested by the invariant question tag (*right*) and a four second pause (line 2) that follows it. Since the operator fails to respond to these cues, the customer states a direct question (line 3), which receives a negative response with no accompanying explanation.

The operators whose communicative behaviour resembles the first style (Style 1 above, overlapping with stereotypically masculine features and exemplified in the above excerpts come out as fact-oriented, yet the views they present are framed as categorical and authoritative. They fail to read the customers' emotional states and to respond accordingly.

In the second style (cf. Style 2 above) identified in the CC exchanges, the operators' communicative behaviour combines stereotypically feminine and masculine features: besides being informational and fact-oriented it is also involved (referring to operator's own experience), empathic (understanding the emotional state of the customer), and caring (for the feelings of the customer). Excerpt 5 exemplifies an exchange in which the operator is oriented towards solving the customer's problem but at the same time remains a truly involved interlocutor:

Excerpt 5 (DYED HAIR)
1   C: You know what, I have dyed my hair today and now I should probably cut it=
2   O: = What happened? Please tell me everything. What colour did you want to get?
3   C: My hair is dark brown and I wanted to get blond, well not really too blond. I just don't know
4   whether I kept the dye on for too long and now it looks uneven, you know. Did I do something
5   wrong?
6   O: Are you naturally brunette? that is you were born
7   C: // yes, yes naturally.
8   O: Naturally, yes? Can you please tell me what dye you used? Do you happen to still have the box at
9   hand ?=
10   C: = NO::, no, I don't have it but [it was]
11   O: [you remember, yes↑]
12   C: very light blond↑
13   O: Mhm, ok, and the brand?
14   C: Uhm, it was… colour naturals ↑
15   O: Mhm, right, good and it was very light blond, right?
16   C: Yes, yes and now my hair looks very strange. What should I do now?
17   O: You know what↑ well, I must admit that changing brown hair into blond can be a bit difficult at
18   first because it should be made fairer by two shades at most so that's why your hair did not turn
19   out the way you wanted. This is neither yours nor the dye's fault, no, you just
20   C:
     // yes↑
21   O: you just need to dye it one more time but not now, you should let your hair [rest]
22   C:
     [yes]

The customer's problem, stated in line 1, is responded to both in the involved and the informative way. The answer starts with the involvement aspect in which the operator assures the customer he/she is fully tuned in to hearing about the misfortune (*What happened? Tell me everything*). Though the customer has already verbalized the problem (line 1), the operator is willing to listen to a detailed version of the incident, which, as

Tannen (1989) explained, creates intimacy. The second part of the operator's response is information-oriented and carried out in the form of a direct question (*what colour did you want to get?*). In lines 4 and 5 the customer poses a direct, highly emotionally-charged question which, although initially ignored, is returned to (by the operator) in line 19. The customer is reassured that he/she is not to be directly blamed for the hair dye confusion. It is interesting to note how the operator remains actively involved in the dialogue with the customer throughout the whole exchange. The customer's answers are acknowledged (lines 8, 13, 15) before another question is asked. The exchange does not resemble a typical institutional exchange (Q-A framework) as the operator extensively relies on the pre-questioning format (e.g. line 8) as well as tends to clarify the inquiry (line 6). The operator actively pursues involvement with the customer, as manifested, for example, by encouraging the customer to recall the type of the product (line 11). This encouragement is interactionally realized by an overlap and the operator's rising intonation. Lines 17-19 again reflect the fact-oriented yet empathic exchange where the operator reiterates the facts and the error made by the customer, but is trying to understand the customer's emotional state by not holding his/her accountable for the problem (*This is neither yours nor the dye's fault.*).

In another part of the same exchange the customer explicitly informs the operator about how he/she feels after the failed attempt to dye his/her hair (line 1 below). The operator, beginning the answer with the *involved* pre-answering phrase (*I'll tell you what*), informs the customer what he/she should do next. The exchange takes on a quasi-therapeutic tone when the operator offers the unsolicited comforting closing comment (line 6 below):

Excerpt 6 (DYED HAIR)

1   C: You know, now I am feeling down because it looks like it was
2   O: // I'll tell
     you what, now you should
3   dye it a darker colour and then after some time when you want to go
     blond again you will have
4   to decolour it first.
5   C: Mhm, ok, you know what, it's ok
6   O: // you really did everything ok, it just
     that the dye did not take.

In another exchange, the customer is trying very hard to convince the operator to let him/her take a fish tank on board a plane.

Excerpt 7 (FISH TANK)

1   O: Just a moment, did I understand you correctly? You're planning to carry a fish tank with water and
2   the fish.
3   C: Well, yes! That's why I think the best solution is to have it with me all the time. I just don't know if it
4   would fit in the overhead compartment or if it would be necessary for me to buy additional tickets for
5   the next seats.
6   O: Unfortunately I am sorry to say but the fish tank itself cannot be treated as a carry-on item. What's
7   more, it is absolutely impossible to carry a water-filled tank as there is a risk that the water would spill
8   out or it may get smashed. Not only would this be unpleasant for you but it could also pose a threat for
9   the safety of your fellow passengers, couldn't it?
10 C: You see, you look at it in a typical clerk-like manner. But for me this fish tank is really important
11 Please, believe me, it's not some sort of a whim. I do need to take it with me! I will be absent from home
12 for almost half a year!=
13 O: = mhm.
14 C: Who am I to leave the fish with? Taking care of it is not that easy at all!
15 O: I'm sure it isn't!
16 C: Can you imagine that my own brother took care of it for only 2 weeks, only 2 weeks, do you get it? I
17 come back and what do I see? My eyes welled up with tears when I saw that only half of the fish
18 survived.
19 O: Yes, it must have been very distressing.
20 C: And do you know what the fish tank looked like? You can't even imagine it, it was a total shambles!=
21 O: = Yes, I agree, it must have been a very upsetting experience. I can see that you are very attached
22 to your fish and that's why I can offer the best solution to this situation. Please call the cargo
23 department at [phone number], you will receive all the necessary information there.

The operator takes the customer's seemingly bizarre request very seriously. In making sure the problem has been understood correctly, the operator makes a statement (line 1-2) instead of a question which does not index the customer's plan of travelling with a fish tank as a kind of eccentricity but as a fact. The request must be refused. Yet, contrary to the pattern typical of Style 1 (above), the negative response (i.e. refusal) is informative (*no* + why) as well as appealing to the customer for understanding (*unpleasant for you; couldn't it?*). During the whole interaction the operator actively listens to what the customer is saying. This is manifested by the use of minimal responses (line 13), mirroring comments (line 15) as well as empathic comments (line 19) which point to the operator's understanding of the emotional state of the customer. Each of the customer's statements is commented on by the operator in a reflective manner. Even though the customer's problem is unusual, a solution is still offered. Significantly, the proposed solution (focus on information) is preceded with a mirroring comment (focus on involvement) (lines 21-23).

The style described above as Style 2, combining masculine and feminine features, largely overlaps with the style prescribed for CC operators. The masculine features provide for the effectiveness of the service. However, the feminine features are indispensable for the provision of personalised care. The latter gives the company in question the 'competitive advantage' (Czerniawska 1998) over others in that it establishes the customer's personal/emotional bond with the company and contributes to the company's humanistic image (cf. Freemantle 1998).

Significantly, while some stereotypically feminine features seem perfect for CC communication, others would be *counterproductive*: (1) emotional (= over-expressive of own emotional states); (2) talkative (= verbose; occupying too much conversation time) (3) pursuing many topics in one conversation; (4) talking simultaneously with other speakers.

It is also noteworthy that the operator's explicit reference to their *own* experience, which is often understood as framing empathy, may have different functions. For example, the cosmetics company consultant who said "I know from my own experience that..." *shared* with the customer her experience of being a customer herself, i.e. put herself in the position of the customer in this particular situation. This statement can be construed as an act of self-disclosure from the operator as the experience she shares with the customer belongs to his/her private sphere. On the other hand, the bank consultant, who assured the customer that the money she/he deposited in the ATM will not be lost said "It has never happened to us, *I* have not witnessed such a case...". It is worth underlining that the function of *I* is defined by the preceding (institutional) *us* making the declaration more precise.

6. Conclusions

The communicative style preferable in the context of CC service can be described as a 'both...and' style: an ideal CC worker possesses a mixture of communicative features stereotyped in Poland as feminine and masculine. Importantly, feminine and masculine features become salient (and indispensable) depending on the type of task to be tackled and the personality of the customer. Although the communicative behaviours which are stereotypically feminine (though not labelled as such by trainers) feature as core prescriptions for CC performance (thus they are valorised), many CC operators have been found to fail in applying them in their interactions with customers.

It seems to be an accepted idea nowadays that communication is a skill to be taught, learned and improved (Cameron 2000b: 38). For one thing, communication is to be mastered for the sake of eliminating conflicts and providing for smooth co-existence. Thus, advice literature is based on the idea that the origins of problems frequently lie in communication breakdowns and that people's communication skills might (and should) be improved.

Much in the same vein, the idea that communication is a 'transferable' skill is also the basis of training in many contexts in which conversation is the tool for achieving commercial ends, for example at call centres. If communication at CCs involves both feminine and masculine skills, the question remains which skills are more easily trainable. Addressing this question is only one of the possible suggestions for further study.

Transcription conventions

C – customer
O – operator
? – punctuation for intonation
↑ – rising intonation, 'intonation spike'
:: – elongation of the sound
(3) – timing in seconds
Here – increase in volume or emphasis
[ ] – overlap
// – interruption
= – equal signs indicate the so-called *latch*. i.e. neither gap nor overlap in talk

Notes

[1] Kwiatkowska (1999) suggests that the co-existence of the two subtypes in the self-stereotype of a woman testifies to an ongoing social change which men either do not notice or do not accept.

[2] At the same time no effort was done to restructure the division of household work (Glass and Kawachi 2002).

[3] Women's unemployment rate was 20,3 in 2003 (cf. men's: 18,4) (source: Grotkowska *et al*) and 19,1 in 2005 (cf. men's: 15,9) (source: Skrzek-Lubasińska 2006).

[4] The area of outsourced services is relatively small, constituting about 10-15 per cent of the whole call centre market (Katarzyna Swatowska, marketing director, Call Center Poland, p.c.). One of the reasons is the relatively low CC brand awareness among Polish business people. Moreover, companies still find it difficult to trust outsource CC providers about handling their customers or information. (Katarzyna Swatowska, p.c.).

[5] Cameron (2000b) has pointed out that "the philosophy of 'customer care' may even lead to the redefinition of routine service work as a therapeutic activity in its own right" (2000b: 40).

[6] In the local Polish context, the average of CC operator is a woman aged 23-26 – in the opinion of trainers, young operators prove better than older ones for at least one reason: Young people are more frequently computer literate. (Katarzyna Swatowska, p.c.).

[7] Today's trainers in good communication suggest that self-awareness in the key to successful communication – it teaches people to be open in disclosing their own as well as perceiving others' emotions better.

[8] Next to the personality characteristics qualifying for the job, such as self-confidence and composure, being very assertive is expected of the CC operator. This happens to be a particularly difficult task to Polish trainees as most have been socialized into believing that modesty is the highest virtue and that boasting or showing off is contemptible.

[9] The idea that a woman should be 'useful' referred not only to her behaviour in general, but also to her communicative functions (for a discussion see Kiełkiewicz-Janowiak 2005).

[10] Polish society has traditionally been oriented towards positive politeness. Therefore, in the process of socialisation there has been more emphasis on developing strategies for saving the positive face of the interlocutor.

[11] Interestingly, our study of language stereotypes in Poland suggests that women are convinced of their possessing special communicative skills. For example, women themselves admit to their tendency to interrupt others, while stressing that this is motivated by their engagement in the conversation, especially as they have 'the ability to read between the lines'.

[12] The excerpts are English translations of the original exchanges, conducted in the Polish language.

References

Cameron, D. 2000a. "Styling the worker: Gender and the commodification of language in the globalized service economy." *Journal of Sociolinguistics* 4.3: 323-347.

—. 2000b. "Good to talk? The cultural politics of 'communication'." *The European English Messenger* 9.1: 38-42.

—. 2000c. *Good to talk? Living and working in a communication culture.* London: Sage Publications.

Czerniawska, F. 1998. *Corporate speak: The use of language in business.* London: Macmillan.

Donawerth, J. 2002. "Nineteenth-century United States conduct book rhetoric by women." *Rhetoric Review* 21.1: 5-21.

Drew, P. and J. Heritage, eds. 1992. *Talk at work: Interaction in institutional settings.* Cambridge: Cambridge University Press.

Fodor, E. 1997. "Gender in transition: Unemployment in Hungary, Poland and Slovakia." *East European Politics and Societies* 11.3: 470-500.

—. *et al.* 2002. "Family policies and gender in Hungary, Poland and Romania." *Communist and Post-Communism Studies* 35: 475-490.

Freemantle, D. 1998. *What customers like about you: adding emotional value for service excellence and competitive advantage.* London and Santa Rosa, CA: Nicholas Brealey.

Glass, C. and J. Kawachi. 2002. "Winners or losers of reform? Gender and unemployment in Hungary and Poland." *The Hungarian Review of Sociology* 7.2: 109-140.

Glick, P. and S.T. Fiske. 1997. "Hostile and benevolent sexism." *Psychology of Women Quarterly* 21: 119-135.

Graff, A. 2003. "Lost between the waves? The paradoxes of feminist chronology and activism in contemporary Poland." *Journal of International Women's Studies* 4.2: 100-116.

Graham, H. 1983 'Caring: A Labour of Love'. In *A Labour of Love: Women, Work and Caring.* Eds. J. Finch and D. Groves. London: Routledge & Kegan Paul, 13–30.

Grotkowska, G., M.W. Socha and U. Sztanderska. 2005. "Elastyczność zatrudnienia a bezpieczeństwo socjalne na rynku pracy. Doświadczenia Polski." Published by Międzynarodowa Organizacja Pracy 2005 at: http://www.ilo.org/public/english/region/eurpro/budapest/download/e mpl/flexibility_poland_polish.pdf

Hartman, J. 2004. "Poza panem i sługą", czyli demokratyczne myślenie o sprzedaży" [Beyond master and servant, or democratic thinking abort sales], *Marketing w praktyce* 11. (Also at:

http://www.iphils.uj.edu.pl/~j.hartman/t.php)

Hauser, E. 1995. "Traditions of patriotism, questions of gender: The case of Poland." In *Post communism and the body politic*. Ed. E.E. Berry. New York/London: New York University Press.

Hochschild, A. 1983. *The managed heart: The commercialisation of human feeling*. Berkeley: University of California Press.

Holmes, J. 1998. "Women's talk: The question of sociolinguistic universals." In *Language and gender: A reader*. Ed. J. Coates. Oxford: Blackwell Publishers, 461-483.

Kiełkiewicz-Janowiak, A. 2002. *'Women's language'? – a socio-historical view: Private writings in early New England*. Poznań: Motivex.

—. 2005. "The socialisation of women in nineteenth century New England." *Homo Loguens (Zeszyty Naukowe NKJO Szczecin)* 1: 63-82.

— and J. Pawelczyk. 2004. "Globalisation and customer service communication at Polish call centres". In *Speaking from the margin. Global English from a European perspective*. Eds. A. Duszak and U. Okulska. Frankfurt am Mein/Wien: Peter Lang, 225-238.

— and J. Pawelczyk. 2006. "Gender stereotypes in language use: Polish and English." In *IFAtuation: A life in IFA. A Festschrift for Professor Jacek Fisiak on the Occasion of His 70th Birthday*. Ed. K. Dziubalska-Kołaczyk. Poznań: Wydawnictwo Naukowe UAM, 349-383.

Kwiatkowska, A. 1999. "Siła tradycji i pokusa zmiany, czyli o stereotypach płciowych" [The power of tradition and the temptation for change, or about gender stereotypes]. In *Męskość- kobiecość w perspektywie indywidualnej i kulturowej* [Masculinity – femininity: individual and cultural perspectives]. Eds. J. Miluska and P. Boski. Warszawa: Wydawnictwo Instytutu Psychologii PAN, 143-172.

Land, H. and H. Rose. 1985. "Compulsory altruism for some or an altruistic society for all?" In *In defence of welfare*. Eds. P. Bean, J. Ferris and D. Whynes. London: Tavistock, 74-96.

Marody, M. and A.G. Poleszczuk. 2000. "Changing images of identity in Poland : from self-sacrificing to self-investing woman?" In *Reproducing gender. politics, publics and everyday life after socialism*. Eds. S. Gal and G. Kligman. Princeton: Princeton University Press, 151-175.

Ogórek, S. 2006. "W infolinii ma być miło i do tego na temat" [A hotline should be nice and to the point]. *Puls biznesu*, 21-08-2006, p.22.

Paoletti, I. 2002. "Caring for older people: a gendered practice." *Discourse & Society* 13.6: 805-817.

Skrzek-Lubasińska, M. 2006. "Sytuacja kobiet na rynku pracy" [The situation of women on the job market], published by Fundacja Kobiety dla Kobiet at: http://www.femina.org.pl/index.php?option=com_content&task=view &id=76&Itemid=35

Rogoziński, K. 2000. *Nowy marketing uslug* [The new marketing of services]. 2nd edition. Poznań: Wydawnictwo Akademii Ekonomicznej w Poznaniu.

Talbot, M.M. 2000. "'It's good to talk'? The undermining of feminism in a British Telecom advertisement." *Journal of Sociolinguistics* 4: 108-119.

Tannen, D. 1989. *Talking voices. Repetition, dialogue, and imagery in conversational discourse.* Cambridge: Cambridge University Press.

Taylor, S. and M. Tyler. 2000. "Emotional labour and sexual difference in the airline industry." *Work, Employment & Society* 14.1: 77-95.

Urgeson, C. 1987. *Policy is personal: sex, gender and informal care.* London: Tavistock.

Varey, R. 2002. *Relationship marketing: Dialogue and networks in the E-commerce era.* Chichester: John Wiley & Sons.

Walczewska, S. 1999. *Damy, rycerze, feministki: Kobiecy dyskurs emancypacyjny w Polsce* [Ladies, Knights and Feminists: Women's Rights Discourse in Poland]. Kraków: eFKa.

Wierzbicka, A. 1985 "Different cultures, different languages, different speech acts." *Journal of Pragmatics* 9: 145-178.

CHAPTER SIX

BORROWING AND SWEARING: INDIRECT CONSTRUCTION OF GENDER AT A HUNGARIAN WORKPLACE

NÓRA SCHLEICHER, BUDAPESTI KOMMUNKÁCIÓS ÉS ÜZLETI FÖISKOLA

Abstract: A number of recent studies have examined the relationship of language and gender at workplace settings or studied the gendered nature of workplaces themselves. However, the majority of this work has been done in the Anglo-Saxon world. My research explored the communicative gender construction of managers at a Hungarian workplace setting. In the present paper I would like to give a short overview of this research focusing on two chosen examples of strategic language use affected by specific conceptions of gender. In one case the frequent use of English borrowings while speaking Hungarian was identified as a strategic attempt at creating the image of expertise. In the other case the unusually frequent use of swear words was interpreted as an effective way of linguistically constructing the quality of honesty. Both strategies were used by female managers and were the result of specific and different meanings attached to male and female managers, that is, specific gender conceptions. With the help of the research results, I would like to prove that it is more useful to conceptualise gender as a field or domain filled with community-specific meanings about 'man' and 'woman' than as an attribute of people.
Key words: *gender, language use, workplace, community of practice, borrowing, swearing.*

1. Introduction

Gender and language researchers have been interested in workplace interaction for quite a long time. (e.g. Holmes 2000; McElhinny 1998; Kendall & Tannen 1997; Coates 1995; Tannen 1994b etc.) Research has focused mostly on the interaction styles of males and females in managerial positions or in other professional occupations (e.g. physicians, teachers, etc.), and more recently also on the gendered nature of workplaces themselves. However, most of the results come from research carried out in the English-speaking world. Previously, no research had been done on the relation of gender and language at a Hungarian workplace setting. My research addresses this area.

I was interested in how the language use of Hungarian managers represents and constructs their gendered identity at the workplace.

As the concepts I work with, that is: language, gender and workplace, are all polysemic categories, their examination requires more precise definitions of the terms. While defining my use of these concepts, I shall also outline hypothesised specificities relating to the national context of the research.

First of all, when I talk about examining language, I am not interested in the abstract structure of 'la langue' (cf. Saussure 1916), but in its use in given contexts and settings, that is the 'la parole' side of language. Nor am I specifically interested in the highly systemic nature of parole itself, which has been discovered by studies oriented mostly by ethnomethodology. What I focus on instead, is the action we carry out by and through talking. (cf. Austin 1962)

As a consequence, I shall not focus on the systemic, structural, grammatical differences between Hungarian and other languages. Although Hungarian is a language which does not mark gender linguistically, and in other studies this specificity might lend itself to a gender focused analysis, in my research this phenomenon would only interest me if, in a certain context, it was used purposely to carry out a given action (e.g. in an ambiguous sentence purposely playing with hiding the gender identity of its subject or object).

By my second concept, gender, I mean a socially constructed part of our multi-faceted identity, which is fluid and flexible, can take up different meanings in different contexts, and is combined in highly diverse ways with other aspects of identity, such as age, nationality, ethnicity, class, etc. My conceptualisation of gender is informed by trends in postmodern feminism (cf. Butler 1999).

Gender has taken on different meanings in different ages and cultures. Thus, gender identity in Hungary, while in itself diverse and constantly changing, differs in a systemic way from gender identity in Western Europe and the United States. This is mostly the result of the legacy of forty years of state socialism, characterised by an almost complete employment of the female workforce combined with a widely available, though bad quality child care service and a state feminist ideology resulting in a relatively high number of token women in politics combined with a general denial of human rights and freedom. As a result, feminism in Hungary was thought to be just one of the many deceiving ideologies of those in positions of power. Steps, that in western feminist thinking would have been considered advantageous for women, were taken as oppressive actions forcing women into work, taking away from them the opportunity of staying at home with their children, and the ridiculous propaganda of the tractorist girl was unveiled as the crude reality of women being forced by necessity to do hard and unhealthy physical labour. 18 years after the transition, feminism is still very weak in Hungary and gender constructions are still affected by memories of the past.

Finally, by my third concept, workplace, I mean the primary linguistic setting of the interactions studied (cf. Hymes 1972). When I talk about its organisational aspects, I accept Boden's definition which claims that "organisations are taken to be locally organised and interactionally achieved contexts of decision making and of enduring institutional momentum" (1994: 19) That is, interactions at the workplace are, on the one hand, influenced by the specific characteristics of the setting and, on the other hand, create these characteristics and thus the organisation itself.

While workplace in general was identified as the primary linguistic setting of the research, the two actual departments under investigation were identified as two different communities of practice, as they satisfied all the criteria set for such communities by Eckert & McConnell-Ginet (1992) who promoted the utilisation of this concept in gender and language research.

In the majority of modern capitalist workplaces, communication is characterised by interaction between people who are neither strangers to each other nor close friends or relatives. Thus, as neither anonymity nor close relations protect the communicators, communication involves more risk. This is strengthened by the fact that workplaces are, in most cases, hierarchically organised and work carried out by the employees are evaluated regularly. (Kendall & Tannen 1997: 81)

If we add to this that, according to certain studies, in managerial positions talking makes up 57-89% of work time (cf. Boden 1994: 51) and the majority of work is effectively done through talking, it becomes clear that how this talk is done is a high-stakes game. We can also hypothesize that interactants pay more conscious attention to their communicative behaviour at the workplace than in certain other settings, for example when communicating with friends or strangers. Erving Goffman's famous theory on impression management is an excellent heuristic tool to be applied to the workplace setting (Goffman 1959).

Specificities relating to the fact that the research was carried out at a Hungarian workplace would be too numerous and far-reaching to be discussed within the scope of this paper. Research in this area indicates, however, that the situation of working women in Hungary is not better (but rather worse) than that of their western colleagues. The existence of the glass ceiling has been repeatedly proved and masculine norms prevail at most workplaces. (cf. Nagy 2001, Frey 2002)

In the research I carried out, I studied the interrelation of the above described three categories. Researching gendered workplace interaction thus means, firstly, examining what role language use plays in the construction of gender, secondly, what is the role of gender in the use and interpretation of language and, thirdly, how the specific workplace context in which the interactions take place affects this relation.

The study of this relationship requires the employment of theories with a potential of being able to bridge the gap between the macro level, where gender as a social category can be found (together with other collective categories like class, ethnicity, etc.) and the micro level, where language use can be effectively studied. (The meaning of linguistic utterances is always context-dependent and contexts of these utterances can only be studied at the micro level.) My thinking about the relationship of gender and language use was thus helped by sociological theories which managed to find the passage between the two levels. In my analysis, I relied on symbolic interactionism, especially the ideas of George Herbert Mead (1973) and Erving Goffman (1959, 1986) who managed to bridge the gap between the collective and the individual level, while also proving that communication, interaction between people plays an especially important role in the formation of identity (thus gender identity as well). On the other hand, Pierre Bourdieu's (1991) theory on the unequal distribution of linguistic capital helped to conceptualise communicative power from a societal point of view, which, in turn, was conducive to a better understanding of gender inequality in communication as well.

2. The research

In studying the relationship between gender and language use at the workplace, my actual research questions were the following: How do women and men communicate at the workplace? How do they present and effectuate their power in leading positions? How does their language use affect their workplace evaluation? What can be said about the gendered nature of the CofPs where interactions take place and how does this affect the first three questions?

To answer the above questions I spent three months at two functional units, the marketing and the operations department of a medium-sized, privately owned Hungarian factory, in 2002. (Hungarian does not refer here to the ownership structure of the company, but to the nationality of the employees and the language of the workplace).

3. Methods

Aiming at studying the context dependent meaning of language use and its role in identity formation leads quite directly to the employment of the qualitative research tradition. To study meaning construction in the two chosen CofPs, I used the method of participant observation. I spent three months at two departments of the company in the role of "observer as participant" (Atkinson & Hamersley 1998) or, from another viewpoint, as "peripheral member" (Adler & Adler 1994) of the groups. The subjects of the research knew that I was present as a researcher interested in communication at the workplace. However, they did not know that I was focusing on the relationship of gender and language. I observed the employees during work hours, went to have lunch with them, spent two full days with them at a conference in the countryside, shadowed the two department heads for a few days, etc.

During the last third of the observation period, I tape-recorded certain speech events which I later transcribed and analysed with the method of conversation analysis. I also conducted semi-structured interviews with all members of both CofPs. Finally, I prepared the sociometric analysis of both CofPs.

Observation helped to understand the context of the interactions under scrutiny and thus led to a more valid interpretation of the actions carried out through and by talking, and of the meanings created in the interactions. Conversation analysis was useful for a meticulous and detailed analysis of the interactions which, due to the temporary nature of talk, observation itself would not have made possible. Interviews were used to get a glimpse at the stereotypes about males and females, male and female leaders, as well as to explore folk-linguistic opinions about 'male and female communicative styles'. Sociometric analysis was helpful in mapping sympathy and antipathy within the CofPs, in identifying central and peripheral members and gaining information about group opinion linked to work related success and leadership qualities of the group-members. The combination of the above methods resulted in rich and varied data, the analysis of which hopefully led to a valid interpretation of 'what was going on' in the two CofPs.

The flow of communication could be examined from the point of view of the speaker, in which case we are interested in his/her intention, that is, what he/she wants to do with what is being said. We could also examine the message and its meaning. Or we can look at the process from the viewpoint of the receiver of the message, in which case we are interested in his/her interpretation of what is going on. The speaker's (often unconscious) intention(s) is very difficult to reveal as the researcher cannot look into the mind of the speaker. The message, according to my approach, has no meaning independent of the communicating actors and the wider context of the interaction. As a result I was focusing mostly on the receiver and on his/her observable reactions and verbalised interpretations (as manifested in the interviews and in the sociometry) of what the 'other' did by communicating.

4. The two CofPs

The marketing department had 18-21 employees (there was some fluctuation) during the period under investigation. It had 4 male and 14-17 female employees. The head of the department was a 34-year-old woman. All the employees were white, upper-middle or middle-middle class people doing white collar jobs. The majority of the employees were young (late 20s, early 30s), unmarried women with a college or university degree. Four women and 2 men were working in managerial positions. The employees earned good salaries, did interesting jobs and were generally satisfied with their workplace. They worked in one, big American style room (with the exception of the head of the department, who had her own room) and knew each other quite well. With the exception of one person, they had worked together for at least a year.

The operations department had 17-19 employees in the same period. There were 9-11 women and 8 men, all white, middle-middle or lower-middle class. The head of the department was a 47-year-old man. The average age was somewhat higher (42 years, as opposed to 34 years at the marketing). Most of the employees were married; the majority of them had children as well. Only 60 % had college or university degrees, the rest of them had secondary education. All of them did white collar jobs, but many of them worked in routine administrative positions. Only one of the women had a managerial position as opposed to 3 men. Salaries were lower than at the marketing department, the work less challenging and satisfying. Most of the employees were dissatisfied with their workplace.

The employees of the department knew each other, but as they worked in 5 separate rooms, interactions between them were less frequent and group cohesion was lower.

Although the scope of this paper does not allow for a detailed analysis of the two communities, I should mention that the two CofPs differed from each other along many different lines, including interaction and leadership styles, norms and attitudes relating to work, as well as to gender. Interestingly, though, stereotypes about 'man' and 'woman', 'male and female leaders', as well as folk linguistic ideas about how 'men and women talk' proved to be very similar in the two communities.

5. Two examples

To show some possible ways of gender construction at the examined workplace, I have chosen to describe two of the observed linguistic strategies which, according to my intention, will shed light on the relationship of gender and language and has thus the potential of grounding theoretical conceptualisation of this relationship.

5.1. 'I'm not just a little blond girl'. Construction of expertise: the use of English borrowings in Hungarian

The first linguistic strategy I'd like to describe was most typically used by the female head of the marketing department, the 34-year-old Klári. During the period under investigation, Klári reported to the director-general, the only person above her in the hierarchy, and managed the work of approximately 20 people. She is a very pretty, elegant, young woman who emphasizes her femininity by her dress and behaviour. She has kind manners and does not normally emphasize her hierarchical power with interactional tools.

In spite of this, she is not very popular in her CofP. The sociometric analysis indicates a peripheral position in the group and both observational and interview data confirm that her subordinates do not like her very much. On the other hand, her subordinates consider her very good in her job, a truly successful manager who has the prospect of a big career ahead of her. In what follows, I would like to show how this evaluation is related to communicative strategies and conceptions of gender.

I quite soon noticed that, while the language of the examined workplace was exclusively Hungarian, quite a few English words were used in the marketing department and Klári was the one who used these English terms and expressions most often. This did not go unnoticed as other people, both from within and outside the CofP, called my attention to this phenomenon as well. The following is a typical excerpt from a meeting organised and headed by Klári. The other participants were all members of the marketing department. They were product group managers, one level below Klári in the hierarchy. The language of the meeting is, as always, Hungarian. I call attention to the words borrowed from English with bald type:

Transcription conventions:
[xxxx] simultaneous speech
= latching
(.)   pause lasting less than 1 second
(2) pause in seconds
(...) untranscribable material
<xxx> remark of transcriber

Excerpt 1.
Róbert: na it a szörvisziz <**services**> megkapja a maga magas pontszámát
Kati: Ez a hármas (...)? [szöpláj csén]<**supply chain**>
Róbert: [e- egyes] a kategória?
Kati: [tréde marketing menedzser?] <**trade marketing manager**>
Klári: [mindenkinek egyes] nem? hát [felhasz]nálói tapasztalatok kellenek
Kati: [nem csak a](2) hát ez a wörkin
<**working**>(...) lídin edzs <**leading edge**>
Klári: [(...)]
Róbert:[(...)]az   egyes   az   az,   hogy(1.4)[láttam   már   kompjútert]
<**computer**>
Klári: [jó, de nem (...)]
Kati: szöpláj csénes <**supply chain**> kettes, kontróler <**controller**> kettes,
brend menedzser <**brand manager**>
Nelli: =kontróler <**controller**>? olyan hármas mint a szél
Róbert: nem nem nem hát
Nelli: nem?
Róbert:(...) az hogy exelt ismer, az egy dolog
Nelli: jó
Kati: brend menedzser <**brand manager**> kettő, (...) asszisztens ő a
hármas? vagy
Klári: miért nem csak felhasználói ismeretek ezek? A wörkin nolidzs
<**working knowledge**> ájtíben <**IT**> az programokat ír
Róbert: nem, az a lídin edzs <**leading edge**>
Kati: az a hármas
Klári: az a lídin edzs <**leading edge**> ? A lídin edzs <**leading edge**> az az
aki aki olyan profin csinálja, hogy ő a tanácsadó

Kati: aki a mászter <**master**>
Róbert: hát ő írja a programot, igen

We can see that the English words in this excerpt, used without any problems by all participants, can be considered technical terms of their profession. While *computer, brand manager, controller* and to a lesser extent *supply chain* are quite widely used terms at the company and in the business world in general, and can be considered to be on the way to becoming integrated into the host language, that is, into Hungarian, *working knowledge* and *leading edge* are felt to be English words, the meaning of which are not normally known for a Hungarian native speaker who does not speak English.

What is the function of the use of these borrowings? The use of these words come naturally to these managers whose university education included the reading of English language literature, and many of whom spent more or less time in an English language environment, either studying abroad or working for multinational companies where the language of the company was English. The English words come to their mind first and, as everybody understands it, they do not make any effort to find the rarely used or non-existent Hungarian equivalent of the terms.

However, such English terms are not used with equal frequency by everybody, especially when speaking to an audience outside the CofP where knowledge of English is presumably much lower.

I would like to argue that the fact that Klári uses these borrowings most often, and uses it not only within the CofP, but also speaking in front of an audience who might not understand these terms, serves a special function strongly related to the issue of gender. Susan Gal in her study of a German-Hungarian bilingual community in Oberwart, Austria, convincingly proves the relationship between language choice (in her case the most frequent choice of German over Hungarian among the women of the community) and the social position of women in the community (Gal 1978). Although, in the case of Klári and her colleagues, we cannot talk about code switching between Hungarian and English, as the English words used are borrowings, fitted into the Hungarian sentences both on the phonetical and morphological level, the reason behind the choice of English borrowings is to some extent similar to the choice of German over Hungarian in Oberwart. German as well as English carries higher prestige than Hungarian and this can be used strategically by the speakers.

Klári is the only woman in the board of managers and the youngest of all of them. The role of the 'leader' in Hungary, as well as elsewhere, is traditionally a masculine position. Women often have a hard time to being accepted as leaders. Janet Holmes (2006) in her plenary lecture at the

IGALA 4th conference claimed that women in such positions have four options: 1. they conform to masculinist norms; 2. they select a woman friendly CofP; 3. they strategically integrate authoritarian with relational discourse and; 4. they challenge masculinist norms and explicitly feminize work.

As I see it, Klári's strategy is a special version of option 3.

As I mentioned previously, her communicative style can be characterised by the use of stereotypically feminine strategies, thus option 1. does not apply to her. The marketing department can be considered a relatively woman friendly CofP (option 2), this, however, cannot be said about the whole company or the board of managers. Klári definitely does not choose the 4th option either as the following anti-woman quotes from her prove it quite convincingly: "*women are more precise, more ordered and thorough, but boys are more creative, groundbreaking thoughts come mostly from boys, they are better analysts and less interested in small details.*" and "*Me too, I employ men because women go away to give birth.*".

Under option 3. Holmes identifies the roles of the 'Mother' and the 'Queen' as metaphors describing the strategic combination of relational and authoritative discourse.

Klári does not choose either of these. Instead she constructs herself as an expert.   The use of English borrowings (especially from the terminology of management and marketing) is one of the linguistic strategies serving this purpose. (The use of long, complicated, foreign words is another.:cf. "*The optimization of category profitability based on multifunctional knowledge is a necessity.*" ["*Szükséges a **multifunkcionális** ismeretekre épülő **kategóriaprofitabilitás optimalizálása.**"*]).

She realizes that she has a problem as a top manager. Talking about one of her (male) fellow managers, she says: "*It took me a year to make him believe that I'm not just a little blond girl.*" But she also says: "*To be a woman is a disadvantage until her professional expertise is discovered. From then on it's an advantage.*" Thus she explicitly states that having yourself accepted as an expert helps to overcome the disadvantage caused by the fact that you are a woman.

That her strategy is partly successful is proved by the opinion of her colleagues exemplified by the following quotes:

"I consider her extremely energetic, dynamic; **professionally her knowledge** is absolutely **well founded**."

"Perhaps she puts the human factor in the background a little bit, with her it's always the **work** which is **in the foreground**."

> "I consider her **absolutely good professionally**, but she doesn't really care about us as human beings"

She is thus successful in having herself accepted as an expert while her colleagues feel that she does not really care about the people. This latter fact explains her low sympathy rating in the sociometric analysis. Let me sum up my argument:

Klári is a woman in a top managerial position.

Expertise, competence necessary for being accepted as a good boss are traditionally considered to be masculine characteristics.

Klári's communicative style is stereotypically feminine, but she uses a high number of English borrowings in her speech.

The use of English borrowings helps to construct the quality of expertise.

This in turn helps her to be accepted as a boss in spite of the fact that she is a woman.

5.2. 'I eat the boys by the kilo'. The construction of honesty: the use of swear words

While Klári could not gain the sympathy of her fellow workers, my second example describes a linguistic strategy used by a woman who is the most popular member of her Cof P. Nelli (28), who also works for the marketing department, is product group manager, head of a group of four women. She reports to Klári. In her appearance she is emphatically feminine. Her communicative style is relation oriented, she never emphasises her hierarchical role or power with interactional tools.

According to the results of the sociometric analysis she has a central position in the CofP. She received the highest number of votes in questions aiming to map up sympathy relations within the group. At the same time she is considered to be a successful boss.

Her communicative strategy is again close to what Holmes (2006) identifies under option 3. as strategic integration of authoritarian with relational discourse. However, her style is even further from that of the 'Queen' or 'Mother' than Klári's. The most typical communicative feature that she is famous for in the CofP is one which is generally described as a masculine strategy. This is the frequent use of swear words. The following examples were noted down in my research diary, all used by Nelli in front of many other members from inside and occasionally also outside her CofP. (Due to the special nature of swearing, English translation was done freely, giving an approximately similar version of the communicative act in English to the one in Hungarian)

"What's this shit?" (Ez mi a szar?)

"I'm pissed off with him." (A tököm tele van vele!)

"I'll ask him/her where the hell he/she is." (Meg fogom kérdezni tőle, hol a picsában van.)

"Fuck, I don't know his/her phone number!" (Baszd meg, nem tudom a telefonszámát!)

"What the fuck?" (Mi a fasz?)

"Róbert is an asshole!" (Róbert egy nagy gyökér!)

"Bloody hell!" (A kurva életbe!)

I should add that the use of swear words is not typical among the white collar workers of the company and during the observation period I noted only one other person using such terms, interestingly also a woman in her early fifties.

Nelli is very much aware of the presence of this feature in her communication which is proved by the following excerpt.

Excerpt 2. (in English translation)
Éva?: ha ha ha ha ha <laughing>
Nelli: I keep on struggling with it a little longer and (1) **the tape-recorder will in a second record such a (1) well Hungarian (.) swear words ehm vocabulary** that (...) <others laughing>
Éva: This i:s will you comp- compare it after ? That

Excerpt 2. (in the original Hungarian)
Éva?: ha ha ha ha ha
Nelli: még egy kicsit küzdök itt a vérbe (?) és (1) a magnó mindjárt olyan izé magyar (.) káromkodás ö szókészletet fog felvenni hogy (...)<közben nevetés>
Éva: ez a: összehas- összehasonlítod utána? hogy

The combination of stereotypically masculine and stereotypically feminine strategies does not go unnoticed as it is proved by the following contradictory quotes by Nelli's colleagues:

"Nelli was **extremely feminine;** she had to be told to keep back a little."

"Nelli is a **democratic leader,** but she also tries to be **firm.**"

"Nelli's communication is **masculine,** she is very direct, says what she thinks."

Women leaders using a stereotypically feminine, relation oriented communicative style are often accused of being manipulative, not saying what they really think (Tannen 1994a). This could be one of the reasons why Klári was not a popular member of her CofP. As one of her colleagues said: *"as if everything had a choreography around her, there were a lot of formalities, humbug, a lot of eye-wash."*

I would like to argue that, by the frequent use of swear words, Nelli effectively constructs herself as an honest, sincere person who says directly what is on her mind. The following quote by her colleague explicitly creates the link between Nelli's communicative style, focusing especially on her frequent use of swear words, and her character:

"Nelli is very **loose-tongued,** she dares to say things, **swears a lot, doesn't hide her opinion.** She is **more human** than many others at the firm."

Nelli's strategy proves to be very successful. She is considered to be a very good boss and at the same time she is liked by her colleagues. Let me again sum up my argument:

Nelli is a woman in middle managerial position.

She uses a mixture of stereotypically feminine (indirectness) and stereotypically masculine (swearing) communicative strategies.

Indirectness, in the case of women, is often associated with manipulation.

Swearing helps to construct the quality of honesty.

This, in turn, helps Nelli to be accepted as an honest person who is liked and respected by her colleagues.

6. Conclusion

Gender and language studies focused for quite a long time on the differences between how women and men communicate. As many recent studies have proved convincingly, we cannot talk about feminine and masculine styles in general (although studying linguistic ideologies helps us to identify stereotypically feminine and masculine communicative styles). (cf. Bergvall, Bing & Freed 1996; Bucholtz, Liang & Sutton 1999; Hall & Bucholtz 1995; Eckert & McConnell-Ginet 2003) There is a wide variety in the styles of women, as well as similarities in how certain women and men speak. Gender does not determine our language use. The above conclusion has been confirmed by my research results as well. While many differences have been identified between the styles of women managers, there were men and women managers who used almost identical styles.

Recent literature in gender and language studies claim that gender is not reflected in language use, but is actually created by it. My findings seem to modify this approach slightly.

I would like to argue that direct construction of gender, that is the construction of a certain femininity or masculinity, is relatively rare, most often taking place during conversation in mixed pairs or groups focusing on building romantic relationships. Such situations are relatively rare in the context of the workplace. This, however, does not mean that gender plays no role in these situations. I hope to have proved that gender has an indirect effect on communication. People construct certain qualities, like expertise or honesty, qualities which themselves are gendered. Honesty is an important quality to be constructed for a woman who can otherwise be easily accused of manipulation. Expertise is a quality useful for a woman who wants to be accepted as a leader while male leaders need it much less as the meaning of maleness includes in itself the concept of expertise by default.

Gender construction thus takes place indirectly. It leads to the conclusion that, from a theoretical point of view, it is more useful to conceptualise gender not as an attribute one has or does, but rather as a domain filled with meanings (specific to the given communities of practice) about 'man' and 'woman'. If, for example, this field contains meanings identifying expert and leader with male but not with female, then women in leadership positions are forced to react in some ways to this situation. (We should add that the domain is, of course, full of meanings about other collective categories like age, ethnicity, profession, etc., which get combined with each other in highly diverse and community specific ways.) Thus these meanings affect both linguistic behaviour and the interpretation of the linguistic behaviour of speakers moving within this field.

To sum it up, neither our biological sex nor our gender (conceptualised as an attribute we obtain through socialisation) determine language use. In most cases gender is not constructed directly through language use either.

Language use plays an important part in constructing certain characteristics like honesty, expertise, courage, etc., characteristics which themselves are gendered. Gender is thus indirectly constructed and should be conceptualised not as an attribute of people, but rather as a field containing meanings of 'man' and 'woman'.

I hope to have proved the above conclusions by the analysis of two different communicative strategies of two of the observed women and the interpretation of these strategies by their colleagues. In one case, while the language of the conversation was always Hungarian, the frequent borrowing of English words characterising the woman's speech played an important part in the specifically gendered construction of the quality of expertise. In the other case, the frequent use of swear words characterising the language use of another woman helped in constructing the quality of honesty also in a highly gendered way.

References

Adler, P. and P. Adler. 1994. "Observational Techniques". In *Handbook of Qualitative Research*. Eds. N. Denzin and K.Y.S. Lincoln. London: Sage, 377-402.

Atkinson, P. and M. Hammersley. 1998. "Ethnography and Participant Observation. In *Strategies of Qualitative Inquiry*. Eds. N. Denzin and K.Y.S. Lincoln. London: Sage, 110-136.

Austin, J. 1962. *How to Do Things with Words*? Oxford: Oxford University Press.

Bergvall, V.L., J.M. Bing and A.F. Freed, eds. 1996. *Rethinking Gender and Language Research. Theory and Practice*. London/New York: Longman.

Boden, D. 1994. *The Business of Talk. Organizations in Action*. Cambridge: Polity Press.

Bourdieu, P. 1991 [1977]. *Language and Symbolic Power*. Cambridge, Massachusetts: Harvard University Press.

Bucholtz, M., A.C. Liang and L.A. Sutton, eds. 1999. *Reinventing Identities. The Gendered Self in Discourse*. Oxford: Oxford University Press.

Butler, J. 1999 [1990]. *Gender Trouble. Feminism and the Subversion of Identity*. New York: Routledge.

Coates, J. 1995. "Language, gender and career." In *Language and Gender. Interdisciplinary Perspectives*. Ed. Sara Mills. London: Longman, 13-30.

Eckert, P. and S. McConnell-Ginet. 1992. "Communities of Practice: Where Language, Gender, and Power All Live." In *Locating Power. Proceedings of the 2nd Berkeley Women and Language Conference.* Eds. K. Hall *et al.* Berkeley: BWLG, 89-99.

— and S. McConnell-Ginet. 2003. *Language and Gender.* Cambridge: Cambridge University Press.

Frey, M. 2002. "Nők és férfiak a munkaerőpiacon". In *Szerepváltozások. Jelentés a nők és férfiak helyzetéről 2001-ben.* Eds. N. Ildikó, P. Tiborné and T.I. György. Budapest: Tárki, 9-29.

Gal, S. 1978. "Peasant men can't get wives: language change and sex roles in a bilingual community." *Language in Society* 7: 1-16.

Goffman, E. 1959. *The Presentation of Self in Everyday Life.* Garden City, New York: Doubleday.

—. 1986[1974]. *Frame Analysis. An Essay on the Organization of Experience.* Boston: Northeastern University Press.

Hall, K. and M. Bucholtz, eds. 1995. *Gender Articulated. Language and the Socially Constructed Self.* London: Routledge.

Holmes, J. 2000. *Gendered Speech in Social Context. Perspectives from Gown and Town.* Wellington: Victoria University Press.

—. 2006 "Did anyone feel disempowered by that?" Gender, leadership and politeness." Plenary lecture at the *4th IGALA Conference: International perspectives on gender.* Valencia, 8-10 November, 2006.

Hymes, D. 1972. "Models of the interaction of language and social life." In *Directions in Sociolinguistics.* Eds. J. Gumperz and D. Hymes. New York: Holt, Rinehart and Winston, 35-71.

Kendall, S. and D. Tannen. 1997. "Gender and Language in the Workplace". In *Gender and Discourse.* Ed. Ruth Wodak. London: Sage, 81-105.

McElhinny, B.S. 1998. "I don't smile much any more": Affect, Gender, and the Discourse of Pittsburgh Police Officers." In *Locating Power. Proceedings of the 2nd Berkeley Women and Language Conference.* Eds. K. Hall *et* al. Berkeley: BWLG, 386-403.

Mead, G.H. 1973. *A pszichikum, az én és a társadalom.* Budapest: Gondolat.

Nagy, B. 2001. *Női menedzserek.* Budapest: Aula.

de Saussure, F. 1997[1916]. *Bevezetés az általános nyelvészetbe.* Budapest: Corvina.

Tannen, D. 1994a. *Gender and Discourse.* New York/Oxford: Oxford University Press.

—. 1994b. *Talking form 9 to 5. Women and Men in the Workplace.* New York: Avon Books.

Chapter Seven

'*I'll Be a Rooster Crowing in the Hen Coop but You'll Be a Hen and I'll Be Bothering You*': The Male Sexual Identity in Cyprus Verbal Dueling

Elli Doukanari, University of Nicosia

Abstract: This study constitutes a sociolinguistic-ethnographic investigation of the display of Greek-Cypriot male identity in Kipriaka chattista (Cyprus rhyming improvisations). More specifically, the study investigates how male sexuality is constructed in this poetic form of verbal play. The data consist of video-taped and tape-recorded performances of chattista. Supportive evidence is also elicited from conversational discourse. The study demonstrates how the Greek-Cypriot man projects images of his sexual male existence with an abundant use of figures of speech. The results indicate that through this traditional genre, the Greek-Cypriot man, displays himself as the superior male in opposition to the female, as the amorous/womanizer, and as the protector of family honor. These projected sexual identities are socially and culturally bound. I argue that, just as the Cypriot society places constraints upon females to control their sexuality (Doukanari 2007), the society also places a burden on males. The Greek-Cypriot man struggles to demonstrate manliness with emphasis on his sexuality, while at the same time he must defend his manliness by protecting his honor, which is directly affected by the sexual behavior of the females in his family or his opponent's sexual verbal insults.

Key Words: *Gendered identities, male sexuality, Cyprus verbal dueling, figures of speech, discourse analysis, honor, respect.*

1. *Chattista*

Kipriaka Chattista or *Chattismata* constitute a traditional poetic genre characteristic of Cyprus. They are spontaneous couplets, improvised impromptu, performed in front of an audience. These improvisations, which are either sung or recited, usually lead to verbal dueling between two or more individuals, especially men. The aim of each singer is to top his opponent by proving that he is the best, in order to gain the approval and admiration of his audience. Chattista may take place in various social occasions such as family and friendly gatherings, weddings, and organized competitions sponsored by municipalities and radio stations during various public festivities. This genre is preserved even among Cypriots of diaspora. There are different types of chattista depending on the situation in which they take place, the purpose they serve, and the way they are used. For more information on chattista, see Doukanari (1997).

2. The investigation of male sexual identity in the Greek culture

Previous research has emphasized that Greeks primarily display gendered identities, which are tied to social and cultural constraints (e.g. Campbell 1964, Cowan 1990, Doukanari 1997, Herzfeld 1985, and Seremetakis 1991). In chattista, numerous aspects of Greek-Cypriot male identities are revealed; e.g. the best singer, the brave lad, the physically powerful, the knowledgeable/witty (Doukanari 1997). This paper focuses on one aspect of male identity displayed by chattista performers, namely male sexual identity.

In the Greek cultures, sexuality becomes central to the definition of gender and is directly associated with the values of honor and respect. Women's sexuality has direct implications on male and family honor (Argyrou 1996, Campbell 1964, Herzfeld 1985) and may even extend to national honor (Doukanari 2007).

In reference to the Sarakatsani community, a shepherd community in rural Greece, Campbell (1964) argues that it is imperative for men to protect the honor of their women which include the wife, mother, sisters and daughters. In that shepherd community, women are believed to continually threaten the honor of men. This is attributed to the nature of women's sexuality. The way a male behaves or presents himself is based on a system of social values considered prerequisites of ideal manhood – namely, honor, strength, and pride. Males and females are constantly evaluated by the community. A man is evaluated as to whether he is justified about what he has said and done, and whether he has displayed manliness (*andhrismos*) in defending his honor. Although women's roles such as household keepers and mothers are oppositionally complementary to men's, a woman's display of identity is submerged to the more dominant identity of man. As Campbell (1964: 57) states, in the Sarakatsani community, "The male sex is held to be unambiguously superior not only in power but also in worth to the female, to which the stigma of original sin is closely attached. The female is a constant threat to the honor and integrity of the male, and must be disciplined and dominated."

The issue of male honor associated with female sexuality has also been emphasized in other studies of Greek culture. Herzfeld (1985) reports that, in a community of the Greek island of Crete, to which he assigns the pseudonym Glendi, one of the traits of a man who is "good at being a man", is to be able to protect his family from sexual and verbal threats. Cowan (1990), in her study of the Sohoians, a community in Greek Macedonia, reports that the honor of males is directly affected by a woman's uncontrollable display of sexuality. By maintaining control of her sexuality, a woman shows respect towards the males in her family. Similarly, Argyrou (1996) observes that in the Greek-Cypriot culture, the honor of a husband or a father is affected by the actions of the women in the family who are expected to protect their chastity or sexuality. A man's honor is a prerequisite in order to be accorded respect by the community. This is based on the Cypriot cultural belief that a man must first be respected by his family if he is to be respected by the society. And a woman's control of her sexuality is one indication of respect towards her male relatives.

The issues that the above studies address are also reflected in this study; That is, the male sex is portrayed as being superior to the female. Also, men make claims about women being a threat to males' honor or the women being a temptation to men. As will be shown, in Section 5 below, reference to a woman's sexuality (be it a mother or a lover), becomes an offense for the honor of the opponent.

In Doukanari (2007), I discuss the issue of sexuality in the Greek-Cypriot culture as it is defined in chattista with focus on female sexuality. The results of that study indicate that while men preserve traditional ideologies in regard to female sexuality, women's improvisations show evidence of modern views and attempt through re-evaluation and negotiation to overturn pre-existing taboos about controlling female sexuality. Based only on the results of Doukanari (2007), one may conclude that women's attempts to overturn traditional ideologies regarding sexuality are indications of only women being oppressed by the society, and that men are not burdened with societal constraints. That is, one may view only women being victims of taboos imposed by the society to the advantage of men. Taking the 2007 study as a point of departure, this paper moves one step further to investigate the other side of the coin, by focusing on the display and perception of Greek-Cypriot male sexuality in chattista.

By looking at sexuality from another perspective, this study aims to give a more holistic picture of Cypriot sexual identities. Three types of prominent male sexual identities are revealed; i.e. the superior male as opposed to the female, the amorous/womanizer and the protector of family honor. Another important issue emerging from this study is that, just like the Cypriot culture places constraints upon women to control their sexuality (Doukanari 2007) it also places constraints upon men. To display manliness, a man undergoes a test. He must engage in competition and struggle to emphasize his sexual existence, while he must simultaneously struggle to protect and defend his honor, which is threatened by the sexual behavior of women in his family, or by his opponent's sexual verbal insults. The male performer of chattista is always evaluated by the audience as to what he has said. Through a skillful rhetorical argument, and with an abundant use of figurative speech, men project a whole image of male sexual existence. At the same time, they reveal social and cultural expectations.

3. Figures of speech and the display of male sexual identity

I have previously identified certain strategies that singers use while composing their improvisations. The most predominant strategy employed in chattista is the projection of masculine superiority. This strategy is enacted through rhyming language with the complex use of verbal and non-verbal devices. Among the devices used by male performers to negotiate masculinity are: Thematic choice, figures of speech, antagonistic evaluation, adversative imperatives, negation, figurative terms of address and non-verbal signs of masculine presentation (Doukanari 1997: 234-246).

Figures of speech are the most prominent devices used by the singers of chattista, to give their audience a vivid iconic image of their masculinity. For this reason, the analysis focuses on figures of speech. According to Stankiewicz (1960), in poetry, themes are frequently developed and interpreted by means of other themes. This is often achieved by the use of tropes, especially of metaphor, which develops the meaning according to semantic similarity. Stankiewicz's view also applies to chattista, which are oral poetry. Thus through the strategic use of metaphors, synecdoche, assonance and alliteration, chattista performers present a sexual masculine self. The ways in which figures of speech are strategically used to project male sexuality are demonstrated in Section 5 below.

4. Methodology and data collection

The study constitutes an ethnographic/sociolinguistic approach and investigates the display of sexuality in performance, taking into account the specific event, and the participants' socio-historical backgrounds, relationships and alignments toward each other. A large amount of data has been collected from private and public settings, such as weddings, festivals, friendly gatherings among Cypriots of Diaspora and Cypriots living in Cyprus, as well as ordinary conversations. All the data were transliterated and transcribed based on Doukanari's (1997) transliteration and discourse transcription conventions. For the analysis of chattista, as well as ordinary conversations, I employ an interactional discourse analysis based on Chafe (1980), Doukanari (1997), Gumperz (1982), Schiffrin (1994), and Tannen (1981, 1984). The significance of this method is that it enables the discourse analyst to investigate the actions the performers take to create meaning, present identities and express ideological, social and cultural values or taboos. In addition to discourse analysis, I have consulted informants, including the participants, through free interviews often based on the playback of problematic segments (Tannen 1984). This served as additional means of investigation and assisted me in the clarification or verification of my findings.

In this paper, the primary focus is on one event, a friendly gathering among Cypriots in Maryland, USA. During the particular friendly gathering, the participants ate and drank to the point where they arrived at a state of mirth and heightened emotions. At a particular point, they were encouraged by the others to compete with chattista. This setting simulates a natural environment for chattista to take place (Doukanari 1997). Caraveli (1985: 261) emphasizes that ritual celebrations involving performance, called *glendia* are formalized arenas "for the expression of individual identity and the negotiation of community boundaries." The advantage of concentrating on this particular event is that the dynamic and interactive nature of chattista, as well as the negotiation of masculine identity, is perceived more vividly. In addition, this particular friendly gathering is the most private event in my data, in which the participants are relatives and friends. Therefore, the display of sexual identities is more abundant and includes more aspects of sexuality. In such types of events, unlike public events, there are no constraints on the performers in terms of time-limitations and turn-taking. Also, because the issue of sexuality may often be associated with taboo language, in such a private setting, the singers are not subjected to language censoring.

5. Analysis, results and discussion

This section illustrates how Greek-Cypriot men present a masculine aspect of selfhood in chattista, namely their sexual identity. As mentioned above, the focus of analysis is on figures of speech since they constitute the most prominent device used to project male sexual identities and the device that reveals social values and taboos culture-specific of the Greek-Cypriot society. However, when figures of speech are discussed, the reader will notice that other devices are mentioned. This is because discourse devices are not clear-cut or independent from each other. Figures of speech cannot be discussed in isolation from other devices that are embedded or coexist with them.

The analysis that follows also demonstrates how male sexual identities are constructed in the Cypriot culture through individual and collective effort. Although the paper focuses primarily on male talk, female talk is not excluded from the discussion since women also become active in the construction of male identities. It is important to note that although some of the examples used are also provided in Doukanari (2007), in this study I employ a more detailed linguistic analysis focusing on male sexuality and the strategic use of figures of speech. The examples are analyzed either as individual entities where men project images of male sexuality, or as several verses in an interaction in order to demonstrate how sexuality is negotiated by men; i.e., how men project their own masculinity while they belittle their opponent's. Throughout the analysis, certain aspects of masculinity for Greek men are revealed. Each time men reveal their sexual male image, they also reveal ideological, social and cultural expectations. Thus, identities are constructed by drawing on an array of social ideologies (Doukanari 2007, Eckert and McConnell-Ginet 2003, Hall and Bucholtz 1995). As Herzfeld (1985: 232) states, "The negotiation of personal identity always also entails the testing of social values".

Note that the original text appears transliterated in *italics*. An idiomatic translation follows in regular fonts. The discourse transcription conventions are based on Doukanari (1997). CAPS mark very emphatic stress. Colon (:) indicates lengthened vowel sound. (Words) within parenthesis indicate ellipsis or paraphrases for clarification. [Brackets] are used for comments on quality of speech and context.

5.1. The display of male sexual identities in chattista

The examined data indicate that the most prominent male identities related to sexuality are:

- The superior male as opposed to the female
- The amorous man/womanizer
- The protector of family honor

5.1.1. The superior male as opposed to the female

One aspect directly associated with male sexuality is simply being the male as opposed to the female. The man often presents himself as the male who makes sexual advances toward his opponent to whom he assigns the female role. Being masculine is presented as a positive attribute whereas being feminine is presented as a negative attribute. The example below taken from the particular friendly gathering demonstrates how masculine identities are negotiated with male-female sexuality as the main point of argument. The antagonists are 45-year old Mihalis and 33-year old Adhamos.

Example A – The superior male in contrast to the female: The rooster/hen metaphor

1. Adhamos: *O: O: i:se axiolipitos mazi mmu pu terkazis,*
   Oooh   Oooh you are pitiful (since) you have to match (rhymes) with me,

2.   *mazi mmu pu terkazis,*
   (since) you have to match (rhymes) with me,

3.   *O: Enna se kamo petinon mes ton ghuma na krazis,*
   Oooh I'll make you a rooster crowing in the hen coop,
   (i.e. a creature with a bad voice)

4. Elli, Miltos: [laugh]

5. Adhamos: *mes ton ghuma na krazis,*
   crowing in the hen coop,

6. Elli: [laughs]

7. Mihalis: *O: dge yo enna 'me petinos mes to ghuma na krazo,*
                 Oooh and I'll be a rooster crowing in the hen coop,

8.   *mes to ghuma na krazo,*
                 crowing in the hen coop,

9.   *O: dge su enna: 'se ornitha dge yo enna se pirazo,*
                 Oooh but you'll be a hen and I'll be bothering you,
                 (I'll be making sexual advances toward you)

10. Audience: [laugh, applaud]

In the above ritual argument that takes place between the two men, male identity is defined through a comparison of male sexuality with female sexuality. Each man metaphorically refers to male and female animals, associating himself with what he believes are the *positive* aspects of animals, and his opponent with the *negative*. The metaphoric use of names of animals to describe people is also reported by Brandes (1980) in his ethnographic study about the men of Monterros, a pseudonym of a township in Eastern Andalusia, Spain.

Notice how skillfully the negotiation of male identity takes place. In this example, Adhamos calls Mihalis a rooster "I'll make you a rooster crowing in the hen coop" (line 3), which implies that Adhamos is such a good singer that as compared to him, his antagonist will sound as bad as a rooster crowing. Mihalis accepts his role as a rooster, but focuses on another aspect of roosterness; i.e. being masculine: "I'll be a rooster crowing in the hen coop, but you'll be a hen and I'll be bothering you" (lines 7-9). By this metaphor, Mihalis associates himself with a rooster, a male, and his opponent with a hen, a female, and implies that "I'll be a rooster, but at least I'll be a man! But you'll be a hen and I'll be making sexual advances toward you". Thus not only does Mihalis emphasize his male identity, (he is a rooster), but at the same time he neutralizes his opponent's masculinity by giving him a female identity (he is a hen).

Mihalis' metaphor associates maleness with *positive* and femaleness with *negative* attributes. According to Lakoff & Johnson (1980) cultures give different priorities to *up and down orientation*. The way concepts are oriented and the orientations, which are most important, vary from culture to culture. Thus Mihalis' ideology as a male Greek-Cypriot is that maleness is *up* and femaleness is *down*, since a rooster, being a male, makes sexual advances towards a hen, a female. The association of femaleness with negativity in reference to metaphoric uses of animals is also reported by Campbell (1964). The Sarakatsani men are associated with sheep, which are considered God's animals, whereas women are associated with goats, the animals of the devil that Christ has tamed for the service of man.

5.1.2. The amorous man/womanizer

Another aspect of masculine identity directly associated with male sexuality is the image of the amorous man and the womanizer. Greek-Cypriot men project their masculinity by presenting themselves as amorous in two different ways:

- As the sexually-active man
- As the man who cannot resist temptation. In this case, the woman is presented as temptation.

5.1.2.1. The sexually active man

The first image of the amorous man is the male who is sexually active. The performer displays himself as amorous by making reference to male-female sexual relationships and by boasting about women. The male is projected as a womanizer, a great lover, a man that is loved passionately by women. The other singer disqualifies his opponent's amorous presentation by offending his opponent or the women he fools around with, often with the use of vulgar language. The examples below (B and C) demonstrate how 79-year old Pappus, meaning grandpa in Greek, projects his masculinity by appearing as an amorous man and a womanizer, and how his opponent, 33-year old Adhamos, neutralizes Pappus' masculinity. In Example B, Pappus, who is the opponent's wife's grandfather, refers to a woman that presumably fell passionately in love with him:

Example B – The amorous: The sexually active man

1. Pappus: [With deep and loud voice accompanied by excessive hand gestures]
Efilun ndin, dge lalen mmu. dhakka me na poniso,
I was kissing her, and she was telling me, bite me 'till I hurt,

2.   *na me pona i vukka mu, na me sse lizmoniso.*
so my cheek will hurt, (and) I won't forget you.

3. Audience: [laugh]

4. Andrulla: *En ulla erotika tu Pappu*
                 Pappu's songs are all love songs

5. Elli: *Ne, ne, ne erotiaris.*
                 Yes, yes, yes he's amorous.

6. Audience: [laugh]

Pappus achieves a special effect in his chattisto (lines 1 & 2) by the
passionate way he recites it (i.e. with deep and loud voice, and with
excessive hand gestures), and by using alliteration and repetition.
Alliteration is the "repeating and playing upon the same letter, a figure of
speech in which consonants, especially at the beginning of words, or
stressed syllables are repeated" (Cuddon 1976: 27). Here, Pappus repeats
and plays with the sound /m/ which occurs twice in the first stich and three
times in the second. He also uses repetition of the phrase *na poniso* ('till I
hurt), line 1, making only a slight change, the parallel construction *na me
pona i vukka mu* (so my cheek will hurt) line 2, in order to emphasize the
woman's passion while they were kissing. A woman falling passionately
in love with him is a compliment for a man. What makes Pappus' chattisto
even more amusing is that although he is an older man, he tries to project
his male image of being a womanizer and a great lover.

The audience's evaluative comments about Pappus' verses confirm
that they have received the portrayed image. It is important to emphasize
that the audience members who explicitly acknowledge these masculine
attributes of the amorous man and the womanizer are women. With their
comments, the two women help build up Pappus' male image. This is an
indication that it is not only men who help construct male identities, but
women as well. The construction of identities is both the result of
individual and collective effort on the part of both genders. But the most
important point deducted from the audience's recognition and acceptance
of the male images projected, is that the audience shares "frames" (Tannen
and Wallat 1993) based on similar expectations of what are ideal
masculine attributes in the Greek-Cypriot culture. In other words, the
audience as members of the society reveal the cultural expectations that it
is positive for a man to be amorous. This serves as evidence that society
places a burden on men to display manliness by emphasizing their sexual
identity.

Adhamos, following the discussion of the audience about his
opponent's self projection of being an amorous person, is urged to answer

Pappu back in order to persuade the audience that his antagonist is not actually the man that he claims to be. After a few attempts, Adhamos comes up with the following chattisto in order to neutralize Pappu's amorous presentation of masculine identity:

Example C – Negation of the amorous presentation

1. Adhamos: *tin mavrin tin kolomavrin tin trizolaomenin*
the dark, that jetblack and female lunatic

2.   *Evastas tus dge yirizes dge piennen gordomeni,*
You were holding (hands) and going around
(with such women) and (that woman) was walking
proudly (swaggered),

3. Audience: [laugh]

4. Adhamos: *dge pu na xeris yero mu pu 'tan xikolomEni.*
and how would you know my old man that she was
bottomless (i.e. so sexually active that she lost
her bottom).

5. Audience: [laugh, applaud]

By using alliteration similar to his antagonist's, i.e. by repeating and playing with the same stressed syllable (*-meni*), Adhamos creates an effective chattisto to humiliate Pappus' masculinity. The feminine participles *trizolaomeni* (thrice crazy), *kordomeni* (swaggered) and *xikolomeni* (bottomless), function as adjectives and describe the characteristics of the woman that Pappus is hanging around with. The first two adjectives lead to the third *xikolomeni* (bottomless). In the Greek-Cypriot culture, a woman sexually active with a lot of men is not an ideal woman to go around with or to get married to (see also Argyrou 1996 and Doukanari 2007). In this example, the participle *xikolomeni*, literally "bottomless", is used metaphorically to mean a woman very sexually active with a lot of men. Through alliteration and metaphor, Adhamos tops his opponent by nullifying his opponent's masculinity as a womanizer. This is a ritual insult for Pappus because for a real "macho" man, it is not a challenge to go out with women who have been very sexually active with a lot of men. Also, the fact that Pappus does not know that the woman is very sexually active, "*dge pu na xeris yero mu putan xikolomeni*" (and how would you know my old man that she was bottomless), line 4, is another strike against his masculinity; i.e., the fact that Pappus is not aware of what kind of reputation the women that he goes out with have, is an indication that he is naïve and ignorant, has no wits, and therefore he is not a man. From the above exchange of chattista between Adhamos and Pappus, we can deduct that the man's amorous and sexual presentation is negated if the woman involved is sexually active with a lot of men (Doukanari 2007). I would like to add here that Adhamo's implied message about his antagonist being ignorant and naive, as well as his reference to Pappus as *yero* (old man), belittles even more Pappus' masculinity as a womanizer and a great lover.

5.1.2.1.1. The amorous/womanizer and the… "gambler"

In Example D below, Pappus projects once more his masculinity as a womanizer. But interestingly enough, he combines his sexuality with the identity of the gambler! He addresses now his chattisto to a woman whom presumably he fools around with.

Example D – The amorous and the… gambler

1. Pappus: *Ela po yiro tu vramu dg' ela tu kalamniona*
             Come around the fence and come to the reed grove

2.   *na pkianno ta vizarya su na pezo zia mona*
             to take your breasts to play odd and even

3. Audience: [laugh, applaud]

Pappus tells a woman to come around the fence and go to the reed grove. The reed grove is a synecdoche, "a figure of speech in which the part stands for the whole and thus something else is understood within the thing mentioned" (Cuddon, 1976: 676). Here, the reed grove is the part which symbolically stands for the whole; i.e., represents any secret spot where lovers meet. According to my informants, the reed grove is only one of the numerous secret spots that in the Greek-Cypriot culture lovers could meet, at least at Pappus' younger times. Secret spots could also be among others the village mill – *milos*, a well – *pighadi*, a water fountain – *vrisi*. These meeting places are abundantly referred to in Greek folk poetry.

Pappus continues with a very playful and creative stich: "*na pkianno ta vizarya su na pezo zia-mona*" (to take your breasts to play odd and even), line 2. In this metaphor, the performer identifies the woman's breasts with dice, by which he plays odd and even, giving a vivid iconic image of himself playing around with them like throwing dice. The word *vizarya* is a compound, a unit consisting of two or more bases. Pappus takes the words *vizya* (breasts) and *zarya* (dice) and creates a new word, the compound noun *vizarya*. More specifically, he creates a "blend" [1]. In this metaphor, the performer's choice of the second word *zarya* to create a blend with *vizya* is interesting for its complex linguistic creativity. The word *zarya* shares the sounds /z/ and /a/ with *vizya*, and consists of the ending -*arya* added to the word *vizya* to make a diminutive out of it [2]. But more importantly, if we look at the etymology of the word *vizarya*, we can appreciate the social significance of Pappu's vocabulary choice. Creating a blend with the particular words *vizya* and *zarya*, Pappus manages to intertwine and project two vivid images of his masculinity; (a) as a womanizer and (b) as a gambler, (another masculine attribute projected in chattista performances). The gambler is portrayed in other examples from my data as well. However, this is a unique example that combines the amorous with the gambler. Pappus' association of sexuality with gambling is not coincidental. His couplet carries a lot of meaning since gambling is a game of taking chances just as life and lovers are based on the chances of fate. Pappus has projected his masculinity here by presenting himself as a playful risky man that takes chances. Herzfeld (1985) also reports that Glendiot masculinity is based upon risks, and one of the risks a man takes is gambling.

5.1.2.2. The male who cannot resist temptation

In the above section, I have discussed the first image of the amorous man; i.e. the male that has sexual relationships with women. The second image of the amorous man depicts women as temptation and himself as the man who cannot resist temptation. In the chattisto that follows (Example E), Pappus projects his image of masculinity by making reference to the fact that no man can resist the temptation of a beautiful woman, not even a saint.

Example E – Men cannot resist temptation

1. Pappus: *Allaxen dge stolistiken o mirodhatos krinos*
             She changed and got all dressed up the fragrant lily

2.   *dge pien mes tin eklishan ston Ain Konstandino*
             and she went inside St. Constantine's church

3.   *tin oran pu tu kondepsen endgisen tis dge dginos*
             At the moment that she came close to Him, even

He touched her!

4. Audience: [laugh]

Line 1, *Allaxen dge stolistiken o mirodhatos krinos* (She changed and got all dressed up, the fragrant lily), constitutes a metaphor where a beautiful woman is identified with a fragrant lily; thus the woman is associated with temptation. Pappus continues that the woman went to St. Constantine's Church and when she approached St. Constantine, He touched her as well), line 3. The stich *tin oran pu tu kondepsen endgisen tis dge dginos* (when she approached him He touched her as well) is a synecdoche, where St. Constantine, the part, (i.e. one man out of all men), stands for the whole (i.e. represents all males). This stich is also a metaphor. A saint in the Greek Orthodox religion is the representation of purity and resistance to temptation. Here, however, Saint Constantine, as a male, touches the woman. This, of course, implies that the "touching" is not so innocent. Through this metaphor, the performer (Pappus) gives a symbolic justification for touching a woman – that even a male saint cannot resist the temptation of a beautiful woman.

This chattisto extends and reflects the cultural perception that Greek-Cypriot men are thought to have difficulty resisting the temptation of any beautiful woman. This finding is in agreement with other studies which discuss the issue of temptation on the part of males in the Cypriot culture. Sant Cassia (1981) asserts that in Cyprus the notion of temptation is based on the cultural belief that a man cannot resist the temptation of having a sexual relationship with a woman. Loizos (1975) points out that the men of Kalo village in Cyprus treat life with a Wildean realism which says that men can resist everything but temptation. Although Loizos refers to the issue of politics being the temptations men are faced with, which threaten the solidarity of the village, his report on the notion of temptation confirms the existence of the Cypriot cultural belief that men cannot resist temptation. The fact that women are considered temptations to men also applies to the Greek culture at large. Campbell (1964), for example, finds that in the Sarakatsani community, women are perceived as sources of temptation for men. Not only are women considered creatures of the devil, but because of the nature of their sexuality, they are believed to continually threaten male honor.

Pappus' couplet obviously reflects the idea that the society justifies a man for his lack of control in the face of temptation due to the nature of his sexuality. This may lead to conclusions that the blame and burden is placed on women, who are always perceived as temptations to men. Such a conclusion may be drawn from my previous study on female sexuality

(Doukanari 2007) as well as from the above mentioned studies. However, if we look into this matter more deeply and from the men's point of view, we may see a burden placed upon men as well. That is, in the Cypriot culture, men are constantly evaluated for the ways they demonstrate manliness (Argyrou 1996, Doukanari 1997, Loizos 1975) either based on their actions or their words. Therefore, they must constantly demonstrate manliness through verbal and non-verbal actions, by emphasizing the nature of their sexuality. There is in a sense a pressure on men to convince the society that they are "real men", otherwise, their manliness will be in question. And I ask. If men did not feel the pressure of safeguarding their sexuality, would they really feel the need to constantly proclaim it? – And more importantly by engaging in competition in the presence of an audience?

5.1.3. The protector of family honor

The identity associated with the woman being depicted as temptation and the man who cannot resist temptation leads to another male sexual identity displayed in chattista performances, which is the protector of family honor. The male is expected to protect the honor of his family and especially the honor of the females in the family. Many chattista are insults against the opponent's mother. Whatever women do that offends their honor, strongly reflects on the males of the family as well, because this means that the males have not protected their family honor by looking after their women. In Example F, Pappus recites a chattisto to his opponent in order to offend Adhamos' family honor.

Example F – The mother's sexual behavior: The son's lack of honor

1. Pappus: *I mana su dg' i mana mu epian is ton milon,*
                  Your mamma and my mama went to the mill,

2.   *i mana mu irten ghliora i mana su ivren filon.*
                  my mamma came back quickly, (but) your mamma
                  found a lover.

3. Audience: [laugh, applaud]

4. Elli: *Bravo Pappu?*

5. Audience: [laugh]

Pappus plays with the utterances *i mana mu* (my mamma) and *i mana su* (your mamma). By repeating these phrases which are very similar in sounds, Pappus creates alliteration (a type of parallelism) by repeating and playing upon the same consonant sound *m,* which is found in the words *mana* (mama), *mu* (my), and *milon* (mill). At the same time, Pappus creates an assonance, by repeating the same vowel sounds a, i and o. Thus, Pappus achieves a particular effect of euphony, while at the same time he mockingly provokes his opponent. The combination of alliteration and assonance and Pappus' choice of the words *milon* (mill) and *filon* (lover), provides his antagonist and the audience with a vivid iconic image. As mentioned above, the *mill* is considered in the traditional Greek culture as one of the many secret places at which lovers may meet. Here, Pappus has created a synecdoche, where the *mill* stands as part of the whole; i.e. as one of the many secret places where lovers meet, as well as a metaphor. The *mill* here does not have its literal interpretation of an establishment equipped with machinery to grind grain into flour or meal. Rather, it is understood as one of the many secret lover-spots that presumably Adhamos' mother meets her lovers, according to Pappus' chattisto.

Thus, through the strategic combination of alliteration and assonance, Pappus addresses a ritual insult against his opponent's mother: *i mana mu irten ghliora i mana su ivren filon* (my mamma came back quickly but your mamma found a lover), line 2. By using this insult about his antagonist's mother, Pappus automatically offends his opponent's honor, and therefore, his masculinity. If one's mother finds a lover, it is the man's fault because he has not protected his family honor by looking after her. Thus Pappus here projects his own masculinity while belittling his opponent's (Adhamos'). This chattisto implies: "I'm a better man than you are because I have my honor; I've looked after my mother and she hasn't found a lover. But you are not much of a man, because you allowed for your mother to find a lover". The phenomenon of projecting one's own masculinity while at the same time putting down the opponent's by creating insults against his mother is also reported by Abrahams (1983) and Labov (1972) as a practice of African-American boys and men, and by Dundes, Leach and Ozkok (1989) on Turkish teenage boys.

Chattista about mothers may not necessarily include only insults directly offending one's honor. Even the idea of talking against the opponent's mother is enough to offend the honor of the opponent. Chattista about mothers may be just playful nonsense rhymes such as the following distich that Adhamos creates in response to Pappu's insulting couplet:

Example G – A mother's private part: An attack on family honor

1. Adhamos: *I mana mu dg' i mana su, ivrasin ena fesi,*
   my mamma and your mamma found a fez,

2. *dg' evalan ndo sto ngolon tis, dge en mbori na shesi.*
   and they stuck it up her (your mamma's) ass, and she
   cannot shit.

3. Audience: [laugh, applaud]

This couplet reveals that just by referring to a private part of the opponent's mother's body (her bottom) in a vulgar way, is enough to attack one's opponent's masculinity. Adhamos makes his chattisto even more offensive by using the word *fesi* (fez). His choice of the Turkish word *fesi* is probably done to achieve a rhyming effect with the verb *na shesi* (to shit), but in addition, as several of my informants have indicated, another issue may be implied with the word "fez". The Greeks and the Turks have a history of not being in good terms for hundreds of years. Following the war in 1974, a part of Cyprus is still under occupation by the Turkish army. Therefore, choosing a fez, which is a very distinctive characteristic of the Turkish culture, to be the object that was placed in the ... bottom of the opponent's mother, makes the insult even more offensive. The choice of the word *fez* reveals the cultural expectations of a Greek-Cypriot, that it is inappropriate to use an enemy's attire in any way.

These two examples (F and G) indicate that Greek-Cypriot men portray themselves as protectors of family honor through chattista, which is a traditional genre. In Doukanari (2007), I demonstrate that this type of identity is also displayed in conversational non-traditional discourse and that women's sexuality is not always restricted to family honor –it can even extend to the nation's honor. In this study, national honor also becomes an issue. The fact that the enemy's object is placed in the opponent's mother's bottom (Example G above) is an attack not only on the opponent's family honor, but also on his national honor. This finding confirms Herzfeld's (1986) suggestion that Greek identities should be defined with more emphasis on national identity.

It is deducted from the above examples that Cypriot men are expected to meet the demands of the society. And one of the constraints society places upon a man is to protect the honor of the females in his family. The demand on men to indicate masculinity by protecting their family honor is also confirmed by others. Herzfeld (1985) finds that a Glendiot man is "good at being a man" if he is able to protect his family from sexual and verbal threats. Campbell (1964) argues that it is imperative for Sarakatsani men to protect the honor of their family by protecting the honor of the women. Zoras (1975) also points out that the issue of honor is often reflected in Greek love songs.

In his study on Cypriot weddings, Argyrou (1996) describes how a Greek-Cypriot father or husband must make sure that his honor is not offended by the actions of the women in his family and emphasizes that the ideology of honor is associated with the value of respect. That is, to gain the respect of the community, a man must first be respected by his family. One indication that the man of the household is taken seriously is for the wife to make sure that the daughter's chastity is protected. Other studies of Greek culture view the respect of a woman towards the males of the family as it is expressed by the way she shows obedience to the males (Campbell 1964), or the ways she displays her sexuality (Cowan 1990), or the way she shows tender care to the males of the family (Doukanari 2007, Seremetakis 1991).

5.2. Evidence of Masculinity in Ordinary Conversations

I have found that the way Greek-Cypriot men project their masculinity in chattista is similar to the way Greek men tease each other in ordinary conversations. I provide one example from another conversation that was tape-recorded during an Easter party to illustrate that the way men project their masculinity in Kipriaka chattista is similar to the way they project their masculinity in teasing sessions of ordinary conversations; thus, whatever is projected in chattista performances is in essence a reflection of the reality of culture. In the following example, Hristos (an Athenian Greek) starts teasing his brother-in-law Stavros (a Greek-Cypriot). This gives Stavros the opportunity to top Hristos by projecting his masculinity.

Example H – Male sexuality is positive: The male-goat metaphor

1. Hristos: *Forese to kapelo eki pera. O* [laughs] *traulos eki pera?*
   He wore the hat over there, the [laughs] male goat over there?

2. Andrulla: *O traullos* [laughs]
   the male goat [laughs]

3. Stavros: *En idhes t' appidhima du traullu. Kalamara.*
   You haven't seen the hump of the male goat. Kalamara.

4. Miltos: [laughs]

Hristos starts teasing Stavros by mocking him about the "cool" hat he is wearing at the time, and calls him *traulos,* which in the Greek-Cypriot dialect, means "male goat". Although Hristos is an Athenian Greek, rather than using the standard Greek word for male goat which is *traghos,* he uses the Greek-Cypriot word *traullos,* with his standard Greek accent (*traulos*). Hristos is married to a Greek-Cypriot and is familiar with the dialect; therefore, his use of vocabulary from this dialect is not surprising in such a teasing situation. Metaphorically used, the word *traullos* carries a bad connotation and implies usually an older man, who is low-bred, boorish, rude, vulgar, deceitful and evil, which goes after very young women.

Stavros immediately picks up on the metaphoric use of *traullos* and accepts his characterization as a male goat; but he accepts what he thinks is a *positive* attribute of a male goat; i.e. masculinity. Stavros uses that to top Hristos by projecting his own male image while simultaneously nullifying the evil attribute that Hristos has metaphorically assigned to him. He identifies himself with a male goat, which as a male, makes sexual advances toward females. By uttering "You haven't seen the mount of the male goat kalamara", Stavros implies that "I am a male goat, a macho man, and since you are not much of a man, I'll hump you to show you what being a male goat means".

In addition, Stavros addresses Hristos as *kalamara.* In ordinary situations, the word *kalamaras* is often used by Cypriots to distinguish the origin of a Greek from mainland Greece as opposed to a Greek from Cyprus. When used in teasing situations among friends, it is usually interpreted as a nickname to make a joke. However, in a conflict situation, the word *kalamaras* may be interpreted as a personal insult. In regard to its origin, the word *kalamaras* has two main interpretations: (a) it refers to educated Greeks since in the older times Greeks were using *kalamari* (a kind of an ink-pen) to write on paper, thus the expression *harti ke kalamari* (paper and ink-pen); (b) it refers to Greek fishermen who fished a lot of *kalamari,* which also means "squid".

It is believed that the word *kalamaras* lost its good connotation and acquired a bad meaning in the army context due to the fact that sometimes Greek-Cypriot soldiers were trained by mainland Greek army officers. Since military training requires strict discipline and differences in power positions due to the different rankings, in conflict situations, a Greek officer was referred to by Cypriot soldiers as *kalamaras.* In addition, Argyrou (1996) points out that, Greek army officers are considered by Greek-Cypriots to be deceitful because through witticisms, false promises and sheer lies, they seduce "innocent" Cypriot girls and then desert them. This is more likely to be the interpretation of *kalamaras* that Stavros wants to assign to Hristos. Remember that Hristos has earlier offended Stavros with the use of the word "traullos", which carries similar connotations with the word "kalamaras"; i.e. someone who is boorish, vulgar, evil and deceitful. Thus, Stavros returns the attack on Hristos and presents him as a worthless man because of the way he seduces women; i.e. seducing women through deception—not through real male presentation.

In sum, in the above example (H), taken from a teasing situation in an ordinary conversation, Stavros projects his sexual image while at the same time he belittles his opponent's, through the metaphoric use of the male animal (goat) in a way similar to the rooster chattisto, Example A above. This indicates that Greek-Cypriot men project their masculinity through language in ordinary discourse, in a similar way that they project their masculinity in chattista, which is traditional poetic discourse. As stated in Doukanari (2007), the sexual identities projected in chattista performances are in essence reflections of the reality of culture. Thus, in Danforth's (1982) sense, chattista performances constitute a symbolic system or a type of language and reveal information about culture. However, the sexual actions and images the participants project in chattista are not always taken as actual actions or properties of self. They are rather expressions of "symbolic identities" (Herzfeld 1986). The participants tie themselves to particular stereotypes of sexual identity, which is socially and culturally defined.

6. Concluding remarks

In an attempt to give a more holistic picture of Greek-Cypriot sexuality as it is displayed in chattista performances, I have taken the Doukanari (2007) investigation one step further. Whereas in that paper the focus of analysis has been on the display of female sexuality, in the present study, the focus is on the display of male sexuality. Even though in both studies the opposite gender is not excluded, the results of each study give more information on the gender primarily investigated. By putting the results together, a more complete and objective picture of Cypriot sexual identity is revealed.

The analysis in this paper has identified several aspects of male sexual identity projected in chattista performances. The Greek-Cypriot man displays himself as the superior male in opposition to the inferior female; as the amorous/womanizer and even the womanizer/gambler who is sexually active and cannot resist temptation; and as the protector of family and even national honor. Each time men reveal their male sexual image, they also reveal ideological, social and cultural values. The male performer of chattista is always evaluated by the audience as to what he has said and done. Through skillful rhetorical arguments, using insults, a whole image of male sexual identity determined by culture is projected, in an abundant use of figurative speech, such as metaphor, synecdoche, alliteration, and assonance.

The most important information elicited from this study is that, just like society places constraints upon women to control their sexuality (Doukanari 2007), society places constraints upon men to vividly proclaim their male sexual existence if they are to be taken seriously and be accorded respect by their community. As a result, men tie themselves to particular stereotypes of sexual identity which is socially and culturally prescribed in order to satisfy society's demands. Thus, in regard to sexuality, there is a cultural expectation and a burden not only on women, but on men as well. The Cypriot man has to engage in competition and constantly struggle through hard negotiations to demonstrate manliness. While a woman must control her sexuality, a man must display his male sexual identity. One way to accomplish his male presentation is by giving emphasis on his sexuality, while at the same time he must defend his manliness by protecting his honor, which is directly affected by the sexual behavior of the females in his family or by his opponent's sexual verbal insults. Supportive evidence elicited from the audience responses in chattista performances, from ordinary conversations and free interviews, leads us to similar results and confirms that the symbolic sexual identities displayed in chattista, although a traditional genre, are not far away from the reality of culture, its expectations and boundaries.

Acknowledgements

I would like to acknowledge all the people and organizations that helped me with my work: All my participants and informants; the Cultural Center, Larnaca; Sigma Television Station, Nicosia; Radio Capital, Limassol; Foto Larko, Larnaca.

Notes

[1] According to Quirk and Greenbaum (1973: 448), "In a blend at least one of the elements is fragmentary when compared with its corresponding uncompounded word form", e.g. brunch is derived from breakfast and lunch, smog is derived from smoke and fog.

² Note that –ario, the singular form of –arya is a literary ending and one of the uncommon diminutive endings (Triandafyllidis *et al* 1988: 124). Nevertheless, it is used by Pappus who has no formal education. Literary words or endings are the ones that entered the Greek language as a result of diglossia. This language situation emerged in the 19ᵗʰ century through scholars, who used an artificial variety of the Greek language (Katharevusa), other than the language of the people (Dhimotiki), to express their scholarly ideas. For more information on Greek diglossia, see among others: Babiniotis 1979, Browning 1982, Doukanari 1991, Ferguson 1959, Herzfeld 1982, Householder 1974, Kazazis 1976.

References

Abrahams, R. D. 1983. *The Man-of-Words in the West Indies: Performance and the Emergence of Creole Culture*. Baltimore, MD: The Johns Hopkins University Press.

Argyrou, V. 1996. *Tradition and Modernity in the Mediterranean: The Wedding as Symbolic Struggle*. Cambridge: Cambridge University Press.

Babiniotis, G. 1979. "A linguistic approach to the language question in Greece." In *Byzantine and Modern Greek Studies*. Oxford: Basil Blackwell, 1-16.

Brandes, S. 1980. *Metaphors of Masculinity: Sex and Status in Andalusian Folklore*. Publications of the American Folklore Society, vol. 1. Philadelphia: University of Pennsylvania Press.

Browning, R. 1982. "Greek diglossia yesterday and today." *International Journal of the Sociology of Language* 35: 49 - 68.

Campbell, J. K. 1964. *Honour, Family, and Patronage: A Study of Institutions and Moral Values in a Greek Mountain Community*. New York: Oxford University Press.

Caraveli, A. 1985. "The symbolic village: Community born in performance." *Journal of American Folklore* 98: 259 - 286.

Chafe, W. L., ed. 1980. *The Pear Stories: Cognitive, Cultural and Linguistic Aspects of Narrative Production*. Norwood, NJ: Ablex.

Cowan, J. K. 1990. *Dance and the Body Politic in Northern Greece*. Princeton, NJ: Princeton University Press.

Cuddon, J. A. 1976. *A Dictionary of Literary Terms*. Garden City, NY: Doubleday.

Danforth, L. M. 1982. *The Death Rituals of Rural Greece*. Princeton, NJ: Princeton University Press.

Doukanari, E. 1991. "Greek diglossia to Greek dimorphia: A new dilemma for linguists and teachers." In *Linguistics and Language Pedagogy: The State of the Art, Georgetown University Round Table on*

Languages and Linguistics. Ed. James E. Alatis. Washington, D.C.: Georgetown University Press, 509-527.

—. 1997. *The Presentation of Gendered Self in Cyprus Rhyming Improvisations: A Sociolinguistic Investigation of Kipriaka Chattista in Performance*. Georgetown University Ph.D. Dissertation. Ann Arbor, Michigan: UMI Dissertation Services.

—. 2007. "Female sexuality in Greek-Cypriot chattista: Traditional ideologies re-evaluated and negotiated." In *International Perspectives on Gender and Language*. Eds. J. Santaemilia, P. Bou, S. Maruenda and G. Zaragoza. Valencia: Universitat de València, 105-124.

Dundes, A., J. W. Leach and B. Ozkok. 1989. "The strategy of Turkish boys' verbal dueling rhymes." In *Directions in Sociolinguistics*. Eds. J.J. Gumperz and D. Hymes. Oxford: Basil Blackwell, 130-160.

Eckert, P. and S. McConnell-Ginet. 2003. *Language and Gender*. Cambridge: Cambridge University Press.

Ferguson, C. A. 1959. "Diglossia." *Word* 15: 325-340.

Gumperz, J. J. 1982. *Discourse Strategies*. Cambridge: Cambridge University Press.

Hall, K. and M. Bucholtz, eds. 1995. *Gender Articulated: Language and the Socially Constructed Self*. New York and London: Routledge.

Herzfeld, M. 1982. "Disemia." In *Semiotics 1980: Proceedings of the Sixth Annual Meeting of the Semiotic Society of America*. Eds. M. Herzfeld and M. D. Lenhart. New York: Plenum Press, 205-215.

—. 1985. *The Poetics of Manhood: Contest and Identity in a Cretan Mountain Village*. Princeton, NJ: Princeton University Press.

—. 1986. Within and without: The category of "female" in the ethnography of Modern Greece. In *Gender and Power in Rural Greece*. Ed. J. Dubisch. Princeton, NJ: Princeton University Press, 215-233.

Householder, F. W. 1974. *Studies in Modern Greek for American Students III. Greek Triglossia*. Bloomington: Indiana University Linguistics Club.

Kazazis, K. 1976. "A superficially unusual feature of Greek diglossia." In *Papers from the Twelfth Regional Meeting, Chicago Linguistic Society*. Eds. S. S. Mufwene, C. A.Walker, and S. B. Steever. Chicago: Chicago Linguistic Society, 369-375.

Labov, W. 1972. "Rules for ritual insults." In *Rappin' and Stylin' out: Communication in Urban Black America*. Ed. T. Kochman. Chicago: University of Illinois Press, 265-314.

Lakoff, G. and M. Johnson. 1980. *Metaphors we Live by*. Chicago: The University of Chicago Press.

Loizos, P. 1975. *The Greek Gift: Politics in a Cypriot Village*. New York: St. Martin's Press.

Quirk, R. and S. Greenbaum. 1973. *A Concise Grammar of Contemporary English*. San Diego: Harcourt Brace Jovanovich.

Sant Cassia, P. 1981. "Property in Greek Cypriot marriage strategies, 1920 - 1980." *Man* (n. s.) 17: 643-663.

Schiffrin, D. 1994. *Approaches to Discourse*. Cambridge, MA: Basil Blackwell.

Seremetakis, N. C. 1991. *The Last Word: Women, Death and Divination in Inner Mani*. Chicago and London: The University of Chicago Press.

Stankiewicz, E. 1960. "Linguistics and the study of poetic language." In *Style in Language*. Ed. T. A. Sebeok. New York and London: MIT Press and Wiley, 69-81.

Tannen, D., ed. 1981. *Analyzing Discourse: Text and Talk. Georgetown University Round Table on Languages and Linguistics*. Washington, DC: Georgetown University Press.

—. 1984. *Conversational Style: Analyzing Talk among Friends*. Norwood, NJ: Ablex.

Tannen, D. and C. Wallat. 1993. "Interactive frames and knowledge schemas in interaction: Examples from a medical examination/interview." In *Framing in Discourse*. Ed. D. Tannen. New York and Oxford: Oxford University Press, 57-76.

Triandafyllidis M., K. Lakonas, T. Stavrou, A. Tzartzanos, V. Vafis and N. Andriotis. 1988. *Neoelliniki Ghrammatiki (tis Dhimotikis). Anatiposi tis Ekdhosis tou ΟΕΣΒ (1941) me Dhiorthosis*. Thessaloniki, Greece: Instituto Neoellinikon Spoudon.

Zoras, G. T. 1975. *Dhimotiki Piisis. B Ekdhosis*. Athens, Greece: Ekdhosis Gregory.

CHAPTER EIGHT

SELLING AND GENDER: RAPPORT BUILDING STRATEGIES USED BY AMERICAN TV SHOPPING NETWORKS' HOSTS

PILAR GARCÉS-CONEJOS, UNIVERSITY OF NORTH CAROLINA, CHARLOTTE

Abstract: The aim of this paper is to determine whether it is the norms of a given community of practice –that of shopping networks in the United Status of America– and a specific situation –selling jewellery to a mostly female audience– (Mills 2003) or gender that supersede in determining the politeness strategies used by male and female shopping channels' hosts to establish and maintain rapport (Spencer-Oatey 2000) with their audience. Six hours of shows from three different home shopping channels on American television (QVC, the Home Shopping Network and America's Store) were recorded and transcribed to collect data for this paper. Three women and three men hosts are represented in each of the samples. All hosts were selling jewellery to the audience, which was mostly made up of women. The goal of these shows is to present and sell a certain number of items within the hour and to have viewers call in on the "testimonial line".

The findings seem to indicate that all hosts use the same rapport creating strategies, mostly keyed to the establishing of common ground (Brown & Levinson 1987) what could lead us to tentatively conclude that community of practice's constraints on participants' roles override gender in determining choice of linguistic behaviour.

Key words: *teleshopping, customer service, politeness, rapport, male gender, community of practice.*

1. Introduction

This paper investigates the rapport building strategies used by male and female hosts of three American TV shopping channels during their live interactions with customers. In one of the channels' own words, QVC is:

> A virtual shopping mall that never closes... a place where customers can, and do shop at the rate of two customers per second. Themed programs are telecast live 24 hours a day, seven days a week, to 87 million households in the United States.

Rapport has traditionally been associated with female interactive behavior (see Brown 1980; Holmes 1995; Tannen 1992 among others). However, this paper's aim is to test the hypothesis that host role within the interactive television community of practice, a female gendered domain, will override any possible differences attributable to gender in what regards male and female hosts' choice of rapport building strategies in their interaction with customers.

The host/customer interaction can be more aptly described by ascribing it to the category of "service encounter" –a transactional exchange between two parties. Service encounters and rapport have been researched from business, gender studies, communication and linguistics paradigms. Within the business approaches, however, it seems that (a) not enough attention has been given to rapport in service encounters and (b) those studies that have focused on rapport have not dwelt on the linguistic choices of service providers conducing to the establishment and maintenance of rapport, but on customers' perception of rapport. Gremler & Gwinner (2000: 83) carried out an exhaustive compilation and review of studies of rapport and concluded that little attention had been given to rapport in the marketing literature. They identified two empirically distinct dimensions of rapport: "... (a) the customer's perception of having an enjoyable interaction with a service provider employee and (b) to be characterized by a personal connection between the interactants". (My emphasis) They also found a positive relationship between these dimensions of rapport and satisfaction, loyalty intent and word-of- mouth communication. Campbell and Davis (2006) drew on Gremler and Gwinner's study but pointed out that "...the influence of verbal behavior ...has been explored very little in the literature...Nevertheless, verbal choices in communication play a critical role in establishing rapport". To answer the question posited by Gremler and Gwinner (2000: 99): "What specific actions can employees take to encourage rapport development in their customer interaction?" Campbell and Davis (2006) used speech act theory and rapport management (Spencer-Oatey 2000) and concluded "it is clear to us that an individual demonstrates his or her effectiveness as a sales representative by choosing appropriate verbal strategies when interacting with customers". The authors point to the need of future research to explore rapport management between individuals within other workplace contexts

Two studies conducted within the business paradigm analyze the discourse of teleshopping channels' hosts. Stephens, Hill & Bergman (1996) focus on the verbal choices that QVC hosts make to encourage viewers to form parasocial relationships - "... feelings of friendship and intimacy on the viewer's part –with remote personae" (Stephens *et al* 1996: 194)- with them. Stephen *et al* describe four strategies used towards achieving this goal: (a) warm, intimate greetings; (b) personal questions and focus on similarities between host/viewer; (c) questions that encourage viewers to connect the product with their own personal experiences or memories and (d) hosts share their own experiences and attitudes with the audience and relate these to the product being featured. Fritchie and Johnson (2003) analyzed the discourse of HSN and QVC's hosts, co-hosts and callers during shows that featured jewelry. The statements made were grouped into categories that corresponded to Cialdini's (1993, cited in Fritchie and Johnson) persuasion strategies used to influence others to comply: social proof, scarcity, authority, commitment and consistency. Although both studies are insightful, their findings lack the support of a sound descriptive, linguistic model.

Other studies (see Babin & Boles 1998; Bucholtz 1999, 2000; Forseth 2005; Snipes, Thomson & Oswald 2006; Kulik & Holbrook 2000) have examined the relationship between gender and service encounters. Of special relevance for the present analysis are Forseth (2005), Kulik and Holbrook (2000) and Bucholtz (1999, 2000). Forseth (2005) claims that, recently, there have been major changes in the customer-service provider relationship. These are related to a shift of power from the institution (which used to be the dispenser of power) to the person (the service provider, or front liner, who deals directly with the customer) that was brought about by the culture of customer sovereignty (the customer is always right). By foregrounding the person, rather than the institution, gender has been brought to the front stage and gendered scripts and cultural expectations have been activated. Kulik and Holbrook (2000) investigated the effects of racial and gender congruence in service encounters, more precisely on the perceived fairness of outcomes of bank loan applications and resolutions. They found that, whereas gender congruence did not automatically inspire more trust, gender congruence or incongruence did raise expectations about the amount of voice time – i.e. the freedom participants have to communicate their views and provide information during the decision making procedures - that women should experience during the application process: "Women have been socialized to expect a great deal of participation when they interact with a person of their own sex and they respond very negatively when these conversational norms are violated" (Kulik and Holbrook 2000: 395). This factor may have an impact on turn length in the host/customer interactions in the corpus. Bucholtz (1999, 2000) analyzes QVC's host-caller interactions. Through these interactions a community is established (Bucholtz 2000) and within it issues of gender and class become evident. The exchanges reveal the "profoundly gendered" nature of the interaction and through them, callers and hosts "...discursively negotiate their own and each other's identities in relation to idealized positions of upper-class authority and lower-middle class authority" Bucholtz (1999: 350)

In recent years, some scholars (Antonopoulu 2001; Bayyurt & Bayraktaroglu 2001; Economidu-Kogetsidis 2005; Kong 1998; Marquez Reiter 2004; Petrits 2001; Placencia 2001, 2004; Traverso 2006) have examined the pragmatic performance of speakers regarding manifestations of politeness (Brown & Levinson 1987) in service encounters. Chan, Bond, Spencer-Oatey & Rojo-Laurilla (2004) apply Spencer Oatey's (2000) reformulation of Brown & Levinson's paradigm to investigate possible cultural effects on the perceived importance of interactional concerns in service encounters.

Politeness theory (Brown & Levinson 1978/1987) offers the tools to analyze the strategies used by speakers to address the face needs of both their interlocutors and their own. Positive politeness strategies address the positive face needs of the hearer by treating him/her as a member of an in-group, a friend, a person whose wants and personality traits are well known and liked. Negative politeness is oriented towards the hearer's negative face wants, i.e. to maintain claims of territory and self-determination. Negative politeness is avoidance based and is characterized by self-effacement, formality and restraint. (Brown & Levinson 1987: 70).

According to Gremler and Gwinner (2000) rapport building strategies in service encounters can be grouped into four types: (1) customer imitation; (2) employee courteousness; (3) attentive interaction and (4) finding common ground. Types 1, 3 and 4 fall under Brown & Levinson's definition of positive politeness. Type 2 refers to the deferential nature of negative politeness. Thus, the majority of politeness strategies used to build rapport in service encounters can be accounted for in terms of positive politeness. As negative politeness is expected to play a lesser role in service encounters, this study will focus on positive politeness strategies.

The overarching research question of the study is as follows:

RQ 1. Will host role within the interactive television community of practice, a female gendered domain, override any possible differences attributable to gender in what regards male and female hosts' choice of rapport building strategies in their interaction with customers?

The answer to the main research question is contingent on four minor research questions: Since rapport has been traditionally identified with female discourse (Brown 1980; Holmes 1995; Tannen 1992),

Will male hosts use rapport-building, positive politeness strategies less frequently than female hosts?
Will male hosts' choice of rapport-building, positive politeness strategies differ from those used by female hosts?
Will female hosts display a wider array of rapport-building, positive politeness strategies than male hosts?
Will female hosts' turns be shorter than male hosts' turns thus providing customers with more "voice time"?

The present study addresses the need for more sociolinguistic based research of rapport in professional contexts brought up by Campbell and Davis (2006) and follows Mills's (2003: 198) suggestion to the effect that, "It is essential to move beyond polarizing women and men as distinct groups and concentrate more on the way that people 'do gender' in particular communities of practice".

2. The interactive shopping TV community of practice

The notion of community of practice, formulated by Wenger (1998), was expanded by Eckert and McConnell-Ginet (1998) to better account for language and gender research. According to these authors: "… a community of practice is an aggregate of people who come together around mutual engagement in some common endeavor. Ways of doing things, ways of talking, beliefs, values, power relations –in short– practices emerge in the course of their joint activity around that endeavor" (Eckert and McConnell-Ginet 1998: 490).

The volume of business –combined reported sales of almost $9 billion dollars in 2005– and the mediated nature of the interactions make for an interactive shopping TV community of practice that is wide and varied. It includes within it many other smaller communities of practice. Although I focus on the hosts and their audiences, other related communities include the producers of the shows, the filming crews, technical personnel, the models wearing the product, when appropriate. Often, celebrity guests, who sell their product through the networks, appear live on air and assist the hosts. Other manufacturers send product representatives who also appear live on air and help out the hosts with their in-depth product knowledge. There are also higher level producers and technical personnel, product buyers, vendors, customer service and fulfillment staffs and network executives to name just a few.

2.1. The interactive shopping TV service encounter: community and gender

The type of service encounters that make up the corpus are twenty of the live testimonial calls that customers made through an 800 number to comment on the article that was being sold. Testimonial calls are the only direct interaction (apart from e-mail communication) that hosts and most customers ever have

2.1.1. Testimonial calls and community

Although the main goal of testimonial calls is not interactional but transactional, during these calls the shopping community is established and reinforced, and the female gendered nature of the interaction is brought to the foreground. Rapport plays an essential part in both. Bucholtz (2000: 194) sees the testimonial call as a fundamental part of what the teleshopping channel offers its viewers:

> The shopping channel…provides not only membership but relationship by means of the interaction between host and shopper. The telephone conversation is itself the network's pre-eminent commodity… the linguistic exchange comes to displace the economic exchange as the source of pleasure.

Gudelunas (2002: 111) coincides with Butcholtz's (1999, 2000) assessment and points out that a sense of "we-ness", of community, is established through the exchanges between hosts and callers during testimonial calls that is extended to the network as a whole. This sense of community can be established due to the polyloguic nature (Kerbrat-Orechionni 2004) of interactive television service encounters. Most service encounters are dyadic, i.e. they involve only two people that carry out the transaction in relative privacy. Interactive television service encounters involve potentially millions of participants whose felt presence imposes different types of constraints on linguistic choices and allows for the interaction between the host-customer dyad to become strategic as it targets the rest of the viewers at the same time. (Bell 1984)

Similarly, other researchers (Cook 2000; Fritchie & Johnson 2003; Gudelunas 2006; Stephens, Hill & Bergman 1996) describe teleshopping as highly interactive and thus conducive to the development of parasocial relationships. Parasocial relationships are very important for the channels' success as 74 per cent of viewers watch or buy because of their interest in the host and 62 per cent watch or buy because they enjoy their connection with the conversations between hosts and co-hosts or between hosts and call-in viewers. (Fritchie & Johnson 2003: 249). As reported by Grant *et al* 1991 (cited in Stephen *et al* 1996: 195), "10 to 15 minutes of every hour are devoted to on-air conversations between the host and viewers who have called in to make (repeat) purchases" . It is mainly during those service encounters when hosts establish and maintain rapport with their audience.

Bailey (1997: 331) distinguished between *socially minimal* service encounters – which include openings, negotiations of the exchange and closings and whose talk reflects a highly institutionalized character, as described by Economidou-Kogetsidis (2005: 257-258)– and *socially expanded* service encounters, which also include discussion on interpersonal topics. The topics, however, are usually related to the exchange in some way. When teleshopping customers call the testimonial line they have already made the purchase, either during the course of the show or some time in the past. So the exchange becomes socially expanded as different topics related to the purchase, the product line, the difference that the product has made in the customer's life are discussed. Often the hosts ask the customer what they would say to other customers who may be thinking about purchasing that product. In the same line, Bucholtz (2000: 201) points out that the introduction of topics unrelated to the transaction in the telephone conversations conveys a feeling of expanded time which contrasts with the "manufactured urgency" created by the timer on the television screen. This sense of expanded time diverts the attention from the transactional goal of the exchange to reinforce its interactive side, as an illusion of intimacy is conveyed.

Regardless of the illusion of intimacy and friendship created by testimonial calls as they help evoke the "…myth of the old-fashioned, idealized store, where greetings awareness of product and the illusion of friendship were part of the exchange of goods" Gumpert & Drucker (1992 cited in Fritchie & Johnson 2003: 250), their main purpose remains transactional and fulfills two major functions:

(a) They provide word of mouth account to other customers who might be sitting on the fence in respect to a specific article.

(b) By building rapport with the customer, i.e. by creating an enjoyable experience and establishing a personal connection with the caller (Gremler & Gwinner 2000), the host works towards achieving satisfaction and creating loyalty.

Transaction and community become one and the same as customers become members of the community by making a purchase. A community which is, in essence, female.

2.1.2. The interactive shopping TV community of practice and gender

Connecting parasocial relationships and gender, Gudelunas (2002: 108) argues that teleshopping –through the establishing of parasocial relationships among mostly female hosts and audience – may tap into "the rituals of femininity" that date back to the Tupperware parties and other events where women gathered to celebrate and cooperate in the traditional task of shopping.

HSN and America's store's webpages indicate that their audience is 75% female with ages ranging between 25-54 years old and with an average income of $61,000. QVC does not offer as precise information on demographics. As Gudelunas (2002: 106) points out: "QVC is notoriously secretive about their consumer demographics". However, several studies point to the fact that their audience also is overwhelmingly female. (See Bucholtz 1999; Gudelunas 2002, 2006; Frichtie & Johnson 2003). The influence of the audience is evident in the gendered nature of the discourse. According to Bucholtz (1999: 351):

> Hosts speak directly to the camera, addressing the audience as singular you and gendering this virtual interlocutor as female. This orientation to women prevails regardless of the gender of the host or the gender associations of the product being promoted for sale.

Also, the host role is female dominated in the three networks included in this study. Out of the 33 hosts that work for HSN and AS, 27 (82%) are female and just 6 (18 %) are male. QVC seems to be a little more evenly distributed but still female hosts (13- 62%) outnumber their male counterparts (8-38%)

Forseth (2005) argues that the new pervasive philosophy of customer service is that of "modern servanthood" (the customer is always right). Among its important characteristics, being nice, caring, polite and deferential are foremost. Modern servanthood's main goal is to make others feel well and satisfy their wishes. The new philosophy activates scripts and schemata that have been traditionally associated with women, usually hired for positions where they were expected to be "...nicer than natural whereas men were more likely to be recruited to positions where they had to be "nastier than natural" Forseth (2005: 444).

The new customer service philosophy combined with the need to create rapport with customers (as a means to achieve satisfaction, loyalty intent and word-of- mouth communication Gremler & Gwinner 2000) and the "nicer than natural" stance that has been associated with positions customarily filled out by women could be the reasons why interactive television host role is dominated by females. Also, it could be expected that the interaction host/customer- given its goals and main characteristics- should be modeled after what has traditionally been considered "female discourse".

Thus, the interaction on the teleshopping channels would be considered "a gendered domain" (Mills 2003: 194) and the men working in that domain would be expected to adopt an interactive style stereotypically associated with females to succeed professionally, in accordance with the norms of this particular community of practice. Mills (2003: 196) argues that the notion of community of practice is particularly relevant to the way that individuals develop a sense of their own gendered identity:

> ... rather than describing a single gendered identity which correlates with one's biological sex, it is possible within this model to analyze a range of gender identities which will be activated and used strategically within particular communities of practice and which is subject to change.

It is the main goal of this paper to determine whether host role within the interactive television community of practice, a female gendered domain, will override any possible differences attributable to gender in what regards male and female hosts' choice of rapport building strategies in their interaction with customers. Based on the on-going conversation in the literature, synthesized above, it would seem that host role will be the prevailing factor.

3. Method

3.1. Data gathering

Six hour shows were video-and-tape recorded between April and October 2006 and transcribed using the standard orthographic system and a number of conventions adapted from Holmes and Stubbe (2003). Three female and three male hosts were selected, and in order to ensure a homogeneous audience, I chose shows in which all the hosts were selling jewelry products to a mostly female audience. Cook (2000) found that jewelry was the number one product sold by QVC. Clothes, cosmetics and fashion accessories were the other three, thus making for a gendered form of programming. Fritchie and Johnson (2003: 205) report similar results: "Typical television viewers are women, with above average incomes, over 35 years of age, who are purchasing jewelry..."

From the hour-long shows, twenty segments in which the hosts talk live with customers were selected and micro analyzed. Out of those, there were ten male host/female customer interactions and ten female host/female customer interactions. Conversations between callers and hosts lasted from one to four minutes. Hosts usually had to terminate conversations before they were actually over in order to move on to the presentation of the next product. Less frequently, it was the customer who brought the exchange to a close.

Although the hosts must be informed of the demographics of their audience, the only information known about these particular callers was their name and location in the United States –sometimes only the state, and sometimes the exact area within that state– and their gender, which was in all cases female. The host, with no visual or non-verbal cues and very little background information, has to find a way to build rapport with the caller in a very short period of time, in front of millions of viewers. This difficulty is, in part, solved by the institutional nature of the exchange that sets constraints on roles and topics and by the fact that the host relates to the customer not at the interpersonal but at the intergroup level- in as much as s/he is a network's customer. (Gudykunst & Ting-Toomey 1988)

3.2. Data coding and analysis

Based on Brown & Levinson's (1987) positive politeness strategies taxonomy, a coding scheme was developed for the analysis of hosts' turns The turns were divided into utterances. Although Brown & Levinson's approach equates the utterance level with the strategy level (i.e. there will be one strategy per utterance), it has already been pointed out in the literature (see Culpeper 2005; Garcés-Conejos 1995, among others) that two or more strategies can co-occur within the same utterance. Thus, each individual item used in the results computation refers to the occurrence of a particular strategy.

> **Example**: Let me know when you get these home how much you enjoy them, ok Shermilia? (Perry Slater- Ex#4-T# 27)

In the example above, three different strategies would have been recorded (exaggerate interest with Hearer (H henceforth), raise common ground and use in group identity markers)

4. Results and discussion

4.1. First research question

RQ 1. Will male host use rapport establishing strategies less frequently than female hosts?

From a total of 617 rapport-building, positive politeness strategies used by the six hosts in the twenty exchanges analyzed, 309 were used by female hosts and 308 were used by male hosts. The use of strategies is evenly distributed between the two groups. Thus, the answer to the first research question would be negative. Male hosts use as many rapport-building positive politeness strategies as female hosts do. These results coincide with Stephens *et al*'s (1996: 197) claim: "All hosts observed use these [conversational] techniques [to encourage viewers to form parasocial relationships with them] about equally frequently".

4.2. Second research question

RQ 2. Will male hosts choose different rapport-building positive politeness strategies from those used by female hosts?

Both groups used fourteen out of Brown & Levinson's (1987) fifteen positive politeness sub-strategies. "Exaggerate (interest, approval, sympathy with H)" "Use in group identity markers" and "Presuppose, raise, assert common ground" were the three sub-strategies, all found under Brown & Levinson's first super-strategy "Claim common ground", most often used by all hosts. Female hosts used the exaggerate (interest, approval, sympathy with H) sub-strategy 82 times (or 25% of the total strategies used) whereas male hosts used it 89 times (or 28.9%). The sub-strategy "Use in group identity markers" was used 42 times (13.6%) by female hosts and 58 times (18.8%) by male hosts. Female hosts employed the sub-strategy "Presuppose, raise, assert common ground" 49 times (or 15.9%) and male hosts 65 times (21.1%).

Some differences in the use of strategies were observed. Female hosts used the sub-strategy "Notice-attend to H interests, wants, needs, goods" 29 times (9.4%) almost twice as often as the male hosts who only used it 16 times (or 5.2%). Female hosts used the sub-strategy "Intensify interest to H" 18 times (or 5.8%). Whilst male hosts used it only 9 times (2.9%). Male host used joking 8 times (2.6%) were female hosts used it only 2 times (0.6%)

Despite these differences, the total number of sub-strategies found under Brown & Levinson's first super-strategy "Claim common ground" is very similar between the two groups with 249 (80.6%) for the female host group and 272 (88.3%) for the male host group. Both female and male hosts mostly build rapport with the customers by claiming common ground with them. This corroborates Fritchie and Johnson (2003: 252) and Stephens *et al*'s (1996: 197) statement that in order to facilitate liking and increase persuasiveness, hosts are trained to use *similarity* when answering calls, i.e. mirror the caller's style.

More noteworthy are the differences in strategy use between the two groups for the other two sets of strategies found under super strategy II-"Convey that Speaker (S henceforth) & H are cooperators" and super-strategy III- "Fulfill H's wants".

Female hosts show more preference for the sub-strategies found under super-strategy II- Convey that S& H are cooperators". Female hosts used sub-strategy "Assert or presuppose S's knowledge of or concern for H's wants 22 times (7.1%). Male hosts used it only 13 times (4.2%) Important differences are the use by female hosts of the sub-strategy "Offer, promise". They employed it 15 times (4.9%). "Offer, promise" was only used by male hosts 4 times (1.3%). The sub-strategy "Include both S & H in the activity" was used 16 times (5.2%) by the female hosts whereas male hosts only made use of it 8 times (2.8%).

These data seem to indicate that part of the female hosts' television persona is based on conveying to her customers (all female in the corpus) that they are cooperators: the female host is there to help out, work with and guide the customer so that her shopping experience is satisfactory. Although the male hosts do not present themselves as collaborators as often, the total number of sub-strategies in this category employed by both groups is not very considerable (18.1% for the female hosts and 9.1% for the male host group) and should not necessarily have a major impact on the customer's overall experience of the exchange.

In regards to super-strategy III "Fulfill H's wants", the only sub-strategy found under this heading, "Give gifts to H (good, sympathy, understanding, cooperation)" is more often used by male hosts (a total of 8 times (2.6%)) than by female hosts who only use it 4 times (1.3%). As was the case with super-strategy II, the total number of uses of this sub-strategy is very low (1.3% for the female group and 2.6% for the male group) and thus its impact on the customer's experience of the exchange not substantial.

Based on the above data, the response to R2 would also be negative. Both groups female and male favor the same group of sub-strategies found under super-strategy I- "Claim common ground". Both female and male hosts coincide in their choice of the three most frequently used sub-strategies, i.e. Exaggerate (interest, approval, sympathy with H)" "Use in group identity markers" and "Presuppose, raise, assert common ground". Some minor differences were observed in the two groups' use of super-strategies II & III. Due the low frequency of use of these however, their impact was deemed to be minimal in the customer's overall experience of the exchange.

4.3. Third research question

RQ 3. Will female hosts display a wider array of rapport-building, positive politeness strategies than male hosts?

Both groups, female and male use 14 out of the total 15 sub-strategies found under the three super-strategies of Brown & Levinson's taxonomy of positive politeness strategies. Female hosts do not make use of the sub-strategy "Be optimistic" and male hosts do not employ the sub-strategy "Assume or assert reciprocity". In both cases, the other group's usage of the said strategy amounts to 1 time (0.3%)

The answer to RQ3, as was the case with RQ1 & 2, also needs to be negative. Both female and male hosts use the same array of rapport-building positive politeness strategies, albeit –as discussed above- with different frequencies.

4.4. Fourth research question

RQ 4. Will female hosts' turns be shorter than male hosts' turns thus providing customers with more "voice time"?

Female hosts' averaged 15 turns and 205.08 words per exchange. The exchanges in which female hosts participated were an average 114.5 seconds long. Male hosts' number of turns was 14.4. The average number of words they used per exchange was 178.9. The exchanges in which male hosts' participated were an average 112.4 seconds long. In summary, the data indicate that, although the number of turns used by female and male hosts' were almost the same, females were less concise in building rapport with their customers.

RQ 4 was based on the prediction that women's turns would be shorter in order to provide their female customers with more "voice time" as Kulik and Holbrook (2000: 395) had indicated. Our data, as set out above, tentatively contradict Kulik & Holbrook's (2000) findings in the sense that female hosts do not exhibit notable different behavior from their male host counterparts in this respect. Actually, they used more words per turn than male hosts. As we do not have access to customers' assessments of the exchange in terms of outcome and overall experience, it is not possible to conclude whether this has any impact on the rapport level built by both groups of subjects.

5. Conclusions

The answer to the overarching research question of the study –"Will host role within the interactive television community of practice, a female gendered domain, override any possible differences attributable to gender in what regards male and female hosts' choice of rapport building strategies in their interaction with customers?"– was contingent on the answers to the minor research questions discussed above. The data indicate that the male hosts' choice of rapport-building positive politeness strategies is very similar to the female hosts'. Both groups coincided, with minor differences, in the total number of strategies used, the preference for one sub-set of strategies (found under Super-strategy I claim common ground), the wide array of types of strategies used and the averages for number of turns, words and seconds per exchange.

As the frequent use of rapport building strategies has been traditionally associated with female interactional behavior (Brown 1980; Holmes 1995; Tannen 1992), and the number of female hosts and audience considerably surpass that of male hosts and audience, it would seem that male hosts adopt the established patterns of interaction in regards to rapport building of this "gendered domain" that are here perceived as stereotypically female (Mills 2003), i.e. unmarked behavior for the female sex in Ochs's words (1992: 342). Thus, host role within the interactive television community of practice appears to be the determining factor in the choice of rapport building positive politeness strategies by male hosts. Also, these findings seem to corroborate Babin and Boles's (1998) argument that male and female employees can become socialized to behave similarly in their roles as service providers. The work role often overrides behavioral or attitudinal differences attributable to gender, which lends further support to a constructivist (Ochs 1992) rather than essentialist view of gender.

References

Antonopoulu, E. 2001. "Brief service encounters. Gender and politeness." In *Linguistic Politeness across Boundaries. The Case of Greek and Turkish*. Eds. A. Bayraktaroglu and M. Sifianou. Amsterdam, Philadelphia: John Benjamins.

Babin, B.J. and J.S. Boles. 1998. "Employee behavior in service encounter: a model and test of potential differences between men and women." *Journal of Marketing* 62: 77-91.

Bailey, B. 1997. "Communication of respect in interethnic service encounters." *Language in Society* 26: 327-356.

Bayyurt, Y. and A. Bayraktaroglu. 2001. "The use of pronouns and terms of address in Turkish service encounters." In *Linguistic Politeness across Boundaries. The Case of Greek and Turkish*. Eds. A. Bayraktaroglu and M. Sifianou. Amsterdam, Philadelphia: John Benjamins.

Brown, P. 1980. "Why and how are women more polite?" In *Women and Language in Literature and Society*. Eds. S. McConnell-Ginet, R. Borker and N. Furman. New York: Praeger, 111-136.

Brown, P. and S. Levinson. 1987. *Politeness: Some Universals of Language Usage*. Cambridge, UK: Cambridge University Press.

Bucholtz, M. 1999. "Purchasing power: The gender and class imaginary on the shopping channel." In *Reinventing Identity: The Gendered Self in Discourse*. Eds. M. Bucholtz, A.C. Liang and L. Sutton. 348-368.

—. 2000. ""Thanks for stopping by": gender and virtual community in American shop-by-television discourse." In *All the World and her Husband: Women in Twentieth Century Culture*. Eds. M.R. Andrews and M.M. Talbot. London: Cassell, 192-209.

Campbell, K.S. and L. Davis. 2006. "The sociolinguistic basis of managing rapport when overcoming buying objections." *Journal of Business Communication* 43: 43-66.

Chan, S.k-C., M.H. Bond, H. Spencer-Oatey and M. Rojo-Laurilla. 2004. "Culture and rapport promotion in service encounters: Protecting the ties that bind." *Journal of Asian Pacific Communication* 14: 245-260.

Culpeper, Jonathan. 2005. "Impoliteness and entertainment in the television quiz show: *The Weakest Link*." *Journal of Politeness Research* 1: 35-72.

Cook, J.P. 2000. "Consumer culture and television Home Shopping Programming: An examination of the sales discourse." *Mass Communication and Society* 3: 373-391.

Eckert, P. and S. McConnell-Ginet. 1998. "Communities of practice: where language, gender and power all live." In *Language and Gender: A Reader*. Ed. J. Coates. Oxford: Blackwell, 484-494.

Economidou-Kogetsidis, M. 2005. "'Yes, tell me please, what time is the midday flight from Athens arriving?' Telephone service encounters and politeness." *Intercultural Pragmatics* 2: 253-273.

Forseht, U. 2005. "Gender matters? Exploring how gender is negotiated in service encounters." *Gender, Work and Organization* 12: 440-459.

Frithcie, L. and K. Jonson. 2003. "Personal selling approaches used in television shopping." *Journal of Fashion Marketing and Management* 7: 249-258

Garcés-Conejos, Pr. 1995. "Revisión crítica de algunos de los postulados de la teoría de la cortesía lingüística propugnada por Brown y Levinson." *Quaderns de Filologia: Stvdia Lingvistica (Aspectes de la praxi interlingüística en l'àmbit europeu)* 1: 43-61.

Gudelunas, D. 2002. "QVC: Television retail and ritual." *The Journal of American Culture* 25: 105-118.

—. 2006. "Shopping with friends: Audience perspectives on television shopping." *Popular Communication* 4: 229-252.

Gudykunst, W. B. and S. Ting-Toomey. 1988. *Culture and Interpersonal Communication*. Sage Publications, Inc.: Newbury Park, CA.

Gremler, D.D. and K.P. Gwinner. 2000. "Customer-employee rapport in service relationships." *Journal of Service Research* 3: 82-104.

Holmes, J. 1995. *Women, Men and Politeness*. London: Longman.

Holmes, J. and M. Stubbe. 2003. *Power and Politeness in the Workplace*. Harlow, UK: Pearson Education.

Kerbrat-Orecchioni, C. 2004. "Introducing polylogue. *Journal of Pragmatics* 36: 1-24.

Kong, K. 1998. "Politeness of service encounters in Hong Kong." *Pragmatics* 8: 555-575.

Kulik, C.T. and R.L. Holbrook. 2000. "Demographics in service encounters: Effects of racial and gender congruence on perceived fairness." *Social Justice Research* 13: 375-402.

Marquez Reiter, R. 2004. "Displaying closeness and respectful distance in Montevidean and Quiteno service encounters." In *Current Trends in the Pragmatics of Spanish*. Eds. R. Marquez Reiter and M.E. Placencia. Amsterdam: John Benjamins, 121-155.

Mills, S. 2003. *Gender and Politeness*. Cambridge, UK: Cambridge University Press.

Ochs, E. 1992. "Indexing gender." In *Rethinking Context: Language as Interactive Phenomenon*. Eds. A. Duranti and C. Goodwin. Cambridge: Cambridge University Press.

Petrits, A. 2001. "Addressing in Modern Greek: Evidence from a case study in the Athens central market." In *A Reader in Greek Sociolinguistics: Studies in Modern Greek Language, Culture and Communication*. Eds. A. Georgakopoulou and M. Spanaki. Berlin: Peter Lang, 199-222.

Placencia, M.E. 2001. "Inequality in address behavior at public institutions in La Paz, Bolivia. *Anthropological Linguistics* 43: 198-217.

—. 2004. "Rapport-building activities in corner shop interactions." *Journal of Sociolinguistics* 8: 215-245.

Snipes, R.L., N. Thomson and S. Oswald. 2006. "Gender bias in customer evaluation of service quality: an empirical investigation." *Journal of Services Marketing* 20: 274-284.

Spencer-Oatey, H. 2000. "Rapport management: A framework for analysis." In *Culturally Speaking: Managing Rapport through Talk across Cultures*. Ed. H. Spencer-Oatey. London: Continuum, 98-120.

Stephens, D., R. Hill and K. Bergman. 1996. "Enhancing the consumer-product relationship: lessons from the QVC and Home Shopping Channel." *Journal of Business Research* 37: 193-200.

Tannen, D. 1992. *You just don't Understand. Women and Men in Conversation*. New York, NY: Quill.

Traverso, V. 2006. "Aspects of polite behaviour in French and Syrian service encounters: A data-based comparative study." *Journal of Politeness Research* 2: 105-122.

Wenger, E. 1998. *Communities of Practice*. Cambridge, UK: Cambridge University Press.

CHAPTER NINE

'BEAUTIFUL JAPANESE LANGUAGE': WOMEN'S SPEECH IN JAPANESE PRINTED MEDIA

LIDIA TANAKA, LATROBE UNIVERSITY, AUSTRALIA

Abstract: Despite many studies reporting on the diversity of Japanese women's speech and its departures from the actively promoted 'women's language', there is still a traditional perception that there is *a* women's language. Moreover, the societal expectations that adult women speak it are still very strong.

Stereotypical feminine linguistic behaviour, perceived and expected, is emphasized and perpetuated through representations of women's behaviour and their language by the printed media. Given that the Japanese society is changing rapidly, it is important to see whether contemporary texts portray the traditional image of women and their language.

This paper critically analyses self-help books and a magazine to see if stereotypical images of women are still reinforced and what strategies are used to do this. The research also incorporates letters sent to an online newspaper on the topic of women and language. The findings indicate that, while the public perception of women's language indicates diversity, a traditional view still prevails in relation to child rearing. The images of women from the past are reproduced with many of the stereotypes, although the arguments have slightly changed to include personal success and happiness. The texts encourage the use of 'women's language' by direct and indirect associations with 'polite' language.

Key words: *Japanese, printed media, gender stereotypes.*

1. Introduction

An obsession with language in Japan is manifested by the volume of books, magazines and newspaper articles published yearly on topics such as the 'correct' use of honorifics or the speech of women. Particularly conspicuous is the enormous interest in the 'correctness and beauty' of the Japanese language and women's language. While there are many countries that make special efforts to maintain the purity and correct use of language (Joseph 2004), that Japan is paying special attention to women's language is notable.

The existence of 'women's language' or *onna no kotoba* has been challenged by many scholars, in particular by ethnographers and sociologists, who have argued that it is an ideological construct and not a reality. However, allusions to women's way of talking are seen in literary texts of as early as the eleventh century (Endo 1997), and later during Japan's early modernization period (Inoue 2004, 2006; Nakamura 2001; Sunaoshi 2004; Washi 2004). Endo (1997) and Nakamura (2001) write that the concept of a separate women's language was inculcated as early as the fourteenth century. Inoue (2004, 2006), on the other hand, argues that today's *onna no kotoba* was strategically created by Japanese governments through the use of novels and textbooks during the process of modernization.

Almost 150 years have passed since the modernization of Japan, and the world has changed enormously. The status of women in Japan has also improved considerably, although not to the extent of other advanced countries. Many changes have been implemented to improve women's rights, in particular after the Second World War. As a result there are more women receiving higher education, more women in managerial positions and more female political representation, for example[1]. In particular, a growing number of women have become visible in politics and business in the last decades. In a similar way, more women are choosing work over marriage. This change in the attitude of women is being reported in the media to the dismay of many who criticize and lament the loss of values[2]. This phenomenon is reported by Inoue (2004, 2006), who writes on similar reactions by the public in the past towards women's language and indirectly towards their behaviour (Inoue 2006: 57–71).

Despite women's increased status in society[3] in terms of job and education equality, self-help literature on 'beautiful' or 'correct' women's language is still being published; remarkably, none such is published for men. It is important, then, to question the reasons behind this preoccupation with reinforcing and maintaining *a* 'woman's language'.

Cameron (1995) writes that in times of change, stereotypes and beliefs are reinforced in order to contain and slow that change. This might be happening in contemporary Japan. It might be the case that the position of women in Japanese society is improving and there is a sense of crisis; therefore maintaining traditional boundaries is more pressing. Critically analysing the language used in contemporary texts that deal with gender is a way into understanding the expectations and stereotypes that are recreated or created.

The objective of this paper is to explore how 'women's language' or *onna no kotoba* is perceived by ordinary people and to critically analyse recently published texts on Japanese language and women. It takes critical discourse analysis as its theoretical framework, which views language as a primary medium of social control and power (Fairclough 1989; Fairclough & Wodak 1997). This study finds that the perceptions of women's language are varied, but the analysis shows how texts perpetuate and reinforce the existence of *a* 'women's language' via the use of linguistic strategies and by linking the concept of beauty to 'women's language'. In addition, the new message is that the use of 'women's language' will help a woman to attain success on both the professional and personal levels. This new implication is different to the concept of *ryoosai kenbo* 'good wife and wise mother' used in the early twentieth century, which stipulated that women should work hard and save in order to build a modern nation (Bernstein 1991). The new motto is that of happiness and success but on a personal level. These contemporary texts promote the image of women as intelligent professionals and good communicators in their professional and private lives. The association of women's language with high social class of the 1980s (Inoue 2006) appears to have shifted towards more abstract concepts such as success and happiness.

This study comprises a brief description of characteristics of the Japanese language in relation to gender followed by a review of the literature. This is followed by a view of public perception of women's language, the linguistic analysis and finally the discussion.

2. Language and women in Japan

There are many languages in the world that have gender differences according to who the listener or the speaker is. In Japanese, a set of lexical and pragmatic items can be chosen based on the speaker's gender (Kindaichi 1990; Kuno 1973). In standard Japanese, speakers can choose the first person pronoun from *watakushi, watashi, boku* and *ore*. The first two are formal and can be used by both men and women; however, the last two are considered less formal and masculine. Sentence final particles are also chosen according to the speaker's gender. Women's speech is exemplified in examples 1 and 3 while male's speech is shown in 2 and 4. Observe the difference in the forms of personal pronouns, sentence final particles and verbs in the imperative form. Examples 1 and 2 are semantically identical, as are 3 and 4.

| 1♀ | *watashi* | *ga* | *mita* | | *no* | *yo* | |
| | I | S | see-PAST | | FP | FP | |

2♂	*boku*	*ga*	*mita*		*n*	*da*	*zo*
	I	S	see-PAST		COM	COP	FP
	'I saw it, I tell you.'						

| 3♀ | *anata* | *hayaku* | *shite* |
| | you | quickly | do |

4♂	*kimi*	*hayaku*	*shiro*
	you	quickly	do
	'(You), hurry up'.		

In addition, Japanese women are said to speak more politely than men because of their high use of honorifics (Ide *et al* 1986, Ogino 1986), their strategic use of politeness strategies (Takano 2005) and their use of a distinct set of lexical items considered elegant and feminine. Politeness is directly related to the formal speech style, and honorifics are governed by the relationship between the interlocutors and the situation. The question 'Have you/has she/he already seen?' can be said in different ways according to who the listener is and the speaker's gender. Not only are the verb endings different but also the use of honorifics indicates the relationship between interlocutor and referent.

| 5 | *moo* | *mita?* | |
| | already | see-PAST-PLAIN | |

| 6 | *moo* | *mimashita* | *ka?* |
| | already | see-PAST-POL | Q |

| 7 | *moo* | *goranninatta?* | |
| | already | eat-PAST-HONORIFIC-POL | |

8	*moo*	*goranninarimashita*	*ka?*
	already	see-PAST-HONORIFIC-POL	Q
	'Have you/ has she/he already seen (it)?'		

While the semantic content in 5–8 is identical, the different verb forms indicate the relationship between the interlocutors. In 5 the ending of the verb indicates informality. Sentence 6 shows a formal situation where the interlocutors may know each other but are not intimate friends. In 7 the honorific verb form is the same but the ending is in the plain form showing that the interlocutor is close to the listener but the referent is considered to be an outsider and the situation is formal. In 8, the level of formality is at its highest because of the honorific form.

Many studies reporting that women use more honorifics than males (Ide *et al* 1986; Ogino 1986) have been criticised for various reasons. The quantitative study by Ide *et al* (1986), for instance, examined only housewives living in the Kanto urban area. This particular group of people speak standard Japanese and are only a small sample of the whole population (Koyama 2004). On the other hand, the argument of Ide *et al* (1986) was that because Japanese housewives have to develop networks in the neighbourhood, with friends, with other parents and so on, they have to use honorific language (Ide *et al* 1986; Ide 1997). In a similar quantitative study Ogino (1986) found that people with higher education tend to use more honorifics, and in particular that women use them the most. Ogino adds, however, that age is another factor, with college students using honorifics the least. On the other hand, Takano (2005) and others (Abe 2000; Smith 1992) argue that professional background is an important factor to consider, as women in positions of power have learned to use different politeness strategies in order to ease situations of tension.

How *onna no kotoba* is actually spoken seems to vary considerably and depends on age, region, profession, social class and situation. However, the expectations and conceptions seem to remain the same as in the past.

2.1. Background

In language and literature, women have had a special place in Japan because of their influence on written and spoken Japanese (Endo 1997; Nakamura 2004); therefore interest in women's language has always existed and is reflected in the number of studies (see Terada 1993). The earliest systematic study was published in the late 1920s, when many diachronic studies were conducted of particular words and usage in the court ladies' language from the Heian Period (785–1185). The interest in women's language has not diminished since, although the focus has greatly changed. In the 1950s and 1960s many studies looked at honorifics, address terms and male/female differences found in literary texts. In the 1970s and 1980s, the research focus shifted towards spoken Japanese based on questionnaires and interviews. In the last ten or fifteen years the use of real speech and authentic conversations has taken centre stage.

Most research on women and language was based on linguistic interest and studies that took the gender perspective started to appear much later. Undoubtedly, the most influential researcher on women's language and feminism is Akiko Jugaku (1979), the first Japanese to write about the relationship between gender inequalities and language. Unfortunately, most scholars in the linguistic area have not followed her line of research and it is only now that researchers are looking at women's language from a wider perspective (Endo 1997; Inoue 2004; Nakamura 2001; Reynolds-Akiba 1993).

While research on printed media and gender has mainly been conducted in the fields of popular culture (Kinsella 1995; Moeran 1995; Rosenberger 1995) and anthropology (Endo 1997, 2004; Inoue 2004, 2006; Nakamura 2001), linguistic works published in English on written texts are very few, with notable exceptions (Hayashi 1997; Kinoshita-Thomson & Otsuji 2003; Okamoto 1996; Shibamoto-Smith 2004; Ueno 2006).

Kinoshita-Thomson & Otsuji (2003) analysed business Japanese textbooks and reported on the extremely skewed representation of men and women in dialogues: men are portrayed in senior positions and women as mothers or housewives. These textbooks, the authors argue, emphasize stereotypes of male hegemony in the workforce and do not provide any female role models despite the fact that most students of Japanese as a second language are female (Kinoshita-Thomson & Otsuji 2003: 186). Similarly, Hayashi (1995) writes about the use of language in the construction of stereotypical social images of females in women's magazines. She argues that the hierarchical relationship between writers and readers, and the interdependence helps to index Japanese women within the stereotype image.

The following three studies looked at comics and television dramas to see how gender was indexed. Okamoto (1996) analysed comics and TV drama dialogues. Her results showed that women's speech styles are diverse and directly related to their identities. Shibamoto-Smith (2004) found a very different pattern in romance novel dialogues. Her study focused on personal pronouns, terms of address and sentence final particles and her data show that the speech of heroines and heroes follows the prescribed gendered styles. Perhaps one reason for this different finding is that the novels in Shibamoto's study were originally written in

English and in the translation process stereotypes were unconsciously chosen when interpreting and representing the speech of men and women. The dialogues in Okamoto's data were written in Japanese and may reflect more accurately how people speak in real life. Ueno (2006) conducted a similar study to Okamoto; however, she compared comics targeted at younger and older females. She found that dialogues in the former show varied linguistic forms whereas the latter exhibited a more traditional usage. Ueno writes that these comics may send the message that the 'use of feminine speech comes with maturity' (Ueno 2006: 24).

In her comprehensive work, Inoue (2006) explains in great detail about the ideologies that enforced the dissemination of *onna no kotoba* since the early 1900s. She examined self-help books from the early 1900s and the 1980s and wrote that what was dismissed and criticized as 'schoolgirl speech' in reference to the particular speech style of schoolgirls in the late nineteenth century came to represent the voice of the modern Japanese woman. In contrast to the rhetoric used in the early 1900s, the same speech style became associated with upward mobility in the late twentieth century. This change in the perception of women's language has to be seen in the context of the 1980s and early 1990s, when the Japanese economy was at its height and a widespread optimism was shared by everyone. Social mobility was possible if one spoke the 'correct Japanese' (Inoue 2006: 200).

Inoue's viewpoint is an extremely important one because it provides a new interpretation of *onna no kotoba*; however, one cannot dismiss the fact that linguistic variation in any society is a natural phenomenon. More importantly, one should not ignore the fact that social expectations towards the use of language are always present; adult women are expected to speak formal Japanese when the situation dictates. This point reflects the comments by Akiba-Reynolds (1993) on society's expectations.

2.2. Research questions: Analysis of linguistic strategies used in texts

As one of the goals of the critical discourse approach is to look at the opacity of language (Fairclough 1989; Fairclough & Wodak 1997), the focus of this study is on the linguistic devices that refer to women and to the concept of a 'woman's language', using printed media as a source of data. In order to find if gender stereotyping is present in the printed media the following questions were formulated:

1.　　How are men and women referred to linguistically?

2. What traits and characteristics are given to men and women?

3. What are the arguments used to justify the use of 'women's language'?

In addition, readers' letters sent to an online newspaper were added to the study in order to explore ordinary people's understanding of women's language in contemporary Japan and to look at intertextuality.

2.3. Perceptions of women's language by ordinary people

In this section I draw on comments by readers sent to an online newspaper in order to look at ordinary people's perceptions of women and language in Japan. I used two sets of comments sent to the online version of *Yomiuri Shinbun*. This newspaper has a daily circulation of 14 million, and although the readership of the web edition is not available it is expected to be similarly high. In the section called *Ootekomachi*, readers are invited to comment about a particular social issue and to contribute to this 'debate' by sending their opinions and comments.

Although it is impossible to verify the identities of the readers, letters sent to newspapers are a reflection of what ordinary people think and importance is placed not only on authorship but also on readers' interpretations (Inoue 2006). Such letters therefore provide a rich source of data. The first group of comments was sent in response to a reader who wrote that the language of young people was becoming *ranboo* 'rough'. Due to length restrictions, only the translation is provided.

> I am a housewife and I am in my 40s. I find it rather annoying to listen to young women's Japanese nowadays. They use words like *dekai, kuu, ketsu, kane kome, heso.*[4] These are words that emerge in daily conversation and are apparently not used with a particular purpose.
> I also have children who are in their 20s, and I sometimes use expressions such as *choo mukatukundayone* or *yabakunai*[5] when I go out with my colleagues to have a drink. However, I wonder if other middle-aged women talk in a similar manner when no humour or sarcasm is involved; I find it difficult to accept them.

Initially, it appears that the reader is quite annoyed about and critical of the use of 'rough' words. However, the second section contains comments in which she herself admits using them. The reader identifies herself as a housewife and we can infer that she works in some capacity. She criticizes young women for using words traditionally associated with male language. Yet, she admits that she herself uses *rough* words when going out with colleagues in informal situations. This letter seems to represent the conflict and confusion of ordinary women when it comes to *onna no kotoba*. On one hand, they know that rough words should be avoided; however, such words are permitted when humour or sarcasm is involved. It should be noted that style shifts can be used strategically, as shown in some studies where extremely polite and feminine language can be used to convey humour and should be considered as 'play' (Inoue 2006: 264) or as a communicative strategy (Maynard 1991).

Among thirteen responses to this first letter, four mention geographical variations, three indicate that they use some of the 'rough' words depending on the situation, and five people are quite critical about the change in the language use of young women. Here are some examples:

I use *meshi kuini ikou*[6]. But that is between very close friends.

I use both forms (the rough and polite forms). So do my husband and my parents. Depending on the region, the honorific prefix *o* is not used at all. I do not feel any reservations using the words you mention, but I do have problems with *choo mukatsukundayone* or *yabakunai*.

Luckily or unluckily I was brought up to speak good Japanese and I often feel uncomfortable. And of course, I feel very uncomfortable if a middle-aged woman like you uses expressions such as *choo mukatsukundayone* or *yabakunai.*

I am a housewife in my 40s. Recently I feel that the language of young girls has become really rough. I would not like women to use the word *umai.*

The other set of comments is related to language usage by mothers towards their children. Interestingly, there were many more answers (20 letters) to this topic and, except for two people, all were critical of mothers who use *male* language to their children. The first letter reads like this:

Recently, I have noticed the conversation between mother and child in parks, supermarkets and different other places (not that I am listening):
'*omae saa docchi kuitai?*' Which one do you want to eat?
'*ee, kocchika. choo mazusoodakara yametokee*' This doesn't look nice, so don't choose it'. *hayaku nore yo nimotsu omotee kara saa* 'Get one quickly, the bag is heavy'. *hontooni temee toroiyona* 'You are really slow'.
I just could not help but look at them. And the child was really small.
Maybe the mother is nice and firm, even though she uses dirty language. It is not that my language is perfect, but I am shocked. Is it the

neighbourhood that is the problem? I guess some might think, but no. It is a nice place.

In this short letter, we can see a number of aspects related not only to language but to women in general. In the italicised sentences the personal pronouns *omae* and *temee* are considered rude, even for men; the verbs *kuitai, yametokee, nore* and the adjectives *omotee* and *toroi* are also forms considered rough.

The writer says that the mother might be *yasashii* 'nice' even though she uses dirty language, and questions whether the problem is the neighbourhood. These two arguments are used by other readers in response to this letter, which indicates that *onna no kotoba* has other connotations. It not only indexes gender, but also it reflects the person's behaviour, social class and status. Although Japan is thought to be a society of just one class, the middle class, the reality is quite different.

The high number of responses to this letter might be an indication that Japanese women consider motherhood a very important aspect of their identity and are very conscious of their responsibility in bringing up their children using 'correct' Japanese language. Many of the letters mention the words *katei kankyoo* which can be roughly translated as 'family background', stressing the importance of one's social class. It could also reflect that women who opt to have children are more traditional.

We can say that these letters reflect the reality of today's Japan and infer that either language change is occurring and becoming less 'polite' or that diversity existed all along but was ignored; and similarly, that there is still a very conservative and stereotyped approach to *onna no kotoba* when it relates to raising children.

3. The texts: Self-help books and magazines

Two self-help books published in 2005 and an information magazine titled *Kurowassan* (10th June 2006) were analysed for this study. The magazine is targeted at adult women and published bi-monthly. It has a circulation of 303,509-700,000[7] and each issue features particular themes like dieting, saving money, fashion tips and keeping healthy. The theme of this particular issue is *kireina nihongo* 'beautiful Japanese'. Most articles are based on opinions formulated by famous people on the Japanese language. Others are based on a loosely structured dialogue. The third type comprises explanations, rules, examples and a quiz on the 'correct' use of the Japanese language authored by two linguists. Two main articles were analysed for this study. The two self-help books are *Atama no ii onna warui onna no hanashikata (AIO)* 'The speaking of intelligent and foolish women' by Kondo Tamami & Shimada Noriko and *Zettai shiawase ni nareru hanashikata no himitsu (ZS)* 'The secret of speaking that assures happiness' by Sato Tomio. Despite the fact that many other books on the same topic were published the same year, these were selected because of their high circulation. *AIO* was first published in 2003, later revised and reprinted under a different title, and *ZS* had already reached its eighth edition.

The format of *AIO* is explanations of how, when, where and with whom to use different phrases and words. It comprises five chapters with the last one devoted to the application of the rules taught in the book. *ZS* has a different format with six chapters. It starts with explanations about the relationship between language use and human relationships and evolves into how to love and be loved. It gives readers advice on how to improve their language, but does not have a textbook approach.

3.1. How are women and men referred to linguistically?

As explained in the previous sections, the gender of a speaker can be clear in written Japanese without explicit reference to names because of particular linguistic elements. All the texts analysed in this study show gender differences in the dialogues. Male and female lexical and pragmatic elements such as personal pronouns and sentence final particles are used in various forms with varying degrees of explicitness; particularly in *ZS* and *AIO* the examples contain gendered linguistic features (in bold), as shown in the following example.

(ZS:17)
1) ♀ *'Watashiwa kekkoo kirei**dawa**. Sono ue, shigoto mo dekiru**noyo**'*
I am quite pretty **dawa**. And on top of that, I am good at work **noyo**.

According to the writer of *ZS* the most basic female aspiration is to be 'beautiful'. He writes that example 1 represents the thought of most women. In these two sentences a number of elements denote femininity: the first person pronoun *watashi* which is the formal form and is also used by women; the final sentence particles *dawa* and *noyo* are prototypical feminine elements in Japanese and stress the femininity of the speaker.

In contrast, the representation of male speech is shown in example 2. This example, writes the author, is a phrase a man would use when arguing with his girlfriend. Observe the second personal pronoun *omae* and the plain ending of the utterance, which have traditionally been considered male linguistic characteristics. It is also noteworthy that the images of men and women appear in the representation of stereotypical roles: females are irrational and men are always cool-headed.

(ZS:88)
2) ♂ *doushite **omae** wa sunao ni ayamarenain **da**.*
Why can't **you** ask for forgiveness frankly **da**?

In *AIO* the speech of males and females is also shown with traditional characteristics. The next phrase is an example of what one would say when meeting an acquaintance after a long time. It is immediately noticeable that this phrase is uttered by a woman not only by the phrase ending with the particle *wa* but also by other lexical compounds that are accompanied by the honorific prefix *o* – all linguistic elements associated with female speech.

(AIO:49)
3) ♀ *ohisasiburi desu. ogenkisoude naniyori desu**wa**.*
It is a long time since I met you last. It is good that you look fine ***wa**.*

This representation of women's speech is observed in the magazine's articles where conversational elements that denote gender are present in various forms. The example below is an extract from an article featuring a television anchorwoman. She comments that when trying to persuade one's husband to drink less one should be more strategic and be less direct. In this sentence, all the conversational particles associated with female speech are used (*wayo, kashira*). It is unclear if the article is an exact reproduction of the anchorwoman's speech or was solely the writer's work.

(Kurowassan)
4) ♀ *soreja osake o hikaetekuretari shinai **wa yo ne**.*
Then (he) will not abstain from drinking **wa yo ne**.
5) ♀ *daijinano wa, 'otto o aishiteru tsuma' toshite hanasu koto janai **kashira**.*
What is important is to speak to one's husband as a 'loving wife' **kashira**.

3.2. What traits and characteristics are given to women and men?

In this section, I show the characteristics given to men and women and how these images are portrayed in the texts. Stereotypes are created by repeating and emphasizing particular characteristics related to appearance, behaviour and other features. The fact that the same attributes referring to men and women are found across the various texts shows how this stereotyping is recreated (Kinoshita-Thomson and Otsuji 2003). Two main characteristics given to men and women are identified: attributes of personality and behaviour, and particular professions or job positions.

3.2.1. Attributes and behaviour

There are two groups of words that describe the Japanese of men and women, and they are in opposition. *Ranboo* 'rough/uncultured' and *kitanai* 'unclean/dirty' are words describing speech considered uncultured and unfeminine. In contrast, *utsukushii* 'beautiful', *kirei* 'beautiful/clean', *hin ga aru* 'cultured/sophisticated', *joohin* 'cultured' and *kyooyoo ga aru* 'educated' are words associated with women's language and proper Japanese. The words *kirei* 'pretty/clean, *utsukushii* 'beautiful' and *hin ga aru* 'refined/elegant' have been used since the early twentieth century (Endo 1997; Inoue 2006; Nakamura 2001). These associations of beauty, elegance and politeness with women's language and behaviour reproduce and reinforce traditional stereotypes.

There is an implicit understanding in all the texts that all women are or want to be *kirei*. This desire, the authors write, is shared by every woman; however, beauty must come from within. Inner beauty is manifested through one's speech and therefore one has to be beautiful 'inside', they write. The inference here is that beautiful people use *'kireina nihongo'* and that by changing how one speaks the inner-self will gradually improve.

(ZS:20)
'onna wa kirei ni naritai, utsukushiku naritai…
gaiken yori naimen o, hanashikata o kaereba naimen mo henka shiteiku'
Women want to become pretty, they want to become beautiful…instead of (worrying about) the facade, if (they) change their speech their inner-selves will also change.'

A shift of perspective in the concept of intelligence can be observed. From the government's slogan of *ryoosaikenbo* or 'good wife and wise mother' used in the early twentieth century, the new concept emphasizes the woman as an independent person and not in the role of a mother. In addition, different to previous associations of 'women's language' with high social status (Inoue 2006) the new viewpoint is that intelligence is an asset. This new twist might be due to the societal changes in Japan after the economic bubble burst in the early 1990s and the fact that most unmarried women are in the workforce[8]. This fact is reinforced by the settings of imaginary conversations in the workplace.

The featured persons in the magazine *Kurowassan* are all successful career women who give their opinion about communication. They are shown in smart suits which emphasize the image of the successful working woman, and are reported saying that in order to become more 'intelligent' or more 'beautiful' the secret is to talk in an indirect manner. This subtle way of reinforcing stereotypical behaviour (polite and soft way of speaking) is accomplished through advice given to the (female) readers on how to soften their comments using polite language while delivering the intended meaning.

Another important feature in these texts is that a binary concept of behaviour is reinforced. Women's behaviour patterns are depicted through common stereotypes such as that women like gossiping and males are silent and power hungry. Distinctions between female and male behaviour and different logic patterns are explained by one of the authors as due to biological differences in the brain. Other examples of stereotypes abound, such as why men are better at three-dimensional observation and why women are good at details. Some descriptions can be seen below:

(ZS:199)
Shikkari shita otoko hodo guchi o iwanai
The firmer a man the less he speaks.
(ZS:121)
Kanjoo o sutoreeto ni hyoogen dekirunowa josei naradewa subarashii choosho desu. .... Josei rasii josei dearu kotoni motto sekkyokuteki de atte hoshii.
It is an attribute that only women are able to demonstrate their feelings openly...Women should actively try to be more womanly.

3.2.2. Professions and job positions

Stereotypical representations of men and women at work appear in dialogues that are set at work. Females are in secretarial roles while men are in senior positions. This representation is not overt but is hidden in gendered linguistic items in the conversation in the following example. The conversation is based on an imaginary situation where 'I' or the (female) reader meets the section manager. The gender and status differences are indicated in the endings of the speakers' utterances. Those in junior positions use polite forms while those in power use plain forms, which is not reciprocated.

(*AIO* :108)

1 S: ♂   *yaa **ohayoo***
        'Hullo, morning'.
2 I: ♀   *Tanaka kachoo. Ohayoo**gozaimasu**. Kyoo wa sawayakana*
        otenkidesune.
        'Chief Tanaka. Good morning. It is a very nice day today.'
3 S: ♂   ***kimi** no busho ni haittekita shin'in no **ko** ga chanto shigoto*
        *yatteru**kai**?*
        'Is the new girl in your section working well?'
4 S: ♀   *warito hikaemena kata desuyone. nanigoto nimo yukkuri mai*
        *peesu ni ganbatte**masuyo**.*
        'She is a little timid, isn't she? She is a bit slow, but she is
        working fine.'
5 S: ♂   ***sooka**. torihikisaki no kobayashi buchoo, **kimi** wa atta koto*
        *aru**ka**?*
        'Good. Have you met one of our customers, Mr Kobayashi?'
6 I: ♀   *ano kanroku ga ate doudou to **shiterassharu kata** desu ne?*
        'That dignified and stately person?'
7 S: ♂   ***soosoo**. itsumo mezurashii nekutai shiterun **dayonaa** (@@@).*
        'Uh-huh. He always wears interesting neckties.'

The greetings are quite different, as observed in lines 1 and 2. The male senior uses the short form and 'I' (the female) uses the polite form. Next, in line 3, three items denote the speaker's seniority and his gender. The second person pronoun *kimi* is addressed to a younger or subordinate 'you'. This pronoun is used mainly by males. Next, the question ends with the particle *kai*, which is a question particle accompanied with a final *i*. This ending is generally associated with the speech of old people or of older men towards someone junior. Note that two different referents are used towards the same person (the new female young employee), *kata* and *ko*. The male manager refers to her as *ko* or child, whereas 'I' uses the noun *kata*, the formal term for referring to a person. Other elements are the SFP *yone* and the formal endings. More gender characteristics can be seen in line 5, with the second use of *kimi* and the abrupt ending of the question form *aruka*, a form considered masculine. Line 6 follows with the use of the honorific form *shiterassharu* and *kata*; however, in line 7 the same person is referred to with the plain form *shiteru* and the ending *dayona*. *Na* is considered to be a masculine particle and from the context one can assume that there is no forceful meaning.

Through this short dialogue, we can see that the roles of males and females are still very traditional. They might or might not reflect the actual reality in the workplace. However, because this dialogue is imaginary, it shows that these are the representations of women and men that the authors have or that they want to portray. Interestingly, not a single example contained a situation where the female was in a senior position.

3.3. Arguments used to promote 'women's language'

Arguments used to promote the use of 'women's language' contain the concepts of 'beauty', 'intelligence', 'adulthood' and in an indirect way the uniqueness of the Japanese language. The authors in *AIO* emphasize that an 'adult' woman has to learn to speak well and stress that according to how a woman speaks, she can be considered elegant and cultured. On the other hand, the author of *ZS* argues that speaking beautifully is not only for the benefit of the speaker but for the listener as well.

Perhaps due to the changes in the demographics of working women there is an emphasis on women's performance at work. The rhetoric again is centred on human relationships. It is argued that if a woman is good at communication, the relationship with her colleagues and seniors will improve. In order to be a good communicator she needs to be polite, to speak firmly but with a soft voice and so on. Advice on how to be polite is a reproduction of etiquette books published in earlier times.

All the texts have a topic on the proper use of honorifics, which is an indication of their importance and what is considered 'beautiful language'. In the magazine *Kurowassan* two whole sections are dedicated to their 'correct' use. This phenomenon might be related to the complexity of a system that must be consciously learned. Most people who enter the workforce are trained and are expected to have full command of honorifics, particularly when dealing with customers.

Allusions are made to the uniqueness of the Japanese language and to its 'spirit' or *kotodama*, the mythical and magical force that will bring happiness to its speakers. This ideological argument is used to promote the use of *kireina nihongo,* although it is not overt. This argument will not be developed further here, as its complexity is worth another chapter.

4. Discussion and conclusion

The analysis of the texts in self-help books and a magazine shows that gendered stereotypes are still perpetuated and reinforced in overt and covert linguistic forms. Most importantly, the existence of *onna no kotoba* or women's language is referred to as a truthful reality and promoted vigorously. Many of the strategies used for this purpose have been used previously; in particular the association of some key words such as *kirei* 'pretty, clean' and *utsukushii* 'beautiful' to femininity is exploited (Inoue

2006). Similarly, the use of 'genderlects' in dialogues and the roles given to men and women in the texts emphasize the binary differences, which is a practice observed in other types of texts (Kinoshita-Thomson & Otsuji 2003). On the other hand, some of the arguments used to promote the use of *onna no kotoba* reflect some of the societal changes in contemporary Japan.

The most striking characteristic in all the texts is the association of 'beauty' with the language or *kireina nihongo* 'beautiful Japanese', which invariably includes the correct use of honorifics. This allusion is particularly conspicuous because it has some ideological undertones; the emphasis is on the correct use of *standard Japanese* with complete disregard of the fact that many Japanese dialects do not have honorific forms (Koyama 2004). This aspect can be observed in the letters of readers who write of geographical differences and the fact that some words considered vulgar are in fact from dialects. One should not forget that the emphasis in disseminating the idea of *onna no kotoba* is closely connected to the standardization of the Japanese language based on the Tokyo dialect (Koyama 2004). Linguistic evidence shows that regional and social differences as well as situational factors affect women's speech (Abe 2000; Matsumoto 2004; Sunaoshi 2004; Tanaka 2004).

Nonetheless, the idea of a binary differentiation between male and female speech styles is still deeply ingrained in most people. Most importantly, the social expectations that women *should* speak *onna no kotoba* is still widespread in present Japanese society. This is seen in the comments of other readers who are convinced that they use 'women's language' and take a critical view towards women who speak 'rough' language. These women might be class conscious and Tokyo residents, and the use of *onna no kotoba* for them is a sign of social status. The relationship between the prescribed 'women's language' and social class in Japan was explored by Inoue (2006), who pointed out that the self-help books of the 1980s clearly conveyed the idea of upward mobility; if one bought designer goods, went to exclusive restaurants and were also able to speak *ojoosama* 'ladies' language, one's status would certainly move upwards. The belief that all Japanese belong to a middle class has been common since the post-war abolition of class divisions and the nobility. However, because the language spoken in the rich neighbourhoods of Tokyo was chosen as 'standard' Japanese there is still the association of refinement and women's language.

Readers of the magazine also point out the distinction between private and public, which is mentioned in one article in the magazine. The article explicitly states how differently one speaks at home and at work; however, this is completely ignored in the self-help books and no differentiation is made between polite and informal speech styles, emphasizing that women should speak in the polite form. The many examples of imaginary conversations include different settings but there is no attempt to define what formal or informal situations are. It seems that there is some confusion between informal language, *onna no kotoba* and formal language. It is unclear, therefore, if those promoting the use of *onna no kotoba* include all situations or refer only to public encounters.

Polite forms appearing in dialogues in the texts include all the stereotypical pronouns and lexical and pragmatic elements associated with female (and male) speech. By showing the differences of male and female speech in dialogues, gender differences are stressed and the binary concept is reinforced. As written previously, this representation of men's and women's speech is common practice in textbooks (Kinoshita-Thomson & Otsuji 2003) in the roles given in the dialogues. Women are always portrayed in subordinate positions and males in senior roles. This subtle way of showing women and men interacting might be a reflection of society or a deliberate strategy to provide role models and reproduce gender stereotypes.

In a similar way, gender stereotypes of traits and behaviour are reproduced through semantic encoding of key words such as *utsukushii* 'beautiful', *kirei* 'beautiful/clean', *hin ga aru* 'cultured/sophisticated', *joohin* 'cultured' and *kyooyoo ga aru* 'educated'. These concepts are associated with women and their language. Advice on how to be polite and use 'beautiful' language is aimed at promoting the use of polite forms and honorifics. Women who can use *kireina nihongo*, the authors write, are or can become beautiful, refined and successful.

Arguments used in these texts are reproductions of those used in the past; however some changes are observable. There are basic arguments given to justify the merits of using 'women's language': beauty, success, intelligence and adulthood. Every woman, the writers write, has a desire to be beautiful. Becoming or being beautiful will lead to a happy life, not only for oneself, but for others. The new message promotes the use of 'women's language' that encompasses social status, occupation, urban living and intelligence. Contrary to the ideology of a 'good wife and a wise mother' used in the early twentieth century, or the assurance or upward social mobility in the late 90s, the new message stresses success and, indirectly, happiness. This shift creates an image of the modern woman who is beautiful, intelligent, successful, and therefore happy.

Another argument used in the texts is that of Japanese social expectations towards adults, which stresses that women must learn how to use polite forms once they become adults. One of the interviewees in the magazine mentioned that she uses masculine first person pronouns, but only at home. However, she stresses that if a woman used male language at work she would lose trust and not be considered seriously. This comment reflects the high expectations in Japanese society towards adults (Reynolds-Akiba 1993). It should be pointed out again, however, that no similar self-help books on language are available for men. This in itself is an indication that women face stricter and less equal treatment in society.

The online letters provided an extremely interesting overview on the viewpoint of ordinary Japanese towards the use of *onna no kotoba*. While there are readers who recognize geographical and formality differences, the responses towards motherhood and child rearing were particularly remarkable, as more than ninety percent of the letters were critical of mothers using 'rough' language towards their children. The criticism included comments that one's upbringing was essential in speaking 'correct Japanese', while the belief that no one around them spoke in that way was even more interesting. This suggests that *onna no kotoba* indexes not only one's gender but also social class, geographical region, level of education and social status.

Given that women's status in Japan is slowly but steadily improving, there might be a sense of change in the society as a whole. As Freed (2003) and Cameron (1997) suggest, it is perhaps when traditional boundaries become less distinct that people feel uncomfortable and see the need to implement and reinforce stereotypes to maintain gender distinctions. In present Japan, women's increased visibility in important positions might bring a sense of danger to many people. Women's advancement in society might be felt as a threat to the traditional gender roles. Therefore, stressing the need for a woman to be 'womanly', to speak *onna no kotoba* and to behave in the prescribed gender role might be an indication of that feeling of 'gender instability' in the face of societal change (Freed 2003: 714).

Notes

[1] The Japan Institute of Workers' Evolution. Reports retrieved, November 2007, from http://www.jiwe.or.jp/english/situation/situation2003.html.
[2] There are popular books such as *Make inu no tooboe* (Sakai, J. 2006) in which the author humorously writes about married and unmarried women, coining for them the terms 'winner dog' and 'loser dog'. Similarly, according to the White Paper of the Ministry of Labour, there are three types of trends in relation to marriage, work and childbirth: those who want to continue working after birth,

those who prefer to quit their jobs and concentrate on child rearing, and those who want to be homemakers.

[3] Data from the White Paper of the Ministry of Health, Labour and Welfare (2005)

[4] *Dekkai, kuu ketsu* are the rough form of *ookii* 'big', *taberu* 'to eat', *oshiri* 'bottom' respectively. The other words *kane, kome* and *heso* when used without the honorific prefix are considered vulgar and rough.

[5] *Choo mukatsuku* is an expression used by younger Japanese. The expression is composed of the prefix *choo* 'extreme' originally only used with nouns. *Mukatsuku* means 'to feel nauseated, to feel unhappy, to become angry'. The degree of informality is stressed by the direct form *da* and the final particles *yo* and *ne*. Similarly, *yabakunai* is the negative form of *yabai* 'dangerous'. This word was originally jargon used by criminals.

[6] *Meshi* 'food' and *Kuu* 'to eat' are the rough word for *shokuji* and *taberu* respectively.

[7] *Shadan hoojin Nihon Zasshi Kyokai*. Retrieved September, 2006 from http://www.jmagazine.or.jp/index.htmlfile://localhost/F:/Women%20in%20Japan/ Women%20in%20Japan%20Today%202003.htm.

[8] The number of never married female workers has increased since 1997. Retrieved November, 2007, from, http://www.jiwe.or.jp/english/situation/situation2003.html.

Texts used for the data

Kondo, T. and N. Shimada. 2005. *Atama no ii onna warui onna no hanashikata*. [The speaking of intelligent and foolish women].Tokyo: Takarajima.

Sato, T. 2005. *Zettai shiawase ni nareru hanashikata no himitsu*. [The secret of speaking that assures happiness]. Tokyo: 3anet.

Kurowassan [croissant]. 2005. 6:10. Tokyo: Magajin House.

Yomiuri Online. Retrieved 29, July 2006, from
   http://www.yomiuri/com/jp/komachi/reader/200510/200500100059.htm

—. Retrieved 31, March 2005, from
   http://www.yomiuri/com/jp/komachi/reader/200405/20040500063.htm

References

Abe, H. 2000. *Speaking of Power: Japanese Women and Their Speeches*. Munich: Lincoln.

Bernstein, L. G. 1991. *Recreating Japanese Women, 1600–1945*. Berkeley: University of California Press.

Cameron, D. 1995. *Verbal Hygiene*. London: Routledge.

Endo, O. 2004. "Women and words: The status of sexist language in Japan as seen through contemporary dictionary definitions and media discourse." In *Japanese Language, Gender and Ideology*. Eds. S. Okamoto and J. Shibamoto-Smith. Oxford: Oxford University Press, 166–186.

—. 1997. *Onna no Kotoba no Bunkashi*. Tokyo: Gakuyoo Shobo.

Fairclough, N. 1989. *Language and Power*. London: Longman.

Fairclough, N. and R. Wodak. 1997. "Critical discourse analysis." In *Discourse as Social Interaction. Discourse Studies: A Multidisciplinary Introduction*. Ed. T.A. van Dijk. London: Sage, vol. 2, 258–284.

Freed, A. 2003. "Reflections on language and gender research." In *The Handbook of Language and Gender*. Eds. J. Holmes and M. Meyerhoff. Oxford: Blackwell, 670–721.

Hayashi, R. 1997. "Hierarchical interdependence expressed through conversational styles in Japanese women's magazines." *Discourse and Society* 8.3: 359–389.

Ide, S. 1997. *Joseigo no Sekai*. Tokyo: Meiji Shooin.

Ide, S., M. Hori, A. Kawasaki, S. Ikuta and H. Haga. 1986. "Sex difference and politeness in Japanese." *International Journal of the Sociology of Language* 558: 225–36.

Inoue, M. 2006. *Vicarious Language. Gender and Linguistic Modernity in Japan*. CA: University of California Press.

—. 2004. "Gender, language and modernity: Toward an effective history of 'Japanese women's language'." In *Japanese Language, Gender and Ideology*. Eds. S. Okamoto and J. Shibamoto-Smith. Oxford: Oxford University Press, 57–75.

Joseph, J. 2004. *Language and Identity: National, Ethnic, Religious*. NY: Palgrave McMillan.

Jugaku, A. 1979. *Nihongo to Onna*. Tokyo: Iwanami.

Kindaichi, H. 1990. *Nihongo* (vols 1 and 2). Tokyo: Iwanami shinsho.

Kinoshita-Thomson, C. and E. Otsuji. 2003. "Evaluation of business Japanese textbooks: Issues of gender." *Japanese Studies* 23.2: 185–203.

Kinsella, S. 1995. "Cuties in Japan." In *Women, Media and Consumption in Japan*. Eds. L. Skov and B. Moeran. Honolulu, Hawaii: University of Hawaii Press, 220–254.

Koyama, W. 2004. "The linguistic ideologies of modern Japanese honorifics and the historic reality of modernity." *Language and Communication* 24: 413–435.

Kuno, S. 1973. *The Structure of the Japanese Language*. Cambridge: MIT Press.

Matsumoto, Y. 2004. "Alternate femininity: Personae of middle-aged mothers." In *Japanese Language, Gender and Ideology*. Eds. S. Okamoto and J. Shibamoto-Smith. Oxford: Oxford University Press, 240–255.

Maynard, S. 1991. "Pragmatics of discourse modality: A case of *da* and *desu/masu* forms in Japanese." *Journal of Pragmatics* 15: 551–582.

Moeran, B. 1995. "Reading Japanese in *Katei Gahoo*: The art of being an upper class woman." In *Women, Media and Consumption in Japan*. Eds. L. Skov and B. Moeran. Honolulu, Hawaii: University of Hawaii Press, 111–142.

Nakamura, M. 2001. *Kotoba to Jendaa*. Tokyo: Keiso Shobo.

Ogino, T. 1986. "Quantification of politeness based on the usage patterns of honorific expressions." *International Journal of the Sociology of Language* 58: 37–58.

Okamoto, S. 1996. "Indexical meaning, linguistic ideology, and Japanese women's speech." *The Proceedings of the 22nd Annual Meeting of the Berkeley Linguistics Society*. Berkeley: Berkeley Linguistics Society, 290–301.

Reynolds-Akiba, K. 1993. *Onna to Kotoba*. Tokyo: Kuroshio.

Rosenberger, N. 1995. "Antiphonal performances? Japanese women's magazines and women's voices." In *Women, Media and Consumption in Japan*. Eds. L. Skov and B. Moeran. Honolulu, Hawaii: University of Hawaii Press, 143–169.

Shibamoto-Smith, J. 2004. "Language and gender in the (hetero) romance: 'Reading' the ideal hero/ine through lovers'dialogue in Japanese romance fiction." In *Japanese Language, Gender and Ideology*. Eds. S. Okamoto and J. Shibamoto-Smith. Oxford: Oxford University Press, 113–130.

Smith, J. 1992. "Women in charge: Politeness and directives in the speech of Japanese women." *Language in Society* 21: 59-82.

Sunaoshi, Y. 2004. "Farm women's professional discourse in Ibaraki." In *Japanese Language, Gender and Ideology*. Eds. S. Okamoto and J. Shimaboto-Smith. Oxford: Oxford University Press, 187–204.

Takano, S. 2005. "Re-examining linguistic power: Strategic uses of directives by professional Japanese women in positions of authority and leadership." *Journal of Pragmatics* 37.5: 633–666.

Tanaka, L. 2004. *Gender, Language and Culture: A Study of Japanese Television Interview Discourse*. Amsterdam: John Benjamins.

Terada, S. 1993. "Nihongo ni okeru joseigo kenkyuushi." *Nihongogaku* 12.6: 262–313.

Ueno, J. 2006. "Shojo and Adult Women: A linguistic analysis of gender identity in Manga." *Women and Language* 29.1: 16-24.

Washi, R. 2004. "'Japanese female speech' and language policy in the World War II era." In *Japanese Language, Gender and Ideology*. Eds. S. Okamoto and J. Shibamoto-Smith. Oxford: Oxford University Press, 76–91.

CHAPTER TEN

'WAR OF WORDS' ON NEW (LEGAL) SEXUAL IDENTITIES: SPAIN'S RECENT GENDER-RELATED LEGISLATION AND DISCURSIVE CONFLICT

JOSÉ SANTAEMILIA, UNIVERSITAT DE VALÈNCIA

Abstract: Although Spain is a modern, democratic European state, it has yet to come to terms with its multiple identities –whether national, ideological or sexual. Over the last few years, we have witnessed a battery of legal measures and of public and private attitudes which would seem to indicate that all gender or sexual identities have finally been accepted or, at least, respected. A look at different newspapers, however, shows that we are still waging a 'war of words' (Dunnant 1994) –which is part of an on-going private and public debate– over specific and highly ideological terms such as 'abortion', 'homosexuality', the meaning of 'family', or the scope of 'gender violence'. Two obvious conclusions emerge instantly: (a) that, in spite of the fact that the majority of Spanish society wishes to have more freedom, there is still fierce resistance against the recognition of new gender and sexual identities; and (b) that the Church and the extreme right-wing political parties are orchestrating a bitter media campaign to oppose any change in their traditional, reactionary model of family and human relationships.

Gender- and sex-related concerns offer valuable insights into people's attitudes and ideologies concerning modernity, democratization and respect for the lifestyles and identities of others.

Keywords: *Gender legislation, sexual (in)equality, gender, sex, mass media.*

1. Gay-marriage legislation in Spain

Although Spain is a modern, democratic European state, it has yet to come to terms with its multiple identities –whether national, ideological or sexual. Over the last few years, we have witnessed a battery of legal measures and of public and private attitudes which would seem to indicate that all gender or sexual identities have finally been accepted or, at least, respected. Among the different laws that have been passed recently we can mention acts on gender violence (Ley orgánica 1/2004, de 28 de diciembre, de Medidas de Protección Integral contra la Violencia de Género), on effective equality between men and women (Ley Orgánica 3/2007, de 22 de marzo, para la igualdad efectiva entre hombres y mujeres) and on gay marriage (Ley 13/2005 de 1 de julio, por la que se modifica el Código Civil en materia de derecho a contraer matrimonio).

New legal measures continue to be adopted daily in an important social effort towards gender equality. All these measures, and the reactions they provoke, constitute excellent vehicles to explore the individual and social sensitivity towards conflicting and evolving conceptualizations of gender and sex. Studying the discursive limits of key gendered or sexualised terms such as 'homosexuality', 'sexual harassment' or 'spouse' is a privileged weapon to analyze conflict, as gender(ed) conceptualizations are symbolic sites onto which more profound inequalities, frustrations and shortcomings are projected.

In this paper I will critically analyze Spain's gay marriage legislation, particularly its reflection in a variety of contemporary ideological texts. These include newspaper or magazine articles and pastoral or religious publications. We should bear in mind that in these texts language is an indirect or mediated index of reality –it constitutes a representation or a construction of identities, prejudices, (hidden) agendas and stereotypes. Media discourse is powerful, as it creates expectations, imposes socially-accepted images and consistently reinforces constructions of behaviour, endowing them with a commonsensical status. Fairclough (1989: 193) emphasises "the dramatic growth in the importance of the media as an institutional site for political struggle".

For Fairclough (1995: 47), media discourse "should be regarded as the site of complex and often contradictory processes, including ideological processes". Mass media are the contemporary arena on which the fundamental gender(ed) and sexual meanings are (re)negotiated. In this paper I will try to find linguisitc traces of the debate over gay marriage legislation in media texts and religious publications. Ours is a critical discourse approach to gender and language, which sees language as constructing, or challenging, sexual identity categories and also as a fundamental vehicle for social control and for the excercise of power (see Fairclough 1995, Fairclough & Wodak 1997). In particular, when there is a controversial issue at hand (e.g. gay marriage legislation), they serve to orchestrate a 'discourse' vs 'counter-discourse' debate[1], which is profoundly ideological and reaches all segments of the population.

2. Homosexuality: past and present, taboo and challenge(s)

In July 2005 the Spanish Parliament passed a law that grants marriage rights to same-sex couples, including the right to adopt children and to inherit from the other partner. This makes their legal status the same as that of heterosexual couples. It was a long-awaited triumph for civil rights campaigners and for many people who have suffered discrimination and punishments. The gay marriage law decrees that it is deemed just and fair that those of a homosexual identity should have equal access to the institution of marriage, albeit outside of the religious context in which it is traditionally embedded. It constituted a surprise for many, who believed Spain was a highly conservative democracy, but who became one of the first countries in the world to give the same marriage rights to heterosexuals and homosexuals alike. When we ask our university students about this law, most of them state their approval of the new legislation. It is, however, a controversial issue around the world. Everyone has an opinion; some base their beliefs on religious or moral values, while others take a more liberal, humanitarian viewpoint.

One of the immediate linguistic consequences of this law is that it has prompted a few significant terminological adaptations in Spanish. In particular, the terms *marido* ["husband"] and *mujer* ["wife"] have been replaced by the gender-neutral *cónyuges* or *consortes* ["spouses"]. Also, the terms *padre* ["father"] and *madre* ["mother"] have been substituted by *progenitores* ["parents"]. These changes will bring about –undoubtedly through discursive struggle- new moral, sexual, linguistic and legal frameworks to live one's sexual identity, family project or moral universe. Obviously, the passage of a gay marriage law does not amount to encouraging a fierce, compulsory sexual activity, or a sort of promiscuity. Manuel Fraga, an ultra-conservative Spanish politician, who used to be a member of dictator Francisco Franco's Cabinet, and is now the honorary president of the right-wing Partido Popular, even declared on the Spanish state channel TVE-1 that this new gay marriage law "abre la puerta 'evidentemente' a uniones entre miembros de una misma familia y a relaciones de consanguinidad" (17-3-05).

Homosexuality is not a recent invention. According to the *O.E.D.* the word 'homosexual' entered the English language in 1892, and it can be defined as:

> A. *adj.* Involving, related to, or characterized by a sexual propensity for one's own sex; of or involving sexual activity with a member of one's own sex, or between individuals of the same sex.

Whether the term 'homosexual' had been coined or not, *homosexuality* –as well as other sexual identities- has always existed. There have been ancient societies in which homosexuality was accepted or even encouraged. In ancient Greece, for instance, *pederastia* (or 'boy love') was established as a social and educational institution. Under this system, an older man took a young boy under his care to educate, protect, love and for whom he was expected to be a role model in life. Part of this pedagogical system included the young man being sexually penetrated by the older man. In Greece, people did not define themselves in terms of being 'homosexuals' or 'heterosexuals' (see Cameron & Kulick 2003) –in fact, they "did not recognize two kinds of "desire", two different or competing "drives", each claiming a share of men's hearts and appetites" (Foucault 1984: 188), but, rather, they "saw two ways of enjoying one's pleasure, one of which was more suited to certain individuals or certain periods of existence" (*ibidem* 190). People were expected to respond erotically to beauty in either sex.

In Greece the only distinction in sexual relations was between an active (or insertive) and a passive (or penetrated) role (see Cameron & Kulick 2003). The 'passive' role was only acceptable for inferiors such as women, slaves and young males. Although taking the passive role was considered shameful, being attracted to men was often considered a sign of 'masculinity'. Significantly, Greek myths tell of same-sex exploits attributed to the gods, and other key figures in Greek history and literature, such as Achylles or Hercules.

In the modern Western world there seems to be a consensus that homosexuals ought to be respected and receive the same rights, but many believe that same-sex couples should not be granted the right to 'marriage' or to form a 'family'. Depending on where they live, homosexuals can have a hard time at school (this is a common situation in Europe or the US), or can have serious trouble in daily situations (in Eastern European countries, such as Poland or Hungary, where homosexuals are silenced or proscribed), or even face physical or psychological aggression (in Iraq, for instance, homosexuals are killed, tortured or mutilated).

However, although many societies around the world seem to have returned to a liberal view of homosexuality, in many parts of the world homosexuality is still viewed as a taboo. From the most liberal to the most conservative societies, homosexuality as a way of life has never been embraced completely as a social norm. Leading life as a homosexual has always carried a negative connotation and members of the community struggle to be accepted as active and contributing citizens to society rather than being identified only by their sexual preference. Today we acknowledge the brave attitudes of powerful personalities who tried to build a tradition of homoeroticism, such as Sappho, Leonardo da Vinci, Michelangelo, Oscar Wilde, Noel Coward or even David Bowie or Madonna. No matter the antecedents, however, when a topic is taboo, it is generally ignored in social conversations because people do not know how to approach it. For many it is much easier to turn away from a controversial issue than to accept it. There is the feeling that contemporary societies are far more tolerant than those in the past, but we must bear in mind that intolerance and taboo have historically hidden behind the masks of 'morality', 'common sense' or 'law'. In many parts of the world it is dangerous to publicly announce own's sexual orientation to be anything other than heterosexual. Although respectful in other spheres of life, many individuals still believe that feeling a physical attraction to a same-sex person is a malady or deviant behaviour.

When depicted on TV or cinema, homosexuality is very often something exotic or funny. That a gay or lesbian character appears on stage or on TV does not mean that homosexuality is accepted normally by society. The example of the recent Ang Lee's film *Brokeback Mountain* (2005) can be certainly taken as a signal that homosexuality is increasingly being included within the spectrum of sexualities depicted in Hollywood films. But we may wonder as well that if homosexuality really were being incorporated into the mainstream as a fully accepted 'lifestyle choice', would such films as *Brokeback Mountain* be so rare or so controversial? In fact, such a wide coverage of a film due (almost exclusively) to its subject matter signals quite the opposite. Although the film was hailed as progressive, it is still a small concession. The majority of Hollywood films continue to depict heterosexuality not only as the overwhelming societal norm but they also enforce heterosexuality as a means of ultimate fulfilment for the individual. In Gumbel's words:

Hollywood still adheres to the mentality that American audiences look to
their on-screen idols as outlets for their own romantic fantasies and thus
need to think of them as strictly heterosexual (Gumbel 2006).

Stereotypes of the typical gay man or woman that are presented by the
media contribute to society's lack of understanding and acceptance of
homosexuals as individuals. Popular culture perpetuates the stereotype of
male homosexuals as being flamboyant, happy-go-lucky, effeminate and
having careers in fashion and interior design. Female homosexuals are
portrayed as being physically masculine and sharing interests similar to
those of heterosexual males. One of the highest rated shows on US prime-
time television is *Will and Grace*, which is about a homosexual man
(Will), living with a heterosexual woman (Grace). Will does not fit the
stereotypical mould of a gay man; he is masculine, holds a high position at
a reputable company, and his hobbies include those of heterosexual men.
On the British TV, the most popular show is perhaps *Queer Eye for the
Straight Guy*, which features a group of five gay men who help a
heterosexual male fix his appearance and living space. All the characters
depicted are the stereotypical, flamboyant gay males who are experts on
fashion and pop culture. Having a 'queer eye' implies that straight men
cannot have a sense of fashion without a 'queer eye', in other words, the
help of a gay man. The show's title also suggests that homosexual males
are all experts in fashion and culture, and are incompetent in all other
professions.

Negative connotations about homosexuals persist in popular texts, and
are reinforced by the media, religious beliefs, and people of authority who
possess power over the masses, making it very difficult for homosexuals to
rid themselves of labels that denounce their way of life. As most minority
groups, they face name-calling, strict stereotyping, and acts of physical
aggression. Most tabloids still seem to have major problems with
accepting homosexuality. But while this is true, it is also well worth
mentioning that we are observing a certain demystification of gay couples
in the Spanish mass media: the most popular TV series –e.g. *Hospital
Central, Aquí no hay quien viva*– incorporate at least one gay character
who is important in the plot regardless of his sexual inclination. The child
programme *Los Lunis*, on TVE-1, recently broadcast a report called
'Bodas diferentes' ["Different weddings"], where the puppets explained to
3 to 7 year olds the different types of 'marriage', the different rituals, and
so on.

3. 'War of words' over the gay marriage law in Spain: Gender as a site of conflict and ideological struggle

A cursory look at different newspapers and institutional or religious publications shows that we are currently waging a 'war of words' (Dunnant 1994) over specific and highly ideological terms. 'Abortion'[2], 'homosexuality', 'family', 'gender violence' or 'gay marriage' are obvious examples.

3.1. An official discourse of tolerance and sexual equality

The first 'discourse' that is present in this on-going private and public debate over gay marriages is legislation. The 2005 gay marriage law justifies the new legal situation drawing on the fact that societies change and adapt to different models of 'family'[3], and that Parliaments should not ignore reality and act consequentially. The law also adds that society has further come to accept the existence of same-sex couples who lead a normal life based on love and affection. The gay marriage legislation also states that today's society has overcome time-old prejudices regarding same-sex relationships[4].

This law recognises and respects everyone's sexual option, and provides measures for everyone to develop his/her personality and sexual rights in terms of equality with the rest of society. This new official (legal) discourse is reinforced by politicians who are in favour of gay rights and defend a more tolerant attitude towards various minority groups. "Spain is now a more decent country," Prime Minister José Luis Rodríguez Zapatero asserted, "because a decent society is one that doesn't humiliate its members" (Bird 2005). It is a discourse of respect, recognition and tolerance, which is voiced by many individuals, organizations, or newspapers which try to offer a more or less balanced information on the topic. It is, most likely, the silent and anonymous discourse of a majority of the Spanish population.

3.2. A multiplicity of counter-discourses

Against this discourse for social and sexual equality, we can find a multiplicity of fierce 'counter-discourses', basically fuelled by the Church and the ultra-conservative media, whose only objective seems to be to oppose any measure of recognition of the rights of minorities and of social dignity. In pastoral publications and in extreme right-wing-dominated mass media, we see a concerted effort to oppose any form of modernisation or dissidence. Resistance is, then, strong, well organised, highly militant, unrespectful, and bold to the point of racism.

According to Scripture (in *Genesis, Leviticus, Romans* or *Corinthians*), homosexuality is a sin. In particular, in *Leviticus* (18: 22) we can read: "Thou shalt not lie with mankind, as with womankind: it is abomination." Although the Roman Catholic Church tries to soften its view on homosexuality, its official doctrine still reasserts that

> Although the particular inclination of the homosexual person is not a sin, it is a more or less strong tendency toward an intrinsic moral evil and thus the inclination itself must be seen as an objective disorder (Williams 2005).

These words were pronounced in 1986 by Cardinal Joseph Ratzinger, showing his energetic fight against the recognition of civil rights for homosexuals, in particular their access to priesthood and marriage. Since the start of Pope Benedict XVI's reign, "stern opposition to homosexuality in and outside the Roman Catholic Church has quickly become a prime public message for the Vatican" (Williams 2005). The Pope himself insists that "same-sex unions are destroying the concept of marriage and eroding Europe's social identity" (Reuters 2005).

Those views have been amplified by other Church officials. Alfonso López Trujillo, a Colombian cardinal, declares that gay marriage "is a crime which represents the destruction of the world" (*LifeSiteNews.com* 2005). The Catechism of the Catholic Church decrees the unnatural character of homosexual acts:

> Basing itself on Sacred Scripture, which presents homosexual acts as acts of grave depravity,[140] tradition has always declared that "homosexual acts are intrinsically disordered."[141] They are contrary to the natural law. They close the sexual act to the gift of life. They do not proceed from a genuine affective and sexual complementarity. Under no circumstances can they be approved. (*Catechism of the Catholic Church* ¶2357)

An extreme view against homosexuality is harshly expressed by President Robert Mugabe of Zimbabwe, when he declares that "gays and lesbians are worse than dogs and pigs" (Husband 2006).

This gay marriage act is deeply troubling to the Spanish Catholic Church, who sees it as "an assault on holy matrimony" (Popham 2007). But perhaps one of the most interesting –if not troubling– things about this law is that it has prompted a fierce concerted (politico-moral) counterattack by the Church and ultra-conservative groups like the Popular Party. Both reject an act which has been passed democratically. The

Spanish Catholic Church, in particular, has insisted that all Spanish Catholics resist the gay marriage law, as we can read in these grand words found in a report from the Spanish Bishops' Conference:

> Catholics, like all people of upright moral character, cannot be indecisive or complacent in the face of this law, but must oppose it in a clear and incisive way (Shirbon 2005).

Yet beyond the pastoral boundaries of a religious organization, the Spanish Catholic Church has shamefully participated in politics, and has organized a series of massive demonstrations in the streets of Madrid to oppose not only this gay marriage law, but also every single legislative measure which favours progressive ideas (homosexuality, new conceptions of 'family', the introduction of citizenship lessons at school, and so on), thus constituting "the church's biggest political mobilisation since the death of the dictator Francisco Franco" (Nash 2005). Even Christian homosexuals criticised the mobilisation "as an un-Christian act of discrimination against a minority" (Nash 2005).

This concerted action of the ultra-conservative groups and the Church has offended common-sense and constitutes a dangerous collusion between (worldly) political and (spiritual) religious interests. The ultra-conservative lobbies are fuelling an on-going public and private debate on moral matters, and whose sheer immorality has perhaps led the Popular Party to again lose the general elections held in March 2008. This debate, however, has proved highly influential for many common people who, upon hearing the word 'homosexual', evoke automatic associations with sin, vice, dirt, pathology, and so on. The right-wing media newspapers and radio stations (*El Mundo, ABC, La Razón* or *La COPE*) have amplified these prejudices to further their own political interests and oppose the legitimate aspirations of sexual minorities.

And let us remember that possibly the most frequently used 'discourse' to counter homosexuality has historically been that of violence, both physical and verbal. Opposition to same-sex love has produced a great deal of bloodshed in the ancient past (in the Roman Empire, in the Middle Ages, Renaissance, etc.) as well as in the present. In 1979, five teenage boys injured the US writer Tennessee Williams as part of a spate of anti-gay violence. In 1998 Matthew Sheppard, from Wyoming, a young gay college student, was beaten and left to die. In 1999 Jeff Whittington, a gay teenager, was beaten to death in New Zealand. In 2001, Aaron Webster was beaten to death in Vancouver, British Columbia. In 2005 Jody Dobrowski was killed in London by two men who perceived him to be gay. And, unfortunately, this tragic catalogue is far from being closed.

Besides, we have to remember that homosexuality is still punishable by death in Iran, Mauritania, Nigeria, Pakistan, Saudi Arabia, Sudan, the UAE and Yemen.

At a linguistic level, the word *gay* is used as a pejorative adjective by young people, and this also reflects a worrying propensity for homophobia in our societies. 'That's so gay' or 'He's such a fag!' are typical remarks made by British or American teenagers when perhaps watching a TV programme portraying gay characters. Schoolboys would also use phrases such as 'don't be so gay' if they felt that a colleague was not performing their idea of the stereotypical male role. These expressions reflect popular language that appears everywhere. When teenagers use these words, they don't mean 'homosexual' –rather, they mean 'stupid' or 'messed up', to describe something unfavourable or displeasing to them. In Spanish, one of the worst insults is 'maricón' –with practically the same connotations just mentioned, and in Hungarian, for instance, the slang expression for 'gay' (*buzi*) is also used with the meaning of 'stupid' or 'idiot'. Therefore the social stigma of homosexuality is perpetuated through language, as people continue to use openly derogatory terms like 'fag', 'dyke', 'gay', 'queer', or 'bender'.

3.3. The debate over the concept of (homosexual) 'marriage'

A particular area of fierce discursive struggle is the resistance against the concept of 'marriage'. This resistance is evident in the press. There is extraordinary lexical instability over the name of the institution, in an incredibly vast array of qualifications. There are numerous shades of meaning and calculated ambiguities used to refer to same-sex partnerships.

The discursive struggle is particularly prominent in the diverse naming practices which are recorded in media texts. This clearly points to the instability of the legal (sexual) field itself. A cursory look at a few newspaper articles yields an astonishing number of similar (but different) terms: 'gay marriage', 'civil partnership', 'same-sex marriage', 'same-sex wedding', 'same-sex unions', 'lesbian unions', 'male partnerships', 'homosexual marriage', 'civil unions', 'registered partnerships', 'equal marriage', 'same-gender marriage', 'reciprocal beneficiary relationships', 'life partnership', 'stable unions', 'civil pact' and so on[5]. The very same instability can be observed in the Spanish-language media or institutional publications, among which we can cite: 'matrimonio gay', 'matrimonio 'gay'', 'matrimonio civil entre personas del mismo sexo', 'pareja de hecho', 'uniones civiles entre homosexuales', 'matrimonio entre homosexuales', ''boda' homosexual', 'matrimonio homosexual', 'uniones homosexuales', 'unión civil de personas del mismo sexo', 'Contrato de Unión Civil entre Personas del Mismo Sexo' (in Chile), 'uniones de concubinato' (in Uruguay), 'uniones estables entre personas del mismo sexo' (proposed by the Spanish Popular Party), etc. In these lists, we can appreciate a mixture of legal, popular, journalistic, and even political terms. They reveal a variety of ideological standpoints and of attitudes towards the most acceptable linguistico-legal status to be applied to same-sex relationships. We certainly cannot deny the centrality of marriage in our social organisation, or the importance of its legal definition:

> Marriage is a lynchpin of social organization: its laws and customs interface with almost every sphere of social interaction. Its foundational role in defining structures of social institution and citizenship means that definitional authority over what 'counts' as marriage, and who is allowed access to it, has always been intensely political. Systematic exclusion of any group of people from the institution of marriage has been (and continues to be) a powerful way of oppressing that group in terms both of concrete rights and responsibilities and –more crucially still– in terms of the symbolic message that the group so discriminated against is unworthy of equality, and is less than 'human' (Kitzinger & Wilkinson 2005: 132).

In fact, and in point of truth, the only places where these relationships are officially called 'marriage' are the Netherlands (since 2001), Belgium, Ontario and British Columbia (since 2003) and Spain (since 2005). If we search for the definition, 'marriage' is:

> 1. a. The condition of being a husband or wife; the relation between persons married to each other; matrimony.
> The term is now sometimes used with reference to long-term relationships between partners of the same sex. (*O.E.D.*)

As McConnell-Ginet (2006: 228) asserts:

> It is not only legislators, judges, and politicians offering opinions: many ordinary folk are also weighing in on defining marriage. Some say definitional debates are 'just semantics', therefore trivial. Others, on both sides, argue that it matters considerably whether the word *marriage* shall be construed as including or excluding same-sex unions.

Homosexuals are often –via prejudices or unconscious attitudes– considered inferior and marginal. Hypocrisy is a key element here, as in some cases those who say that they accept homosexuality in general, would not accept the idea that one of their sons or daughters were homosexual. But we believe that defending the right of homosexuals to marriage is, from a human rights perspective, relatively easy. Two or three quotes will suffice to prove the point. According to Spain's Gay and Lesbian Federation, "(e)quality is complete or it is not equality. Lesbians and gays want, like any other citizens, to be able to decide freely if they marry, and if so, with whom" (Woolls 2005). With similar simplicity, the Spanish deputy Prime Minister, Mª Teresa Fernández de la Vega, declares that "(t)his measure improves rights and harms no one, absolutely no one, while it does benefit many people" (Shirbon 2005). And the Socialist MP Carmen Montón declares: "It's unfair to be a second-class citizen because of love [...] Spain joins the vanguard of those defending full equality for gays and lesbians" (Reuters 2005).

As with many social issues, there are numerous reasons and arguments against gay marriage but many come from ignorance and intolerance. Religion factors largely into the opinions and beliefs of many when it comes to gay marriage. The *Bible* claims that weddings are religious ceremonies, and therefore, most religious people are against gay marriage. We are to remember, however, that many weddings, over the last twenty years or so, have taken place in city halls or in equally unreligious places.

Religion has certainly been a particularly significant force in the ongoing debate over homosexuality, as the Catholic Church has traditionally held particularly strong views against homosexuality. In July 2003, the Vatican launched a global campaign against gay marriages, warning Catholic politicians that supporting gay marriage was 'gravely immoral'. In a document called *Considerations regarding proposals to give legal recognition to unions between homosexual persons*, the then cardinal Ratzinger insisted on the unnatural character of homosexuality:

> No ideology can erase from the human spirit the certainty that marriage exists solely between a man and a woman, who by mutual personal gift, proper and exclusive to themselves, tend toward the communion of their persons (Ratzinger 2003).

And he also paraphrases the *Catechism of the Catholic Church* when he writes:

> Marriage is holy, while homosexual acts go against the natural moral law. Homosexual acts "close the sexual act to the gift of life. They do not proceed from a genuine affective and sexual complementarity. Under no circumstances can they be approved (Ratzinger 2003).

Although the Church fathers recommend that homosexuals "must be accepted with respect, compassion and sensitivity" (*Catechism of the Catholic Church* 2358), the attitude of the Church establishment seems to create more intolerance against homosexuals, as well as challenges for homosexuals when seeking to gain the same respect and equal rights as heterosexuals. The Spanish Catholic Church is in fact fiercely championing a stern opposition towards any change in the traditional, reactionary model of family and human relationships represented politically by the Popular Party. Without a doubt, the idea of legalizing same-sex 'marriages' is a direct attack on the Church's exclusivity to decide what counts as a 'marriage' and what does not, on who is included or excluded from the institution, on who can be invested with the symbolical values traditionally associated with marriage, and so on. We will summarize here the main arguments used by the Catholic Church to orchestrate a 'war of words' against the institution of 'homosexual marriage':

(1) First argument: Etymology. 'Matrimony' derives from Latin *matrem* (mother) + *monium* (condition). Etymology seems to emphasise woman's right to become a mother within a legal bond, and the aim of marriage is procreation. Until several years ago, at least in Spain, the concept of 'matrimony' gave meaning to the idea of 'family'. Possibly the real argument today lies not in the fact that gay couples should or should not be allowed to marry, but rather whether or not marriage still has a place in today's society. With increasing divorce rates and increasing numbers of one-parent households, people are swaying from the idea of marriage and preferring the idea of cohabiting, something easily done by couples, regardless of their sex and of their religious affiliation.

(2) Second argument: Matrimony as procreation. The main reason for 'matrimony' is procreation, to produce legitimate offspring. Rebating this argument is pretty easy: what happens with older couples who are past their reproductive capacity, or with sterile spouses? And what would we call 'one-parent' families, so common today?

(3) Third argument: Matrimony as a holy union. This may be the real message instituted by the original Church, but today people get married and divorced as if marriage meant nothing in the first place. Marriage is not as sacred as it once was. Marriage vows are still, in English:

'I (Bride/Groom), take you (Groom/Bride), to be my (wife/husband), to have and to hold from this day forward, for better or for worse, for richer,

for poorer, in sickness and in health, to love and to cherish; from this day
forward until death do us part.'

but statistics show that very few people follow these vows.

(4) Matrimony and children. Further arguments against gay marriage
include the idea that children are not raised as well with single-sex
parents. There are, however, many single parents who raise wonderful
children and, conversely, traditionally married couples who neglect their
children shamefully.

(5) Fifth argument: Matrimony and 'gayness'. If a child, so the
argument goes, is raised by gay parents, he or she will grow up to be gay
too. This seems untenable, as there are straight parents who raise
homosexual children, and vice-versa.

(6) Sixth argument: Matrimony and moral norms. According to some
Catholic Church officials, children who are raised by a same-sex couple
will grow within a highly sexualized atmosphere, most likely void of
moral norms. This is a banal argument: a gay couple may be as loving or
as cruel as a heterosexual couple. Love or care are not dependent on sexual
orientation, let alone on being married or not.

By way of summary, let us read the apocalyptic words pronounced by
Bishop Ricardo Blázquez, President of the Spanish Bishops' Conference,
when he said that after the legalisation of gay marriages in Spain, "the
stability of marriage has been gravely injured and tremendous confusion
over marriage and family have been unleashed" (Woolls 2005). And to
finalize the argument, Bishop Antonio Martínez Campo, spokesman for
the Bishops' Conference, declared that the gay marriage law "represents
the disappearance of marriage as the union of a man and a woman … with
grave consequences for society" (Nash 2005).

4. Conclusions

No meaning associated with a word is immutable. A look at various
texts (newspapers, pastoral instructions, public statements, etc.) shows that
at the moment we are waging a 'war of words' (Dunnant 1994) –which is
part of an on-going private and public debate– over specific and highly
ideological terms such as 'abortion', 'homosexuality', 'family', 'gender

violence' or, as in this case, 'homosexual marriage'. Two obvious conclusions emerge instantly:

(a) that, in spite of the fact that the majority of Spanish society wishes to have more freedom, there is still fierce resistance against the recognition of (new) gender and sexual identities; and

(b) that the Church and the extreme right-wing political parties are orchestrating a bitter media campaign to oppose any change to their traditional, reactionary model of family and human relationships.

Gender- and sex-related concerns offer valuable insights into people's attitudes and ideologies concerning modernity, democratization, and respect for the lifestyles and identities of others. In Rubin's words:

> Contemporary conflicts over sexual values and erotic conduct have much in common with the religious disputes of earlier centuries. They acquire immense symbolic weight. Disputes over sexual behavior often become the vehicles for displacing social anxieties, and discharging their attendant emotional intensity (Rubin 1984: 267).

In this way, one may then view the same-sex marriage debate as the latest challenge posed by certain religious and politically conservative groups to oppose change even when the old order is unjustly oppressing marginalized groups, just as women and blacks were oppressed in the past. The Spanish Catholic Church and ultra-conservative groups like the Popular Party are generating a multiplicity of 'counter-discourses' to justify the preservation of certain traditional rights.

No one is harmed by homosexuality, and for that reason, there is no legitimate basis for opposing same-sex marriage. Our generation, and the preceding ones after, will continue to fight for what is right and perpetuate the cycle of tolerance that, despite occasional backlashes, is growing for the homosexual community. Homosexuals are likely to remain a marginalized group for a long time, though it seems that the acceptance of gay marriage and homosexuality will continue to make progressive strides towards a more tolerant society. In the texts we have referred to, lesbians and gays do not ask for 'special rights'. They merely request the same basic human rights that the rest of the population is entitled to.

The very institution which seems to have been reinforced all through this discursive conflict is heteronormativity, an institution which constructs both the heterosexual and homosexual categories. Heterosexuality is considered to be a normal, logical, and unmarked institution that presumes sexual liaison with the opposite sex as the only normal and positive type of sexual behaviour. Our social construction of sexuality establishes heterosexuality as the natural condition, the place where sexuality is spoken from but not inquired into. This makes homosexuality an aberration that must be studied or perhaps tolerated, but not an authoritative place from which one can study sexuality. So-called 'deviant' sexualities have not only incurred name-calling, a form of linguistic abuse, but also physical abuse as well. Lesbians, gays, transvestites, and bisexuals have experienced threats, physical assaults, rape, torture, and even murder throughout history. There are, however, no sticking arguments to suggest that gay couples should not be given the same rights as heterosexual ones. Sex-orientated discrimination is dissipating and gay couples are gaining more recognition. Therefore, with time and political pressure, couples in all countries, despite their sex, should have the same legal standings when it comes to discussing legal rights.

This paper is a first approach to the discursive conflict we are currently experiencing throughout the Spanish state. There is a clash between a (lukewarm) discourse towards modernity and respect for individual identities and lifestyles, and a multiplicity of (vociferous) discourses which emphasize monolithic attitudes and behaviours. Again gender/sexuality constitutes an excellent index of social conflicts, the site of an ongoing discursive conflict which constitutes the very (ideological) essence of our daily lives.

Notes

[1] In this paper, the concept of *discourse* is understood in the Foucauldian sense of "systematically-organised sets of statements which give expression to the meaning and values of an institution. Bdyond that, they define, describe and delimit what it is possible to say and not possible to say. [...] A discourse provides a set of possible statements about a given area, topic, objects, process that is to be talked about. In that it provides description, rules, permissions and prohibitions of social and individual actions" (Kress 1985: 6-7).

[2] See Santaemilia *et al* (2000).

[3] "La sociedad evoluciona en el modo de conformar y reconocer los diversos modelos de convivencia" (Boletín Oficial del Estado 2005: 23632).

[4] "La convivencia como pareja entre personas del mismo sexo basada en la afectividad ha sido objeto de reconocimiento y aceptación social creciente, y ha superado arraigados prejuicios y estigmatizaciones" (Boletín Oficial del Estado 2005: 23632).

[5] In analysing the situation created in the UK with the introduction of 'civil partnerships', Kitzinger & Wilkinson (2005: 144) state: "Anything less than 'marriage' for same-sex couples sends the message that the government sees us as second-class citizens. Indeed, the willingness of governments to grant civil partnerships to same-sex couples seems to precisely *because* they preserve

marriage itself exclusively for heterosexuals. [...] By re-branding as 'civil partnership' a union that is otherwise identical to opposite-sex civil marriage, civil partnerships achieve the symbolic separation of same-sex couples from the state of 'marriage'."

References

Primary sources

Bird, M. 2005. "Church Vs. State". *Time* (Sunday, 7 August 2005)

Boletín Oficial del Estado. 2005. "Ley 13/2005 de 1 de julio, por la que se modifica el Código Civil en materia de derecho a contraer matrimonio" (BOE 2 de julio de 2005)

Gumbel, A. 2006. "Gay rights and wrongs: Hollywood's biggest taboo". *The Independent* (5 December 2006)

Husband, S. 2006. "Civil partnerships: Darling, happy anniversary". *The Independent* (10 December 2006)

LifeSiteNews. 2005. "Top Vatican Cardinal: gay marriaga is "a crime which represents the destruction of the world..." *LifeSiteNews.com* (3 May 2005)

Nash, E. 2005. "Spain's clergy rally support to oppose gay marriage law". *The Independent* (18 June 2005)

Popham, P. 2007. "Old Bat Ears and a Catholic Agenda". *The Independent* (23 February 2007)

Ratzinger, J. 2003. *Considerations regarding proposals to give legal recognition to unions between homosexual persons.* Available at http://www.vatican.va/roman_curia/congregations/cfaith/documents/rc_con_cfaith_doc_20030731_homosexual-unions_en.html

Reuters. 2005. "Spanish parliament OK's gay marriage bill". *Boston Globe* (22 April 2005)

Shirbon, E. 2005. "Bishops order Catholics to resist law on gay marriage". *The Independent* (7 May 2005)

Williams, D. 2005. "New Rules Affirm Pope Benedict's Stance Against Gays." *The Washington Post* (Saturday, 8 October 2005)

Woolls, D. 2005. "Spanish gays get full legal rights". *The Independent* (3 July 2005)

Secondary sources

Cameron, D. and D. Kulick. 2003. *Language and Sexuality*. Cambridge: Cambridge University Press.

Dunant, S., ed. 1994. *The War of the Words. The Political Correctness Debate*. London: Virago Press.

Eckert, P. and S. McConell-Ginet, eds. 2003. *Language and Gender*. Cambridge: Cambridge University Press.

Foucault, M. 1984. *The History of Sexuality. Vol 2: The Use of Pleasure*. Harmondsworth: Penguin Books. Trans. Robert Hurley.

Fairclough, N. 1989. *Language and Power*. London: Longman.

Fowler, R. 1991. *Language in the News. Discourse and Ideology in the Press*. London: Routledge.

Kitzinger, C. and S. Wilkinson. 2004. "The re-branding of marriage: Why we got married instead of registering a civil partnership". *Feminism and Psychology* 14.1: 127-150.

Kress, G. 1985. *Processes in Sociocultural Practice*. Victoria: Deakin University Press.

Land, V. and C. Kitzinger. 2007. "Contesting same-sex marriage in talk-in-interaction". *Feminism and Psychology* 17.2: 173-183.

McConnell-Ginet, S. 2006. "Why defining is seldom 'just semantics'." In *Drawing the Boundaries of Meaning: Neo-Gricean Studies in Pragmatics in Honor of Laurence R. Horn*. Eds. B. Birner and G. Wards. Amsterdam: John Benjamins. Rpt. in *The Language and Sexuality Reader*. Eds. D. Cameron and D. Kulick. London/New York: Routledge, 2006, 227-240.

O.E.D. (Oxford English Dictionary) – accessible online at http://www.oed.com

Rubin, G. 1984. "Thinking Sex: Notes for a Radical Theory of the Politics of Sexuality". In *Pleasure and Danger: Exploring Female Sexuality*. Ed. C.S. Vance. London: Pandora Press, 267-319.

Santaemilia, J. 2000. *Género como conflicto discursivo*. Valencia: Universitat de València.

—. *et al.* 2000. "Lexical Cohesion in Legal Language: Several U.S. Supreme Court abortion decisions". In *Integrating theory and practice in LSP and LAP. Papers from the IRAAL/ALC conference, March 1998: Part 2*. Eds. D.P. Ó Baoill and M. Ruane. Dublin: IRAAL & University College Dublin, 13-21.

CHAPTER ELEVEN

HYBRID OR IN BETWEEN CULTURES: TRADITIONS OF MARRIAGE IN A GROUP OF BRITISH BANGLADESHI GIRLS

PIA PICHLER, GOLDSMITHS, UNIVERSITY OF LONDON

Abstract: The chapter offers a discourse analytic exploration of the topic of arranged marriage, which continues to fuel popular discourses of culture clash in public/media debates on one hand, and academic celebrations of hybrid British Asian femininities in a range of (non-linguistic) research disciplines on the other. My own work with a group of adolescent British Bangladeshi girls seeks to provide a space in language and gender research for the voices of adolescent Asian girls. At the same time I aim to offer to existing cross-disciplinary scholarship on young British Asian identities a discourse analytic focus on the complex negotiations and contestations of ideas, discourses and subject positions that characterise the spontaneous talk of five Bangladeshi girls from London. Whereas my analysis of the spontaneous data highlights the hybrid nature of a modified discourse of arranged marriage which emerges from the girls' negotiations, later interviews with my in-group informant contain a discourse which positions the girls as being torn between cultures. My chapter on the girls' talk about marriage will therefore take a critical and reflexive approach to perspectives of researcher and researched, different sources of data, and discourses of hybridity and culture clash.
Key words: *British Bangladeshi*, *hybridity*, *between cultures*, *arranged marriage*, *girls*.

1. Introduction

This chapter presents a discourse analytic investigation of the negotiation of cultural practices and subject positions in a group of five adolescent British Bangladeshi girls in relation to the topic of marriage. My analysis of the girls' spontaneous talk will focus on what I call a "modified discourse of arranged marriage", which, I argue, emerges locally as a hybrid during the complex interactive negotiations of a wide range of cultural discourses with ethnic, gendered and classed inflections in the girls' spontaneous friendship talk. However, I shall also present an extract from a different source of data, loosely structured interviews between myself and one of the girls. In this extract my in-group informant Hennah appears to challenge my post-structuralist celebration of hybrid British Bangladeshi femininities with regard to the girls' positioning to traditions of marriage.

Language and gender scholars have generated a substantial amount of research on adolescent girls and their friendship or peer groups, focusing both on structural and on discoursal features of young women's talk (Bucholtz 1999; Coates 1999; Eckert 1993; Eckert & McConnell-Ginet 1995; Eder 1993; Goodwin 1999; Mendoza-Denton 1999). Like the extensive body of cross-disciplinary research on young Asian women many of these linguistic studies take a constructionist approach to identity, and some of them also show an interest in exploring gender in non-white groups (Goodwin 1999; Mendoza-Denton 1999; Pichler 2006a). However, language and gender research has, to my knowledge, so far not turned its attention to the talk and the identity practices of British Asian girls. My own work therefore builds on non-linguistic research into young hybrid British Asian identities and the topic of arranged marriage.

Popular media representations of arranged marriage continue to perpetuate the stereotype of the suppressed Asian girl as a victim of culture clash (e.g. Cramb, writing in *The Daily Telegraph* 25/04/2002; Kelbie, writing in *The Independent* 30/08/2006). Early academic work such as Watson (1977) and the Community Relations Commission (1976) did not present an altogether different perspective, describing the situation of second generation Asian adolescents in Britain as being trapped "between two cultures". On the other hand, during the last two decades pathologising culture-clash theories have been challenged both by feminists presenting a structuralist argument focused on racism, gender, social class and education (Amos & Pratibha 1981; Brah & Minhas 1985) and, more recently, by scholars taking a constructionist rather than a structuralist stance. The work of Ahmad (2003), Alexander (2000), Archer (2002 a,b), Brah (1996), Dwyer (2000) and Shain (2003) challenges earlier studies and conceptualisations of British Asian adolescents for their essentialist approach to culture and identity as fixed and static, with "Asian-ness" and "British-ness" as independent, a priori and, moreover, homogenous categories. Frequently this work from anthropology, cultural studies, sociology and education is framed as a 'celebration' of hybridity (Puwar 2003: 31-36), with a particular focus on second and third generation South Asian young women.

This recent, cross-disciplinary research adopts a (feminist) poststructuralist approach to culture, conceptualising it 'not [as] an essence but a *positioning*' (Hall 1990: 226), or, in other words, viewing culture not as a reified, homogenous entity (Bauman 1997: 211) but instead as a 'process' and as 'semiotic space with infinite class, caste, gender, ethnic or other inflections' (Brah 1996: 234, 246). The spontaneous conversational data that I collected from a group of Bangladeshi girls on the topic of marriage contain what I would interpret as rich evidence of the process of invoking, challenging and synthesising cultural practices and discourses with various 'inflections' and thus of the local negotiation of 'cultures of hybridity' (Hall 1992: 310). However, my second source of data, consisting of interviews, suggests that this performative notion of culture and the celebration of cultural hybridity are not always shared by the research participants themselves. My combination of data sources therefore encouraged me to adopt a critical and reflexive approach to the topic of (arranged) marriage, building both on academic theorization and my participants' lived experience of culture and hybridity, and even considering the possible limitations of my linguistic data.

After presenting some background information about my two data sources, the participants in my study and previous research on "arranged marriage" I shall first focus my analysis on the girls' spontaneous talk and then turn to the interviews with my in-group informant. The final section of this chapter will draw conclusions about the girls' positioning in relation to the topic of marriage on the basis of my analysis of these diverse and seemingly contradictory data.

2. Data and participants

The girls in this group, who I shall refer to as Ardiana, Dilshana, Hennah, Varda and Rahima, all attended year 11 (15-16-years old) and formed a friendship group at their single-sex comprehensive school in the East End of London, which recruited students mainly from the surrounding working class areas. Three girls were born in Bangladesh but all of the girls had received between two and eight years of schooling in Britain.

The conversational extracts I present in this chapter derive from the self-recorded spontaneous talk of the girls during their lunch breaks at school. I supplemented these spontaneous conversational data with recordings and notes of several loosely structured interviews resulting from my in-depth, long-term collaboration with one of the girls who helped me to translate the Bengali/Sylheti utterances in the girls' talk. These "interviews" with Hennah not only provided me with valuable ethnographic information about the girls themselves, their families and communities but they also allowed one of the participants to add her own interpretation of the conversational data to mine and encouraged me to reflect on my own stance and perspectives as a researcher.

3. Arranged marriage – a research overview

Ahmad (2003: 44-45) is critical of what she feels to be an 'overemphasis' on arranged marriage in relation to South Asian women in academic work. My own study on young femininities was not led by any a priori interest in the topic of marriage, but instead the topic was positioned as significant by Ardiana and her friends themselves in their group talk. My exploration of these conversational data on marriage, however, benefits greatly from the wealth of previous, non-linguistic research on and with young British Asian women.

Most of this cross-disciplinary research suggests that "arranged marriage" continues to be prominent among second and third generation Asians in the UK, but that it is also undergoing significant changes. However, individual studies vary greatly in how they present this tradition. Although some of the large-scale studies such as Anwar (1998), Ghuman (1994, 2003), Modood et al (1994) emphasise that there might not be any inter-familiar conflicts about the tradition, they tend to take a more critical, or, at least, non-celebratory stance to arranged marriage, arguing that there is 'reluctant obedience, especially among the young Muslims' (Modood et al 1994: 79) to the tradition, or even describing it as 'most troublesome [custom]' (Ghuman 1994: 71). On the other hand, recent long term or small-scale ethnographic and feminist studies by Basit (1997), Gavron (1997) Shain (2003) provide evidence for Brah's (1996: 77) conceptualisation of arranged marriage as a 'joint undertaking between parents and young people'.

4. Talking traditions of marriage:
Young British Asian femininities

4.1. Negotiating hybrid positions – the girls' spontaneous talk

My own conversational data from the group of British Bangladeshi girls appear to confirm Brah's stance, but it also shows the heterogeneity of the practices and positions within the group, and the complex negotiations that are necessary for the girls to achieve a consensus (Eckert 1993) on the topic of marriage. Unlike the cross-disciplinary research on the topic of arranged marriage my aim in this chapter is to focus on the process of these negotiations and identity formations by linking my analysis of discourse to an exploration of lexical and syntactic features, the sequential organisation of the interaction, including pauses, non-verbal signs such as laughter and paralinguistic features like a change of voice.

The following narrative and subsequent discussion of a wedding proposal from the girls' spontaneous talk is divided into three sections. The first section focuses on the girls' accommodation strategies to the discourse of arranged marriage, the second on the girls' resistance against this discourse, and the third section on the evolvement of what I define as a modified discourse of arranged marriage.

(a) Discourse of arranged marriage: accommodation. The story of the wedding proposal reveals a discourse which positions parental choice of children's future spouses as the appropriate form of marriage arrangement (staves 1-9).

Extract 1.1: The Wedding Proposal[1]

(1)
A   .hh >did I tell you something< er [thingie] my brother
D   [what]

(2)
A   came from Bangladesh innit like   (.) a wedding proposal
D   \huh

(3)
A   (-) f[or me]   for me (.) and I was so: shocked they wrote
D   (-) [WHA::T]

(4)
A   a letter to my s- my mum and dad right saying that .hh

(5)
A   *{drawling}* "she's really ni::ce she s- talks politely"

(6)
A   and everything *{swallows}* and I was shocked my brother

(7)
A   (>was like<) my sister was like reading it to me yeah and

(8)
A   she goes "<they want me to be their bride>" and everything

(9)
A   and I was like saying (.)   ["EXCUSE ME-"]
D   wh[o are they]   related to you

(10)
A   =they just live next door to m[y h]ouse in
D   (.) cousins=   [ah]

(11)
A   Bangladesh (.) and they just want **me** (.) as their

(12)
A   son's bride
H   oh [my God]
V   [(Ardiana)] did you see the photo (.)

(13)
A   *{swallows}* I've seen the guy when I went to
V   (that-)*{swallowing}*

(14)
A   Bangladesh [(he is alright)] looking he's alright
?D   [is he nice]
?   (xxx)

(15)
A   looking   [but he's::-] the same height as me EXCUSE ME
H   *{- laughs -}*
?V   *{amused}*[(yeah:::)]

This extract shows the group's familiarity with and acceptance of a discourse of arranged marriage which allocates a significant (matchmaking) role to the two families of the couple-to-be. Although two of her friends express their surprise in stave 3: 'WHAT' and stave 12: 'oh my God', this surprise is directed at Ardiana's (cleverly introduced) news of having received a wedding proposal, rather than at the procedures adopted by the two families. Thus, despite Ardiana's repeated claims that 'she was (so) shocked' (staves 3, 6) her friends display less shock than curiosity about the wedding proposal. They have no difficulties in understanding the reference of the third person personal pronoun 'they' (staves 3, 8, 9, 10, 11), showing no sign of surprise that the authors of the letter turn out to be the parents of the suitor, rather than the young man himself (staves 9-12). Similarly, they do not question the fact that the proposal is not addressed to the bride-to-be but instead to Ardiana's parents (stave 4). Dilshana's assumption that the family of the suitor is in fact related to Ardiana (staves 9-10) signals her knowledge of the cultural practice of consanguineous marriage (Basit 1997; Dwyer 2000; Gavron 1997; Phillipson *et al* 2003). Both Varda and Dilshana express their curiosity about the physical appearance of the young man, asking Ardiana whether she has seen a photo of him and whether the boy is good looking (staves 12 and 134). The enquiries and reactions of Ardiana's friends show that their aim is to find out the particulars of the wedding proposal, but it does not suggests that the girls question the practice of arranged marriage itself. It seems that the girls do not expect to choose their future spouse on their own; instead they align themselves with a discourse where the role of active matchmaking is assumed by the families of the young couple.

(b) Discourse of arranged marriage: resistance? However, the above extract also appears to suggest that there may be some resistance to the discourse of arranged marriage in the group. Ardiana's claims of being shocked in extract 1.1 also serve to introduce her critical position towards this wedding proposal. In stave 9 she raises her volume to protest: 'EXCUSE ME' but is prevented from voicing her objections by Dilshana's question. Significantly, Ardiana's resistance to the wedding proposal does not appear to go hand in hand with a critical position towards the role of her own family in the match-making. Whereas she creates a distance between herself and the groom's parents by subverting their voice when reporting details of the wedding proposal in stave 5, she does not change the quality of her voice when she reports what her sister said in stave 8. The change of voice quality is one possible strategy for a speaker to mark a detachment from the voice that she is reproducing (Bakhtin 1986; Coates 1999; Maybin 2003). In addition, Ardiana does not switch into direct speech in stave 8 as she did when speaking in the voice of her suitor's parents in stave 5. Instead, she uses reported speech 'they want me to be their bride' (rather than 'they want you to be their bride').

However, after being temporarily prevented from displaying her resistance fully by her friends' eager questions about the proposal and the suitor, Ardiana vehemently airs her opposition to the proposed marriage when she switches into a discourse which appears to value love-marriages:

Extract 1.2: The Wedding Proposal - continued:

(15)
A   [but he's::-] the same height as me EXCUSE ME I LOVE
H
?V   [(yeah:::)]*{amused}*

(16)
A   MY BOYFRIEND here right I don't wanna get married to

(17)
A   somebody else I don't /**know**
H   (-)   [(inn]it) (.)
R   (-) innit ma[n]
?V   (-) *{- - - laughs - - -}*

(18)
A   [but then
H   *{amused}*he may be gorgeous but then again he mig[ht have a

(19)
A   again (a] ha-)
H   (a)]   personality like a (.) **ape** or **some**thing=

Ardiana here introduces a discourse of romantic love, which constitutes the popular norm in a large majority of western communities. Initially, it seems as if the other girls were following Ardiana's lead and accepted her switch into a discourse of romantic love (stave 17 'innit man'; 'innit'). Following Ardiana's criticism of marrying a young man she does not know, Hennah provides the reasons for their reservations in staves 18 -19: if a girl does not know her future husband before getting married, she runs the risk of ending up with a husband who may be good looking, but could have a flawed personality. Hennah's joke and the girls' agreement with Ardiana appear to signal the group's unanimous alignment with the tradition of love marriage, and consequently their rejection of arranged marriages. However, on a sequential, micro-linguistic level, the presence of a hesitation in the form of pause after Ardiana's utterance signals that the group's acceptance of Ardiana's switch into a discourse of romantic love is not entirely smooth (see Conversation Analytic work, e.g.

Pomerantz 1984, Levinson 1983: 334 on the significance of pauses as markers of dispreferred seconds).   Moreover, the remainder of the conversation does not provide any further evidence of the group's unanimous resistance to the tradition of arranged marriage and instead highlights a much more complex process of positioning within the group.

(c) Modified discourse of arranged marriage. Ardiana's protest is expressed in her utterance 'EXCUSE ME I LOVE MY BOYFRIEND here right I don't wanna get married to somebody else I don't **know**'. Whereas the first part of the utterance clearly voices a western notion of romantic love, the second can be interpreted as positioning Ardiana in a modified discourse of arranged marriage, emphasising solely her resistance to getting married to somebody she does not know.

I argue that the other girls align themselves only with the latter part of Ardiana's proposition. The third extract of the conversation provides evidence for this claim, showing that the girls do not object to the tradition of arranged marriage per se, but instead resist a particular version of it.

Extract 1.3: The Wedding Proposal - continued:

(20)
A   =YEAH:: [that's] true (.)
D   [yeah]   (.) yeah when they come to England

(21)
A   they just wanna get
H   [(they just]xxx-)
D   yeah they just lea[ve you man]

(22)
A   married to girls from London [because like they are
V   [yeah because of the

(23)
A   Londoni] (.) **yeah** [they are from London they are
V   passport] (.)   [they want their passport
D   (ah[::){*agreeing}*

(24)
A   British] they are British and they wanna come to this
V   inn]it
(25)
A   country as well
V   (-) {*swallows}* they want the passports

(26)
A   so what's wrong with you Rahima
?V   (the British) passport
?   *{dental click}*   *{laughter}*

What the girls *do* challenge in this extract is the tradition of being
married to men from Bangladesh. The interactive manner in which they
formulate this challenge is highly collaborative, mirroring and building on
each others' contributions in a way that Coates (1996, 1999) found to be
characteristic of the friendship talk of white adult middle-class women.
Thus, the girls use many thematic repetitions ('Londoni-British') and
lexical repetitions ('passport'), supportive minimal agreements such as
'yeah' and 'joint constructions involving simultaneous speech' (Coates
1996: 121) as in staves 22 to 24. One explanation for their objection to
men from Bangladesh is based on the girls' view that Bangladeshi men are
only interested in British citizenship and that they leave their wives once
they have established themselves in Britain. All the girls reject their role in
this alleged pursuit: in staves 22-24 Ardiana and Varda collaboratively and
simultaneously express their condemnation of the men's motivation to get
married to girls from Britain because of their British passport. They
receive support from Dilshana, who voices her agreement with their claim
in stave 23.

It is hard to imagine that the girls' concern about their role as potential
gateway to British citizenship has not been affected by a widespread
popular anti-immigration discourse in the UK (see also Ahmad 2003: 48-
49). However, this anti-immigration discourse appears to overlap with a
trend among many young British Asians and a substantial number of their
parents to object to marriages of British girls being arranged with suitors
from the Indian subcontinent (Anwar 1998: 112; see also Gardner &
Shukur 1994; Ghuman 1994; Shain 2003: 90; but for conflicting evidence
see Gavron 1997: 124). On the other hand, connections with Britain are
still valued highly by Bangladeshi families, as the term 'Londoni', which
tends to be applied to people, houses and entire villages that have
connections to Britain (Gardner & Shukur 1994: 147) shows. In stave 23 it
is used by Ardiana to signal her understanding of the value attributed by
many Bangladeshis to a potential link with Britain and therefore with girls
like themselves.

Moreover, when Hennah says that a Bengali groom might have 'a
personality like an ape' (extract 1.2, stave 19), the connotation of the word
'ape' suggests that Hennah expects the men's behaviour to be ill-mannered
or even uncivilised. By referring to Bangladeshi men in these derogatory

terms Hennah's utterance also reveals an influence of a discourse of imperial Darwinism, which allows the girls to establish their own superiority. At the same time the girls reveal their anxiety about feeling alienated from their future husbands' (Sylheti village) background, which they appear to contrast negatively with their own (urban British Bangladeshi) background. This discourse of cultural incompatibility between British Asian girls and grooms from the Indian subcontinent due to cultural and educational differences appears to have established itself recently in many parts of the British Bangladeshi and other British Asian "communities" (Anwar 1998: 112; Basit 1997: 81-84; Gardner & Shukur 1994: 156; Phillipson *et al* 2003: 51; but see also Gavron 1997 for counter arguments). However, I would argue that by engaging in this (essentialist) discourse and by orienting to their own "Londoni" or "British" identities, the girls in this group in fact acknowledge their own hybrid identities, which they position in opposition to the identities of their Bangladeshi suitors.

4.2. Torn between cultures? The interview data

In the girls' spontaneous group talk about Ardiana's wedding proposal popular 'culture clash' discourses therefore at best serve to explain the girls' rejection of grooms from Bangladesh, and not the girls' relationship with their parents or their position to (a modified version of) the tradition of arranged marriage. However, my interview data present a different perspective. I had originally planned these ethnographic-style interviews with my ingroup informant, Hennah, as a means to collect additional information about individual girls, their friendship group, families and wider community. However, in the course of these "interview sessions", which took place a year after the recordings, I was also able to give Hennah feedback on my progressing analysis of the girls' talk, as for example on my interest in the girls' bicultural or hybrid identities. At times Hennah aligned herself with my interpretation by arguing that the girls did have agency in choosing their future husbands or by acknowledging her own ability to, as she said, 'do both', that is, to align herself with what she perceived to be as 'English' as well as 'Muslim' and/or 'Bangladeshi' discourses and practices. However, she also spoke about hardship in relation to coping with different sets of norms (Pichler 2008; forthcoming). The following example will show an instance in which she goes very far in distancing herself from a celebration of 'hybrid identities'.

Extract 2: Torn Between Two Cultures

1) P   the thing is I I do not you know from from like looking

2) P   at **this**   I do not think that it's: like true: .hhh ah:
   H   =yeah

3) P   how a lot of like sociologists have said *{slightly dramatic}*

4) P   "oh you know like .hh erm: .hh it's so: difficult and

5) P   people: and and (.) you know like (.) girls .hh they are

6) P   completely torn between the two cultures"[2] [I]   think
   H   [hhhh]

7) P   that you are doing really /**well (.) you know** with the
   H   *{laughs}*

8) P   two (-) I mean [don't you /think]
   H   *{laughs}* [no nono]   nonono hh you know this

9) P   yeah
   H   yeah   this i- we're (-) there's so much teasing there

10) P   =yeah yeah
    H   yeah   that it makes it look like but it isn't (.)

11) H   honest to God *{almost staccato}*it is **not like** cause if you

12) P   yeah   =yeah
    H   look at Dilshana Ardiana yeah   look at the mess

13) P   yeah
    H   they're in (-)   and look at Rahima .hhh if it was erm:

14) H   (-) if it was OK they wouldn't be torn now (-) do

15) P   yeah
    H   you get me because .hhh   %her parents are really

16) H   angry% they **know** that she's going out with someone .hh

17) P   [yeah]
    H   but she won't tell them .hh [who it] yeah is or who erm

18) H   when he's gonna come for her (like) for good and stuff like

19) H   that and they aks her *{authoritarian}* "**tell** <u>him to come to you</u>

20) H   <u>for good</u> cause (-) I don't like what people are saying to me"

21) P   (-) yeah [yeah]   yeah
    H   (-)   [d'you] get me   and erm: *{laughing}*<u>Ardiana she's</u>

22) P   ye[ah]   yeah
    H   <u>in aboard</u>   [and] Shashima she's already **married** d'you get me

In this extract Hennah objects to my assessment of the girls 'doing well' (stave 7) and my challenge of the 'torn between cultures'- discourse (stave 6). Hennah points out that (at the time of this interview more than ever) several of her friends in the group are in a 'mess' (stave 12): Ardiana abroad (in Bangladesh amongst speculations that she would be "married off") and another friend, Shashima, already having been married (after her parents' discovery that she was dating), see staves 21-22. Interestingly, Hennah also indirectly challenges my interpretation of the relevance of teasing for the group (which I had told her about previously), positioning it as a strategy to cover up difficulties (staves 9-10), rather than as a strategy to resolve difficulties and synthesise different cultural discourses and norms, as I had suggested on the basis of the girls' spontaneous talk (Pichler 2006a, b). Thus, in the extract above Hennah argues that some of the girls in the group are in fact torn 'between two cultures' (Watson 1977), rather than stressing their bicultural or hybrid identities, clearly positioning the different norms on dating and marriage as incompatible and adopting a rather essentialist definition of culture.

My analysis of the interview data elsewhere (Pichler 2008) takes into consideration that interviews, just like conversations, are co-constructed events, in which subjects take on a range of frequently conflicting discourses and subject positions. It is also essential to acknowledge that Hennah's stances and positioning may or may not be representative of the entire group. Nevertheless, I felt that this extract also required me to ask whether Hennah's alignment with this discourse of 'being trapped between two cultures' reveals an experience of a "reality" of the girls' heterosexual relationships outside the context of conversational interaction, which is more difficult to manage than what the spontaneous talk of the girls suggests. In connection with this I felt it was necessary to ask whether a focus on conversational micro-phenomena can wrongly prioritise an emphasis on the participants' agency. Critiques of extreme constructionist approaches to language and identity share their concern about a focus on conversational micro-phenomena which may draw a distorted picture of participant agency. Bonnie McElhinny (2003: 26-27) highlights the relevance of this question for language and gender research:

> People's ability to adapt language readily and rapidly from situation to situation, addressee to addressee, may accord people an unusual degree of agency and flexibility in their construction of themselves in a way that other forms of cultural and actual capital can and do not [...].

In the light of the above quote the girls' difficulties in balancing cultural norms in relation to marriage and dating, which Hennah claims in the interview, could partly be explained by the fact that in the cultural field (Bourdieu 1991) of the girls' wider community, gender norms about heterosexual relationships are considerably less flexible than the diverse and shifting discursive positions which I have identified in their spontaneous conversations.

5. Conclusion

The informal talk about the wedding proposal shows that the girls draw on and negotiate a wide range of discourses and cultural practices in their heterogeneous group. On one hand, the topic of marriage is clearly positioned as very central to the adolescent femininities of Ardiana and her friends, whereas marriage was simply not a topic pursued in the other two non-Asian groups of adolescent girls I was working with at the time. On the other hand, in their spontaneous talk one of the girls briefly adopts a discourse of romantic love and all girls insist on 'knowing their partners', however without necessarily adopting a discourse of premarital dating. At the same time as positioning marriage arrangements as a family undertaking the girls also voice their opposition to marrying men from Bangladesh, by drawing on anti-immigration discourses as well as on discourses of cultural incompatibility and imperial Darwinism.

I would argue that in the girls' spontaneous conversations about marriage ethnic boundaries and cultural differences are frequently constructed interactively and locally (Brah 1996: 163); they mostly remain implicit, as for example when Ardiana objects to her marriage proposal on the grounds of loving her boyfriend. These ethnic and cultural boundaries are constantly de-constructed, re-negotiated and/or synthesised by the girls in their talk, allowing them to engage in 'identity formations which cut across and intersect [...] frontiers' (Hall 1992: 310), that is, in the construction of hybrid identities.

The significance of an essentialised and stereotypical notion of ethnic culture is also acknowledged explicitly on some occasions by the girls in the group talk, as when they position themselves as British and Londoni in opposition to Bangladeshi suitors, and much more frequently so by Hennah in our interviews (Pichler 2008). As Bauman (1997: 209) argues, dominant and essentialist notions of culture(s), equated with discrete and homogeneous ethnic groups, remain relevant aspects in a critical examination of culture as a process, as they 'form [...] part of the discursive competence of citizens from 'ethnic minorities' themselves, and continue [...] to function as one element in the negotiation of difference'. Whereas in some instances Hennah aligns herself with my own celebration of flexible, hybrid cultural practices and identities, in others she relies on much more essentialist discourses of culture and difference. However, these discourses, I believe, can reveal cultural experiences and norms which are much less easily synthesised than the linguistic practices that can be identified in the group's conversational data.

As I argued above, one way to resolve what appears to be a discrepancy between my emphasis on cultural hybridity and Hennah's alignment with a discourse of culture clash is to acknowledge our different foci, my own, initially mostly on linguistic micro-phenomena, and Hennah's, on non-linguistic experiences. Another solution is to refrain both from a re-alignment with the dominant popular discourse of 'being torn between cultures' and from an academic over-romantisation of hybridity (Puwar 2003).

The comparison of my two sources of data suggests that the translation and negotiation between cultural practices and identities which Hall (1992: 310) deems essential for the formation of hybrid identities is not necessarily free of contradictions and conflict (see also Ballard 1994: 31). There is some evidence for this already in the girls' spontaneous talk about marriage, as the group needs to engage in complex negotiations of individual stances and cultural practices to achieve a consensus in the form of what I defined as a modified discourse of arranged marriage. These complex discursive negotiations that the girls carry out locally in their friendship talk possibly reflect some of the issues and difficulties which, as Hennah indicates in her interview, the girls face in relation to cultural norms and practices surrounding dating and marriage outside their friendship group. At the same time, however, I would argue that their spontaneous talk offers the girls a platform to negotiate different traditions of marriage, and therefore not only reflects but also potentially affects discourses and cultural practices of marriage well beyond their adolescent friendship group.

Notes

[1] Transcriptions are based on an adaptation of the stave system (Coates 1996, 1999) and the following conventions.

A	Ardiana
D	Dilshana
H	Hennah
R	Rahima
V	Varda
P	Pia
?	identity of speaker not clear
{laughter}	non verbal information
xxxxxx {laughing}	paralinguistic information qualifying underlined utterance
[.....]	beginning/end of simultaneous speech
(xxxxxxxx)	inaudible material
(......)	doubt about accuracy of transcription
"......"	speaker quotes/uses words of others
CAPITALS	increased volume
%......%	decreased volume
bold print	speaker emphasis
>...<	faster speed of utterance deliver
/	rising intonation
yeah:::::	lengthened sound
-	incomplete word or utterance
=	latching on
(.)	micropause
(-)	pause shorter than one second
(1); (2)	timed pauses (longer than one second)
.hhh; hhh	in-breath; out-breath

[2] Apologies for this generalisation based on Watson's 1977 work

References

Ahmad, F. 2003. "Still in 'In Progress?'– Methodological dilemmas, tensions and contradictions in theorizing South Asian Muslim Women." In *South Asian Women in the* Diaspora. Eds. N. Puwar and P. Raghuram. Oxford: Berg, 43-66.

Alexander, C. 2000. *The Asian Gang.* Oxford: Berg.

Amos, V. and P. Parmar. 1981. "Resistances and responses: the experience of black girls in Britain." In *Feminism for Girls. An Adventure Story.*

Eds. A. McRobbie and T. McCabe London: Routledge and Kegan Paul Ltd, 129-152.

Anwar, M. 1998. *Between Cultures. Continuity and Change in the Lives of Young Asians*. London: Routledge.

Archer, L. 2002a. "Change, culture and tradition: British Muslim pupils talk about Muslim girls' post-16 'choices'." *Race, Ethnicity and Education* 5.4: 59-376.

—. 2002b. "It's easier that you're a girls and that you're Asian': interactions of 'race' and gender between researchers and participants." *Feminist Review* 72: 108-132.

Bakhtin, M. 1986. *Speech Genres and other late Essays*. Ed. C. Emerson and M. Holquist. Transl. Vern W. McGee. Austin: University of Texas Press.

Ballard, R. 1994. "Introduction: the emergence of Desh Paradesh." In *Desh Paradesh. The South Asian Presence in Britain*. Ed. R. Ballard. London: C. Hurst & Co. Publishers, 1-34.

Basit, T. 1997. *Eastern Values, Western Milieu: Identities and Aspirations of Adolescent British Muslim Girls*. Aldershot: Ashgate.

Bauman, G. 1997. "Dominant and demotic discourses of culture: their relevance to multi-ethnic alliances." In *Debating Cultural Hybridity: Multi-cultural Identities and the Politics of Anti-Racism*. Eds. P. Werbner and T. Moodod. London: Zed Books, 209-225.

Bourdieu, P. 1991. *Language and Symbolic Power*. Cambridge: Polity Press.

Brah, A. 1996. *Cartographies of Diaspora*. London: Routledge.

Brah, A. and R. Minhas. 1985. "Structural racism or cultural difference? Schooling for Asian girls." In *Just a Bunch of Girls. Feminist Approaches to Schooling*. Ed. G. Weiner. Milton Keynes: Open University Press, 14-25.

Bucholtz, M. 1999. "'Why be normal?': language and identity practices in a community of nerd girls." *Language in Society* 28: 203-223.

Coates, J. 1996. *Women Talk. Conversation between Women Friends*. Oxford: Blackwell.

—. 1999. "Changing femininities: the talk of teenage girls." In *Reinventing Identities. The gendered Self in Discourse*. Eds. M. Bucholtz, A.C. Liang and L.A. Sutton. Oxford: Oxford University Press, 123-144.

Community Relations Commission. 1976. *Between two Cultures*. CRC.

Cramb, A. 2002. "It was my fault says mother of arranged marriage girl, 16." *The Daily Telegraph* (25/04/2002).

Dwyer, C. 2000. "Negotiating diasporic identities: young British South Asian Muslim women." *Women's Studies International Forum* 23.4: 468-475.

Eckert, P. 1993. "Cooperative competition in adolescent "girl talk"." In *Gender and Conversational Interaction*. Ed. Deborah Tannen. Oxford: Oxford University Press, 32-61.

Eckert, P. and S. McConnell-Ginet. 1995. "Constructing meaning, constructing selves: Snapshots of language, gender and class from Belten High." In *Gender articulated. Language and the socially constructed Self*. Eds. K. Hall and M. Bucholtz. New York: Routledge, 49-508.

Eder, D. 1993. ""Go get ya a french!": romantic and sexual teasing among adolescent girls". In *Gender and Conversational Interaction*. Ed. D. Tannen. Oxford: Oxford University Press, 17-31.

Gardner, K. and A. Shukur. 1994. ""I'm Bengali, I'm Asian, and I'm living here": the changing identity of British Bengalis." In *Desh Paradesh. The South Asian presence in Britain*. Ed. R. Ballard. London: C. Hurst & Co, 142-164.

Gavron, C. 1997. *Migrants to Citizens: Changing orientations among Bangladeshis of Tower Hamlets, London*. Unpublished PhD Thesis, University of London.

Ghuman, P.A. Singh. 1994. *Coping with two Cultures. British Asian and Indo-Canadian Adolescents*. Clevedon: Multilingual Matters.

—. 2003. *Double Loyalties. South Asian Adolescents in the West*. Cardiff: University of Wales Press.

Goodwin, M.H. 1999. "Constructing opposition within girls' games". In *Reinventing Identities. The gendered self in discourse*. Eds. M. Bucholtz, A.C. Liang and L.A. Sutton. Oxford: Oxford University Press, 388-409.

Hall, S. 1990 "Cultural Identity and Diaspora." In *Identity: Culture, Community, Difference*. Ed. J. Rutherford London: Lawrence and Wilshart, 222-237.

—. 1992. "The Question of cultural identity." In *Modernity and its Future*. Eds. S. Hall, D. Held and T. McGrew. Cambridge: Polity Press, 273-316.

Kelbie, P. 2006. "Mother appeals for safe return of daughter, 12, feared abducted by father for forced marriage." *The Independent* (30/08/2006).

Levinson, S. 1983. *Pragmatics*. Cambridge: Cambridge University Press.

Maybin, J. 2003. "Voices, intertextuality and introduction to schooling." In *Language, Literacy and Education: A Reader*. Eds. S. Goodman, T.

Lillis, J. Maybin and N. Mercer. Stoke on Trent, UK: Trentham Books in association with The Open University, 159-170.

McElhinny, B. 2003. "Theorizing Gender in Sociolinguistics and Anthropology". In *The Handbook of Language and Gender*. Eds. J. Holmes and M. Meyerhoff. Oxford: Blackwell, 21-42.

Mendoza-Denton, N. 1999. "Turn-initial no. Collaborative opposition among Latina adolescents." In *Reinventing Identities. The gendered Self in Discourse*. Eds. M. Bucholtz, A.C. Liang and L.A. Sutton. Oxford: Oxford University Press, 273-292.

Modood, T., S. Beishon and S. Virdee. 1994. *Changing Ethnic Identities*. London: Policy Studies Institute.

Phillipson, C., Nilufar A. and J. Latimer. 2003. *Women in Transition*. Bristol: The Policy Press in association with University of Bristol.

Pichler, P. 2006a. "Multifunctional teasing as a resource for identity construction in the talk of British Bangladeshi girls." *Journal of Sociolinguistics* 10.2: 226-250.

—. 2006b. ""This sex thing is such a big issue now": Sex talk and identities in three groups of adolescent girls." In *Sexual Identities and Desires across Cultures*. Eds. S. Kyratzis and H. Sauntson. Houndmills, Basingstoke: Palgrave Macmillan, 68-95.

—. 2008. "Gender, ethnicity and religion in spontaneous talk and ethnographic-style interviews: balancing perspectives of researcher and researched." In *Gender and Language Research Methodologies*. Eds. K. Harrington, L. Litosseliti, H. Sauntson and J. Sunderland. Basingstoke: Palgrave Macmillan, 56-72.

—. forthcoming. *Talking Young Femininities*. Houndmills, Basingstoke: Palgrave Macmillan.

Pomerantz, A. 1984. "Agreeing and disagreeing with assessments: some features of preferred/dispreferred turn shapes." In *Structures of Social Interaction*. Eds. J. Heritage and J.M. Atkinson. Cambridge: Maison des Sciences de l'Homme and Cambridge University Press, 57-101.

Puwar, N. 2003. "Melodramatic postures and constructions." In *South Asian Women in the Diaspora*. Eds. N. Puwar and P. Raghuram. Oxford: Berg, 43-66.

Shain, F. 2003. *The Schooling and Identity of Asian Girls*. Stoke on Trent: Trentham Books.

Watson, J. 1977. *Between two Cultures: Migrants and Minorities in Britain*. Oxford: Basil Blackwell.

CONTRIBUTORS

Elli Doukanari is an Assistant Professor, Intercollege, Cyprus. She has a B.A. in Greek and English Language and Literature, University of Athens, Greece, and an MS and a Ph.D. in Linguistics, Georgetown University, USA. Her interests include: Language and Gender, Discourse and Conversational Analysis, Sociolinguistics, Anthropological Linguistics, Greek / Cypriot Society and Culture and Language in Education. She has published on Greek Diglossia, the Historical Present in women's violence stories and Discourse Analysis in the classroom. E-mail address: edoukanari@yahoo.com.

Stina Ericsson works at the Department of Linguistics, Göteborg University, Sweden. Main interests: language and gender, language and sexuality, semantics and computational semantics, pragmatics and computational pragmatics, information structure, dialogue systems. E-mail address: stinae@ling.gu.se.

Pilar Garcés-Conejos is an Assistant Profesor of Applied Linguistics at the University of North Carolina at Charlotte, US. Her main research interests include intercultural pragmatics, English as a Second Language and English for Specific Purposes. E-mail address: pgblitvi@uncc.edu.

Allyson Jule is a Senior Lecturer in Education at the University of Glamorgan, Wales. She is the author of several books and articles on gender and silence in various classrooms. E-mail address: ajule@glam.ac.uk.

Agnieszka Kiełkiewicz-Janowiak teaches at the Instytut Filologii Angielskiej of the Adam Mickiewicz University, Poznań, Poland. Main research interests: sociolinguistics, socio-historical linguistics, contrastive linguistics, pragmatics, language and gender.

Joanna Pawelczyk is an Assistant Professor at the Instytut Filologii Angielskiej of the Adam Mickiewicz University, Poznań, Poland. Her main research interests are sciolinguistics, language and gender, and lexicography.

Pia Pichler is a lecturer in Linguistics at Goldsmiths' College, University of London. Her research examines the interplay of language, gender, ethnicity and social class in adolescent groups of girls from a range of backgrounds, drawing on situated conversational data as well as on ethnographic-style interviews and integrating linguistic discourse analysis with crossdisciplinary research on adolescent identities. E-mail address: p.pichler@gold.ac.uk.

Joan Pujolar is Director of the Department of Languages and Cultures at the Universitat Oberta de Catalunya. He has published various works on the sociolinguistics of bilingualism and gender, particularly *Gender, heteroglossia and power. A sociolinguistic study of youth culture*. Berlin: Mouton de Gruyter, 2001, and *Language, culture and tourism: perspectives in Barcelona and Catalonia*. Barcelona: Turisme de Barcelona, 2006. E-mail address: jpujolar@uoc.edu.

José Santaemilia is an Associate Professor of English Language and Linguistics at the *Universitat de València*, as well as a legal and literary translator. His main research interests are gender and language, sexual language and legal translation. He has edited *Género, lenguaje y traducción* (Valencia, 2003) and *Gender, sex and translation: The manipulation of identities* (Manchester, 2005). With José Pruñonosa, he is author of the first critical edition and translation of *Fanny Hill* into Spanish (Editorial Cátedra, 2000). E-mail address: jose.santaemilia@uv.es.

Nóra Schleicher received her PhD in sociology at the University of Eotvos Lorand, Budapest. Presently she is head of the Institute of Journalism and Media Studies at Budapest College of Communication and Business. Her main research interest is focused on the relationship of language, power and identity. She has researched and published in the area of bilingualism and gender and language. E-mail address: schleichernora@axelero.hu.

Andrea Simon-Maeda is an Associate Professor in the Career Design Department at Nagoya Keizai University in Japan. She has published articles in TESOL Quarterly, and her research interests include postmodern feminism and critical ethnography in educational settings.She has been teaching tertiary level EFL for over 30 years and is currently writing an ethnographic report of bi/multilingual speakers in Japan. E-mail address: andy@nagoya-ku.ac.jp.

Lidia Tanaka is lecturer in the Asian Studies division of the School of Sociology, Anthropology and Politics at La Trobe University, Australia. She obtained her PhD in linguistics in 2001 and her research interests include language and gender in Japan, Conversation Analysis and the language in interviews. She is the author of *Gender, language and culture: A study of Japanese television interview discourse* (John Benjamins, 2004). E-mail address: l.tanaka@latrobe.edu.au.

INDEX